W0042007

Contributions to Management Science

More information about this series at:
http://www.springer.com/series/1505

Katarzyna Rostek

Benchmarking Collaborative Networks

A Key to SME Competitiveness

Springer

Katarzyna Rostek
Faculty of Management
Warsaw University of Technology
Warsaw
Poland

ISSN 1431-1941 ISSN 2197-716X (electronic)
Contributions to Management Science
ISBN 978-3-319-16735-0 ISBN 978-3-319-16736-7 (eBook)
DOI 10.1007/978-3-319-16736-7

Library of Congress Control Number: 2015937735

Springer Cham Heidelberg New York Dordrecht London

© Springer International Publishing Switzerland 2015
This work is subject to copyright. All rights are reserved by the Publisher, whether the whole or part of
the material is concerned, specifically the rights of translation, reprinting, reuse of illustrations,
recitation, broadcasting, reproduction on microfilms or in any other physical way, and transmission
or information storage and retrieval, electronic adaptation, computer software, or by similar or
dissimilar methodology now known or hereafter developed.
The use of general descriptive names, registered names, trademarks, service marks, etc. in this
publication does not imply, even in the absence of a specific statement, that such names are exempt
from the relevant protective laws and regulations and therefore free for general use.
The publisher, the authors and the editors are safe to assume that the advice and information in this
book are believed to be true and accurate at the date of publication. Neither the publisher nor the
authors or the editors give a warranty, express or implied, with respect to the material contained
herein or for any errors or omissions that may have been made.

Printed on acid-free paper

Springer International Publishing AG Switzerland is part of Springer Science+Business Media
(www.springer.com)

Foreword

This publication was based on the need, which is supporting SMEs in their development and the struggle to survive in the competitive market. In the contemporary world, the speed of change in the economy and the multiplicity of entities operating in the market are a growing challenge for SMEs with limited organizational, financial, and human potential. On the other hand, the small businesses are the strength of the economy, which generates jobs for young people who are able to flexibly switch to a new profile of activity and adapt to changing environmental conditions much faster than large companies. The challenge and the necessity are to ensure that SMEs' functioning is sustainable and the growth opportunities are similar to those in big companies. The author of this publication was faced with such a major challenge.

In this book, consisting of six chapters, the author proposes the concept of organizations network and combines advanced methods of competitiveness analysis with the possibilities offered by the cooperation within the group. The author also proposes the organizational and technical solutions related to SMEs' limitations which the small businesses face every day. Here the insufficient analytical data potential, the potential of the financial and human resources, or the lack of knowledge in the area of advanced methods and management models should be mentioned. The author has used in these solutions the latest achievements of management sciences such as trust management, coopetition, brokering information, knowledge management, benchmarking analysis, or trust management. What is important is that the results of the work have been verified on the basis of research.

It is obvious that not all of the aforementioned challenges are resolved in the presented publication. Some of them are left by the author as open matters for further discussion and research. Therefore, this work opens up new possibilities of creating solutions that will lead to sustainable development of SMEs.

It is also important that the presented concept of organizations network, although dedicated to SMEs, has a much broader application context. This promotes wider than is now the case competitive cooperation, which seems to be an inherent consequence of the faster growing demands of the market and the economy. Hence, it can be recommended reading for all entrepreneurs who wonder how to effectively support the development of competitive strategy in the organization. It will also be interesting for a wide range of faculty and students who deal with the issue of competitiveness. It may eventually be material for discussion for researchers involved in the development of science and practice in the field of competitive strategy.

Koszalin, Poland   Zbigniew Banaszak

Preface

The market for small and medium-sized enterprises (SMEs) worldwide plays a key role in shaping and developing the economy. Performed research shows that the good condition of SMEs affects the state of the overall economy—both locally and globally. Additionally increasing market volatility and phenomena such as reindustrialization of the cities, Industry 4.0, or B4B activity create the need to be better and adapt faster to changes in the market. From this perspective more than ever it is reasonable to effectively support the development of SMEs and improve their competitiveness.

The effectiveness of competing is determined by the ability of the entity to continuously improve through the implementation of innovative changes leading to the achievement of designated purposes (such as increasing profits, reducing the number of leaving customers, raising the quality of products and services). The ability to properly select such changes will bring the expected effects and is determined primarily by market awareness and theoretical and practical knowledge in the field of innovation management. The vast majority of SMEs do not have such knowledge and do not have access to it, which justifies the preparation of support programs for them. The enhancing of SMEs' competitiveness takes place on several areas:

– The substantive—by launching dedicated courses and training
– The economical—by providing sources of financing innovation
– The technological—by lowering the cost of purchase and installation of technological tools

In each of these areas, there are different possibilities for support in the range of abilities and various local and national initiatives or the European and governmental programs. However, as indicated by studies, their availability is varied and insufficient, because most of the SMEs' managers still operate intuitively, focusing on short-term purposes, without the ability to forward plan and predict its effects. In order to achieve the expected efficacy, an approach should be proposed in which

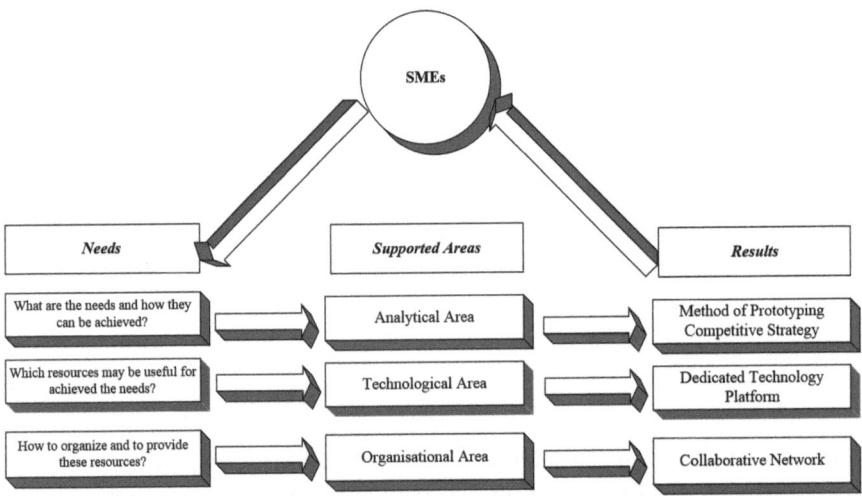

Fig. 1 The approach of competitiveness supporting (*source*: own research)

these three main areas (i.e., analytical, technological, and organizational) of competitiveness support are operating independently, which means that for a trader to take advantage of them, they must be aware of these (Fig. 1):

– What are needs and how can they be achieved?
– Which resources (i.e., technologies, methods, tools) may be useful for achieving these needs?
– What are the ways of organizing and providing these resources?

Against the above there is a need to integrate the areas supporting the competitiveness of SMEs in one complete approach (Fig. 1). Such approaches provide:

– Effective method of prototyping competitive strategy
– Implemented on a dedicated technology platform
– Being economically and organizationally available for SMEs

The proposed approach indicates the need for using the latest achievements of science and technology, while maintaining its organizational and economic availability for SMEs. This in turn implies the need for cooperation of many SMEs to increase their competitiveness potential and the apportionment of liability and the cost of implementation.

SMEs' cooperation cannot be limited only to the sharing of costs. It is also necessary to share the experience, skills, and elaborated patterns of conduct in those areas that are strengths of the company and in return to expect similar support in these areas is the company's weak point. Such a mutually supporting group is called the Benchmarking Collaborative Network (BCN). The monograph is dedicated to its characteristics, organization, and functioning.

Chapter 1 presents the current methods to support the competitiveness of enterprises and their constraints from the perspective of SMEs. Through the content of this chapter, we have sought to answer the questions, what are the possibilities of supporting the competitiveness of SMEs, and why does the typical SME uses these methods very rarely? Typically the financial constraints of small entities are considered as causes of all problems. However, research shows that although they are important, they are not only and often not the most important limitations of SMEs' functioning.

Chapter 2 presents emerging science and business trends and new development directions, which are promising due to the effectiveness of supporting the competitiveness of enterprises. Some of these methods, such as benchmarking and Business Intelligence, are known and have been used for a long time. Usually, this, however, requires such a large commitment of organizational capacity, human, technical, and financial, that its scope of application in SMEs is small. Other methods, such as coopetition and crowdsourcing, still require scientific and practical research in the area of their usefulness for SMEs. Thus, the content of Chap. 2 supports the search for answers to the question, what new methods, techniques, and technologies can and should be addressed in order to promote the competitiveness of SMEs? Certainly, Chap. 2 does not provide a complete answer to these questions, but focuses around these areas of science and knowledge, which have found their use in the proposed concept "Benchmarking Collaborative Network."

BCN concept has been presented in detail in Chaps. 3–5, starting from the method of competitiveness analysis (Chap. 3), through its use in the group of SMEs (Chap. 4), to ensuring its proper implementation through the coordination of the activities in the group (Chap. 5). BCN is described in three areas:

- The analytical—responding to the question of which analytical methods support the development of SME competitiveness strategy, taking into account the shortcomings of the knowledge and skills of their users?
- The technological—responding to the question of how to ensure the availability of such technology and tools of analysis and reporting which are the best for implementing the objectives of the analytical perspective?
- The organizational—corresponding to the question of how to ensure the possibility of achieving the objectives of the analytical and technological perspective and achieve high efficiency in the case of SMEs' limitations?

In summary, the BCN conception, starting from the model and the method of the competitive strategy, also proposes specific methods to implement these solutions in the situation of limitations in knowledge, skills, financial resources, and human resources. This does not mean that the BCN conception proposes unrealistic solutions. Its use is associated with acceptance of collective action, cooperation, and acceptance of responsibility for the results of this cooperation. It is also associated with specific financial burdens which, however, are significantly smaller than in functioning alone. Usability of BCNs has been verified in research groups of

SMEs dental clinics' functioning in a highly competitive and dynamic market. This verification gave as many answers as asking the next questions. Therefore, the proposal presented in Chaps. 3–5 is also an invitation to a discussion of the benefits and risks posed by collaboration between companies, especially being SMEs.

A summary of these elements is in Chap. 6. It also shows the wider context of the application of BCN, which, although designed for SMEs, does not preclude the use of other groups. Hence, BCN can and should be treated not as a closed solution, but as an open conception with many opportunities for practical application.

Warsaw, Poland   Katarzyna Rostek
January 2015

Acknowledgment

I want to thank all the individuals and institutions that have supported me during the work on this publication.

First of all, I want to thank my great mentors for having significantly contributed to the creation of this publication in its final form. They are my scientific tutors in the person of Professor Tadeusz Krupa from Warsaw University of Technology, Professor Zbigniew Banaszak from Koszalin University of Technology, and Professor Janusz Zawiła-Niedźwiecki from Warsaw University of Technology.

This work has evolved over several years and the results have been repeatedly discussed at seminars and conferences. I want to thank very much all my colleagues from the Department of Business Informatics at the Faculty of Management in Warsaw University of Technology. All of them accompanied me in my work with great patience and understanding, serving me the substantive support and practical experience. In particular I would like to mention my great tutors and colleagues: Professor Wiesław Kotarba, Professor Grażyna Gierszewska, Professor Ewa Górska, Professor Irena Hejduk, Professor Jerzy Lewandowski, Professor Ryszard Żuber, Professor Tadeusz Waściński, Professor Stanisław Tkaczyk, Professor Tadeusz Grzeszczyk, Ph.D. Eng. Teresa Ostrowska, Ph.D. Eng. Anna Kosieradzka, Ph.D. Eng. Antoni Rakoczy, Ph.D. Lech Gąsiorkiewicz, Ph.D. Jadwiga Chudzicka, and Ph.D. Eng. Michał Krawczyński.

I thank my family, who provided me comfort and convenience during the work. All of them accepted the temporary loss of wife, daughter, and mother for development of this research and science. I hope that their sacrifice and taken time are not wasted.

I also wanted to thank the Ministry of Science and Higher Education, which has enabled me to do research, thanks to the award of a grant for its implementation (i.e., scientific research financed by funds for science in 2009–2011 as a research project).

In the end, I thank all those who were dividing with me their comments and insights at conferences and scientific events. Their conclusions were extremely helpful in designing this book.

Abbreviations and Notations

AHP	Analytical Hierarchical Process
AM1, . . ., AM4	Stages of the BCM method (Arranging Method)
ASTRA	Strategic analysis that allows to specify the behavior of the enterprise as a whole under the impact of a changing environment
B4B	Business for Business initiative (related to the concept of Industry 4.0)
BCG	Benchmarking Collaborative Group
BCM	Benchmarking Collaborative Method
BCN	Benchmarking Collaborative Network
BI	Business Intelligence
BPM	Business Process Management
BSI	Broker of Strategic Information
CBSI	Contract of Brokering Strategic Information
CC	Cloud Computing
CM1, . . ., CM5	Stages of the MBSI method (Coordinating Method)
DBI	Dedicated Business Intelligence
FHRPM	Fuzzy Hierarchical-Regression Prototyping Method
FPM1, . . ., FPM4	Stages of the FHRPM method (Fuzzy Prototyping Method)
HMDP	Hierarchical Model of Decision Problem
HRPM	Hierarchical-Regression Prototyping Method
IM1, . . ., IM5	Stages of the DBI implementation method (Implementing Method)
MBCN	Model of Benchmarking Collaborative Network
MBSI	Method of Brokering Strategic Information
OECD	Organization for Economic Cooperation and Development
PM1, . . ., PM4	Stages of the HRPM method (Prototyping Method)
ROI	Return On Investment
SME	Small and Medium-Sized Enterprises
SPACE	Analysis matrix of Strategic Position and Action Evaluation

SWOT	Analysis of Strengths, Weaknesses, Opportunities and Threats
α	The confidence level of the research sample
β	The value of the regression coefficient
γ	The confidence interval of the research sample
δ	The threshold value in the decision tree node
ε	The random component in the regression model
ϕ	The significance of the explanatory variable in the regression model
λ	The significance level
μ	The membership function specifying observation's affiliation to a child of decision tree node
η	The population fraction possessing the analyzed characteristic in the research sample
A_k	The kth judgment matrix
$a_k(i,j)$	The degree of importance of the ith element in the relation to the jth element in terms of their impact on the kth element in the judgment matrix
$\hat{A}_{kk}$	The kth fuzzy judgment matrix
$\hat{a}_k(l, m, u)$	l is the lower limit, u is the upper limit and m is the most likely value of importance of the kth element in the fuzzy judgment matrix
C_i	The ith model (competitiveness) criteria
c_i	The value of ith model (competitiveness) criteria
d	The maximum permissible error of measurement
EN	The entropy function value of the decision tree node
F	The F-test statistic
f_k	The certainty degree of the kth decision variant
G_i	The ith intermediate goal
g_i	The value of the ith intermediate goal
G_s	The main goal
g_s	The value of the main goal
H_0	The null hypothesis
l	Lower
n	The sample size (the observations number)
NV	The non-standardized value of the judgment vector
O_{ij}	The ith observation in the jth tree node
o_{ij}	The value of the ith observation in the jth tree node
Q_i	The ith quartile
p	The value of the probability function
$Profit_{avg}$	The average profit value (the main goal in HMDP)
p-value	The test statistic used for testing significance of the null hypothesis
$\hat{R}_k$	The kth fuzzy priority vector
$\hat{r}_k$	The value of the kth fuzzy priority vector
R^2	The R-squared statistic

S_i	The ith strategy variant
SE	The mean square error
SV	The standardized value of the judgment vector
t_i	The ith time unit
TS	The Student's t-test statistic
TT	The test splitting the observations set in the tree node
u	Upper value
V_i	The ith decision variant (the competitive strategy)
V_s	The selected strategy variant (the implementing variant)
W_i	The ith company (clinic)
w_k	The weight of the element is calculated in relation to kth element
$\hat{w}_k$	The fuzzy weight is calculated in relation to kth element
X_i	The ith explanatory variables (independent variables) in the regression model
x_i	The value of the ith explanatory variables (independent variables) in the regression model
Y	The response variable (dependent variable) in the regression model
y	The value of the response variable (dependent variable) in the regression model
Z	A set of constraints (factors that constrain the variants of competitive strategy)
z_i	The value of ith constraint

Contents

1 SMEs and Competitiveness: Facts and Challenges 1
  1.1 Competitiveness: Definition and Evolution 2
  1.2 Competitive Strategy 5
  1.3 Model of Competitiveness 10
  1.4 Methods of Competitive Analysis 15
  1.5 Summarizing: SMEs Significance and Limitations 19
  References 22

2 New Approaches in Supporting to SMEs Competitiveness 29
  2.1 Collaboration and Coopetition 30
  2.2 Benchmarking 33
  2.3 Brokering and Crowdsourcing 37
  2.4 Business Intelligence Technology 41
      2.4.1 Technological Framework 41
      2.4.2 Business Process Management via Business
            Intelligence 44
      2.4.3 In-Memory Analytics 45
      2.4.4 Big Data and MapReduce Model 46
      2.4.5 Cloud Computing 47
  2.5 Trust and Risk Management 48
  2.6 Summarizing: Concept of Benchmarking Collaborative
      Network 51
  References 52

3 Prototyping Competitive Strategy 59
  3.1 Hierarchical Model of Decision Problem 61
  3.2 Hierarchical-Regression Prototyping Method 63
      3.2.1 PM1: Identification of the Competitiveness Criteria 63
      3.2.2 PM2: Selecting the Key Competitiveness Criteria 65
      3.2.3 PM3: Prototyping the Competitive Strategy Variants . . . 68
      3.2.4 PM4: Prioritizing the Competitive Strategy Variants . . . 70
      3.2.5 Summarizing the HRPM Method 72

3.3   Crisp Method: Case Study and Utilities Verification   72
       3.3.1   Step 1: Quantitative Research   72
       3.3.2   Step 2: Research Experiment   73
       3.3.3   The HMDP Model   73
       3.3.4   PM1: Identification of the Competitiveness Criteria   74
       3.3.5   PM2: Selecting the Key Competitiveness Criteria   74
       3.3.6   PM3: Prototyping the Competitive Strategy Variants . . .   76
       3.3.7   PM4: Prioritizing the Competitive Strategy Variants . . .   77
       3.3.8   Verification of HRPM's Utility   79
       3.3.9   Example 1: The Case of Clinic W09   79
       3.3.10   Example 2: The Case of Clinic W03   81
3.4   Summarizing   83
3.5   Fuzzy Hierarchical-Regression Prototyping Method   83
       3.5.1   FPM3: Prototyping the Competitive Strategy Variants
                with Fuzzy Prototyping Goal Value   84
       3.5.2   FPM4: Prioritizing the Competitive Strategy Variants
                with Fuzzy Prototyping Goal Value   85
3.6   Fuzzy Method: Case Study and Utilities Verification   87
       3.6.1   FPM1: Identification of the Competitiveness Criteria . . .   87
       3.6.2   FPM2: Selecting the Key Competitiveness Criteria   87
       3.6.3   FPM3: Prototyping the Competitive Strategy Variants
                with Fuzzy Prototyping Goal Value   87
       3.6.4   FPM4: Prioritizing the Competitive Strategy Variants
                with Fuzzy Prototyping Goal Value   91
3.7   Summarizing: How to Effectively Implement Analytical
       Method?   93
References   94

4   Arranging Benchmarking Collaborative Group   99
4.1   Benchmarking Collaborative Paradigm   100
4.2   Benchmarking Collaborative Method   101
       4.2.1   AM1: Creating the Benchmarking Collaborative
                Group   102
       4.2.2   AM2: Providing the Technology Platform   104
       4.2.3   AM3: Supplying the Source Data   105
       4.2.4   AM4: Providing the Strategic Information   107
4.3   Benchmarking Collaboration: Case Study and Utilities
       Verification   109
       4.3.1   AM1: Creating the Benchmarking Collaborative
                Group   109
       4.3.2   AM2: Providing the Technology Platform   111
       4.3.3   AM3: Supplying the Source Data   115
       4.3.4   AM4: Providing the Strategic Information   118
       4.3.5   Summarizing the BCM Method   121
4.4   Summarizing: How to Effectively Coordinate the Group?   122
References   123

5   Coordinating Benchmarking Collaborative Group   125
    5.1   Model of Benchmarking Collaborative Network   125
    5.2   Method of Brokering Strategic Information   127
            5.2.1   CM1: Arranging the Benchmarking Collaborative
                      Group   128
            5.2.2   CM2: Signing the Contract   129
            5.2.3   CM3: Implementing the DBI System   130
            5.2.4   CM4: Delivering the Services   133
            5.2.5   CM5: Is a Required Change Possible?   134
            5.2.6   STOP: When Is the Time for Termination of
                      Collaboration?   136
    5.3   Brokering Strategic Information: Case Study and Utilities
            Veryfication   136
            5.3.1   CM1: Arranging the Benchmarking Collaborative
                      Group   136
            5.3.2   CM2: Signing the Contract   137
            5.3.3   CM3: Implementing the DBI System   137
            5.3.4   CM4: Delivering the Services   139
            5.3.5   CM5: Finalization of the Experiment   140
    References   140

6   Benchmarking Collaborative Network: Summarizing   141
    References   144

Annex 1. Results of the Survey   145

Annex 2. Results of the Analysis   151

Bibliography   165

Index   167

Chapter 1
SMEs and Competitiveness: Facts and Challenges

There are many known definitions of competitiveness. Both the understanding of this concept and references to management practices evolve over time and in the current socio-economic situation. Although a common definition of competitiveness does not exist, it is possible to identify certain constant features of the competitiveness phenomenon, which are (Gunasekaran et al. 2011; Gu et al. 2012; Kasztelan 2014):

- competitive advantages measured by achieved benefits;
- concerns motivating companies to more efficient actions;
- a lack of space for all the competing enterprises in the market and as consequent consequence:

  - selection (and elimination) of enterprises in the market;
  - enterprise adaptation to changing market conditions.

The first three features are essential determinants of the rivalry mechanism in the competing process—you must strive to be much better, because the market has a limited capacity and not everyone can succeed within it. As a consequence, it is obvious that either an enterprise will obtain a competitive advantage at a level that will allow it to stay on the market, or it will be eliminated (the first consequence from the third competitiveness feature).

The question therefore arises, is there any alternative for this type of brutal rivalry? This is the final point of the competitiveness list—adaptation which provides flexibility to changing market conditions, taking into account the constant deepening knowledge about the market and its requirements, and (as a last resort) also changing the industry. Implementation of this feature requires the involvement of the organizational, technical and analytic potential in the range, which will be presented in next chapters. It is a challenge for today's enterprises and also a chance for achieving sustainable development.

The condition for effective competitiveness is the ability to understand what it is and what impact it will have. Therefore the content of this chapter is to characterize

© Springer International Publishing Switzerland 2015
K. Rostek, *Benchmarking Collaborative Networks*, Contributions to Management
Science, DOI 10.1007/978-3-319-16736-7_1

the concept and to determine methods supporting the enterprises competitiveness in the market (Sects. 1.1–1.4). A summary of the chapter is to identify the typical situation of SMEs trying to survive in the market, having to deal with the ever-increasing dominance of larger, wealthier, better organised and technologically advanced companies (Sect. 1.5). It leads to the conclusion that there is still a gap between the abilities and needs in supporting SMEs and their competitiveness. Hence it is reasonable to search for new methods to meet these needs.

1.1 Competitiveness: Definition and Evolution

Due to its complexity, competitiveness is defined in different ways. These definitions represent the multidimensional development of the concept, progressing with the advancement of science and technology, as well as the increasing level of globalization of businesses, economies and nations. Many researchers claim that the lack of agreement and ambiguity in the definition makes it difficult to effectively support and develop a competitive strategy (Krugman 1994; Anca 2012). Hence the ordering of concepts, classifications and their understanding is one of the major challenges of modern management science.

The subject of competitiveness in relation to rival economic and social players was discussed previously in the eighteenth and nineteenth centuries by the classicists of economics, such as A. Smith (Smith 1776), T. Mathus (Mathus 1798), D. Ricardo (Ricardo 1817), J. S. Mill (Mill 1848).

In the mid-twentieth century, the Harvard School acknowledged that competitive advantage depends mainly on the size of financial and tangible capital (Bain 1956; Mason 1949–1957). It is only to a small extent that it is conditioned by the efficiency and innovativeness of activities.

However, the Chicago School demonstrated that the theories of the Harvard School were not entirely accurate, pointing to business effectiveness as a major determinant of the benefits achieved by enterprises (Bork 1978; Demsetz 1973, 1974, 1979, 1982).

The Evolutionary School has shown that one cannot shape competitiveness in one country without paying attention to the actions of markets in other countries (Thurow 2000). Hence, the Evolutionary School assumed a liberal approach to domestic enterprises and a very restrictive one to foreign entities.

The Ultra-Liberal School pointed out that a state monopoly is harmful for the economy (Armentano 1982). Just as damaging is the artificial suppression of concentration processes by governmental entities. Due to there being natural limits to the expansion of a company, which naturally refrain economic entities from excessive concentration, which generates higher costs than benefits.

In parallel, theories of strategic management were developed. These showed that achieving a competitive advantage is a necessity and requirement for survival. Also the sources of the competitive advantage must be sought in the improving of the individual components of the competitive strategy. Of this group of theories, the following should be highlighted: hypercompetition (D'Aveni 1994; Lee et al. 2010; Kriz et al. 2014), judo (Bowden 2003; Gimeno 2004), or hardball theory (Stalk et al. 2004; Baarslag et al. 2011; Hauptmeir and Greer 2012).

There are currently different theories and approaches being developed that take into account the globalization of economies, the escalation of their deregulation and privatization, acceleration of the development of technologies, also as sovereignty and the dominant role of the consumer. This research has lead to classifying the evaluation and measuring models of competitiveness in two perspectives—micro and macro (Cellino and Soci 2002; Chikan 2008). The micro perspective refers to enterprise competitiveness. The macro perspective means regional and national competitiveness. These perspectives are not separable in a global economy. The subject of research is the relationship existing between them and defining the mutual strength and impact on the results (Fanelli 2003; Herciu and Ogrean 2008).

It has been shown that an increase in the competitiveness of SMEs affects the growth of competitiveness of the economy (Jeppesen 2005; Singh et al. 2008, 2009; Mesquita and Lazzarini 2010). From this follows that SMEs are a group linking micro and macro perspectives. This reinforces the validity of addressing the subject of supporting the competitiveness of SMEs.

In summary historical research concerning the evolution of the concept of competitiveness should be viewed as consisting of four basic elements (Garelli 2012): (1) objectives, (2) resources, (3) choice and (4) efficiency (Fig. 1.1).

Objectives (Fig. 1.1) indicate that competitiveness is not an objective in itself, but a means used to achieve the desired position in the market, to develop the expected margin of profit, the acquisition of a new group of customers, etc. Just as perceived competitiveness may contribute to the actual development of the enterprise (Porter 1987; Yusuf et al. 2004).

Choice (Fig. 1.1) is associated with the fact that competitiveness objectives are achieved thanks to decisions undertaken by the enterprise (Wagner and Schaltegger 2004; Li et al. 2010). Thus competitiveness is the ability to make the right choices and rational decisions, leading to the achievement of the objectives at the intended level and in a timely manner.

Resources (Fig. 1.1) determine and limit the scope and flexibility of decision-making. Their availability and sufficiency is an indispensable aspect of the activities effectiveness that will be implemented as a result of the undertaken decision (Barney 2001; Peng 2001).

Efficiency (Fig. 1.1) is a basic feature identified with the competitiveness concept. It is defined as the ability to operate in a better, more efficient, more

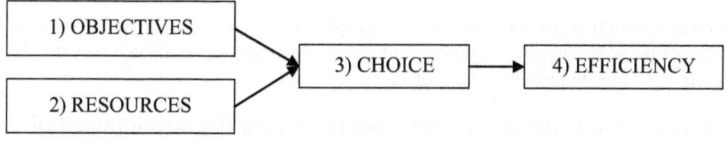

Fig. 1.1 The structure of competitiveness (*source*: own research)

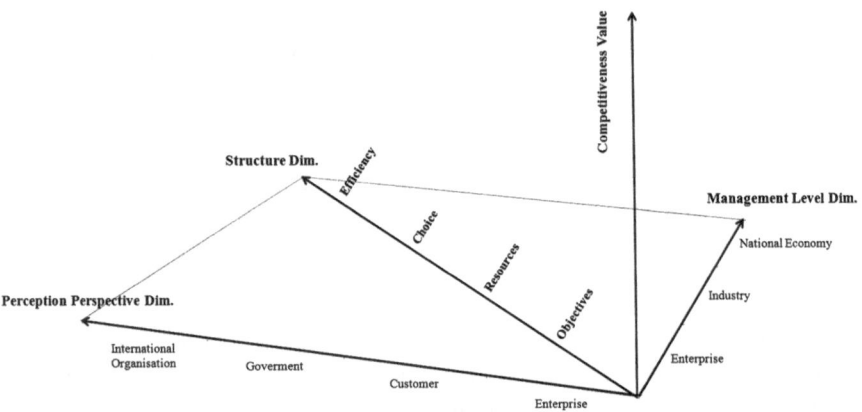

Fig. 1.2 The dimensions of competitiveness definition (*source*: own research)

flexible, or more effective manner as compared to others (Tongzon and Heng 2005; Porter 2011). Efficiency is not a casual occurrence, but the result of skilfully defining the purpose, obtaining adequate resources and making appropriate decisions that lead to the implementation of this purpose.

Such an understanding of competitiveness is referred to at different levels of management (including micro, mezzo and macro levels)—from the company, by industry, up to whole economies and nations. It can also be seen from many different perception and interest perspectives: business, client (receiver), government and international organizations (Fig. 1.2).

In this publication the emphasis is at the lowest level i.e. on the enterprise competitiveness, both in relation to the management level, as well as the perception perspective. From these assumptions it can be implied that the proposed definition of the competitiveness, taking into account its multidimensional structure, should be as follows:

> Competitiveness is the high effectiveness of taken actions, achieved by making the right choices in the area of defining purposes, selecting implementation methods and providing required resources.

Summarizing the evolution of the competitiveness theory indicates the desire to release the global market and lead to a situation where all entities will have the same rights and conditions of competition. As apparent from the definition of the concept of competitiveness, achieving this goal will not be possible without adequate resources and conditions for its implementation. This can be expressed by the following thesis:

> Improving competitiveness requires access to sufficient resources, skills and knowledge in order to define goals, acquire resources and rationally make decisions in a way that leads to obtaining the expected effectiveness of these activities.

Acceptance of this thesis was the main reason for the development of the BCN concept, as an alternative method of meeting the requirements for competitiveness.

1.2   Competitive Strategy

The company, in order to have the ability to compete, must reach the market advantage. In this context the greater importance is strategy planning, which determines the long-term effect of actions, involving the choice of behaviour at the marketplace and to the competitors.

Competitive strategy is a set of moves in the market, which are conscious and thoughtful actions (Barney and Hesterly 2011). This activity is determined by specific structure factors, called competitive criteria. In the resource-based approach, the competitiveness strategy is a set of activities aimed at the development of competitiveness sources i.e. resources, skills and knowledge having decisive impact on the enterprise competitiveness (Pierścionek 2011).

The competitiveness of companies is a property that should determine the process of the formulating competitive strategy (Hitt et al. 2012). It is a cyclical process subjecting to improvement and development over the whole organization lifetime (Fig. 1.3). Its aim is to provide the highest efficiency of decisions and actions aimed at improving competitiveness. This is expressed through a competitive advantage, namely the acquisition of the features that distinguish the enterprise from competitors on the market.

The learning effect in the present cycle is obtained by controlling the efficiency measures of undertaken actions. The basic measure of competitiveness is a competitive position, calculated as a result of competition from one entity in a group of competitors operating in the same market (Porter 1998; Giachetti and Dagnino 2013). This measure expresses the force with which the enterprise is able to interact with their competitors on the market, and therefore also with which it can to shape and to influence on the market. Therefore the main objective of the strategy of

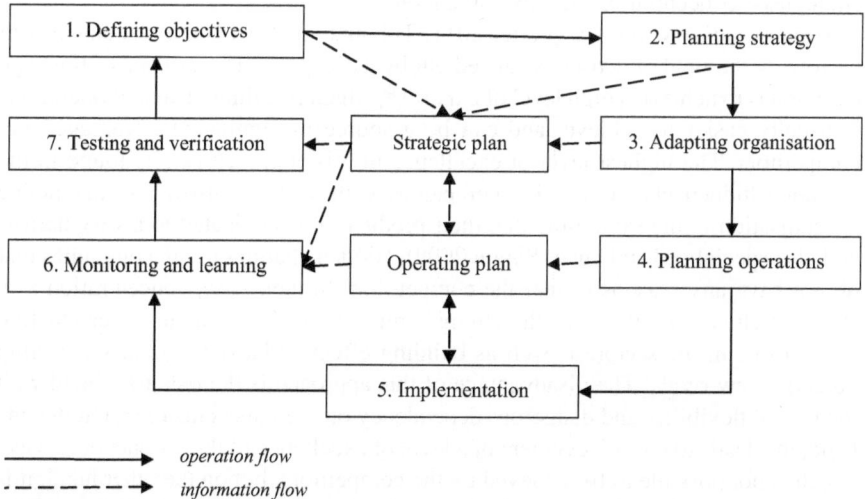

Fig. 1.3 The strategy formulation process [*source*: (Kaplan and Norton 2008)]

Fig. 1.4 Types of
competitive strategy
(*source*: own research)

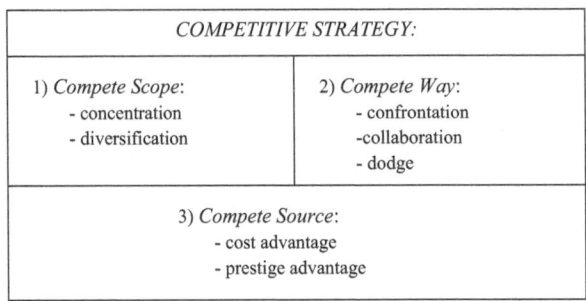

COMPETITIVE STRATEGY:	
1) *Compete Scope*: - concentration - diversification	2) *Compete Way*: - confrontation -collaboration - dodge
3) *Compete Source*: - cost advantage - prestige advantage	

competitiveness development is to provide a plan of action what, with high probability, with well-known constraints and in assumed time, will achieve the expected competitive position.

The strategy effectiveness is a measure of efficiency of such decision making, which form this strategy. The basic outcomes of decisions making up the competitive strategy relate to the three main planes of strategic choice (Porter 1998, 2011) (Fig. 1.4):

- the field of competitive actions—that is the Compete Scope;
- the type of relationship with competitors—that is the answer how to compete, i.e. the Compete Way;
- the source of competitive advantage—that is the characteristics of this what is the compete strength, i.e. the Compete Source.

First plane—*The Compete Scope* (Fig. 1.4) concerns the field of competitive activities of enterprises. It means the same as the conception understood as a market, product, area and scope of activities. In this area, there are two basic strategies—concentration and diversification.

Concentration strategies (Porter 2011; Toh and Kim 2013) are associated with narrowing the field of activities carried out by a company. The essence of this type of action is to achieve a high level of expertise, which in a limited area of operations is usually easier to achieve, and can be a source of significant advantage over competitors. The highest level of excellence in this approach can be found in the so-called hidden champions, i.e. companies with such a narrow and distinctive specialisation at the same time that their production is dedicated to a very narrow and also specialised audience (Simon 2009). Hidden champions are companies that do not have any reasons to fear the competition. In their case, concentration as a strategic choice is related to the strengthening of one's advantage over existing competitors in the sector, as well as building effective barriers of entry deterring potential new rivals. The disadvantage of this approach is the risk associated with the loss of flexibility and dangerous dependency on their specialisation. On the one hand, this leads to the achievement of a level of excellence of the product or service, which is not possible to be achieved by the competitors, but on the other hand, it is easier to become a victim of substitution production, which floods the market today.

Diversification strategies (Bobillo et al. 2010; Liu and Hsu 2011) lead to the expansion of the field of activities by entering new markets and new areas of production. These strategies can be implemented through the development of markets, products and transferring previously acquired skills and accumulated potential to new areas, related to the present ones. They may also take the form of expansion into entirely new markets, not related to the current activities of the company. They favour flexible matching to the needs and expectations of the market. There are, however, certain risks associated with them as well. The threat lies in excessive diversification, the wide range of activities of which hinders both the efficient management on the whole, as well as achieving the necessary level of excellence in their respective fields. A company that operates in a wide variety of areas may gradually lose the effect of internal synergy. It will become increasingly difficult then to utilize the experience and coordinate the allocation of resources. As a result, the company may lose the consistency of its actions, which significantly complicates the implementation of the process of competitiveness management, and above all increases the threat of the competition's efficient functioning.

Second plane—*The Compete Way* (Fig. 1.4) contains the definition of the relationship in relation to competitors. It includes three possible variants of these relationships: confrontation, collaboration and dodge.

Confrontation strategies (Makadok 2010; Adler 2011) represent the concept of business development at the expense of its competitors. Their goal is to defeat the opponent. In an extreme case it leads to the total annihilation and acquisitions of the market in which they operated. The milder form of its aim is to stop the expansion of an opponent or to weaken their position in the market. Aggressive competitive actions have many weaknesses and limitations. Contrary to appearances, not only the defeated competitor suffers the consequences of his defeat. Price and marketing competition often happens to be equally devastating for all competitors. As a consequence, it may lead to facilitating the entry of those competitors who, while not taking part in the competition, did not lose strength and resources. Therefore, all confrontational projects should be treated with caution, preparing them carefully and while in each case assessing the risks and consequences resulting there from.

Collaboration strategies (Allred et al. 2011; Huxham and Vangen 2013) rely on resigning from confrontational attitudes in order to compatibly interact with competitors. Good cooperation can bring synergy, expanding the individual benefits of each of the parties by the results of joint ventures. In this way, you can enhance the competitive position, even to the next, as yet unknown rivals, thus increasing the chance of an effective fight against them and laying the foundation for expansion. The effects of the dissemination of cooperation and overcoming resistance to it are more and more visible in the modern economy. In a growing number of industries and branches of industry the traditional competitive struggle is disappearing, oligopolistic structures are formed, agreements, cooperation networks that eliminate destructive competition. Note, however, that cooperation with competitors is not always beneficial. It may lead to a situation when the partners of the alliance will lose the motivation for aggressive (and disruptive in their nature) and risky development projects. They can become vulnerable to the activities of enterprises with less potential for development, but gaining competitive advantage due to their determination. The danger of cooperation is also linked to the need to open up information and the resources to a partner, never being sure about the durability and effectiveness of joint activities, and even the intents of the ally. This could jeopardize the company's competitive position, depriving it of the specific advantages arising from knowledge or skills. Sometimes corporate identity can be compromised, forced to adapt to the needs and requirements of the partner. However, it appears that in light of current research, this field of competitiveness, particularly in relation to SMEs, is the most promising. Thus, Sect. 2.1—*Collaboration and competition* was devoted to the issues of opportunities of competitive cooperation.

Dodge strategies (Porter 2011) are based on a conscious and planned avoidance of confrontation with a rival, not to provoke him to behave aggressively. It is also the search for safe existence conditions next to the competitor, usually in the immediate vicinity. The classic way to implement this dodging strategy is the self-limitation of the company. It is based on the deterrence of expansion, the resignation from entering the competitors' market, and even regression from markets of particular importance to the competitor; everything and anything in order to protect the company from unwanted confrontation. Evasive strategies are certainly convenient and cheap, but in spite of the submission of security over development, they constitute a real threat. The potential benefits of reducing spending on confrontational activities and reducing the risk of expansive growth is offset by passive strategic posture. If self-restraint will become the norm among strategic actions, then it will significantly hinder, and in extreme cases, prevent the development of the company. Tractability and passive strategy may prove to be serious errors in circumstances where the increasing number of competitors reveal expansive posture and as such can eliminate an operator from the market.

Third plane—*The Compete Source* (Fig. 1.4) relates to the identification of what the company can compete with, that is—the dominant competitive advantages. Competitive advantage applies to companies in respect of which it is intended to act in a confrontational manner. Two basic categories of prestige and cost advantage strategies are highlighted here.

Cost advantage strategies (Chevalier-Roignant and Trigeorgis 2011; Porter 2011) are also called the lowest unit cost strategies. This means that the condition for success is to offer the lowest cost per unit of a product/service in the sector and competitive on the market. Manufacturers who do best in reducing cost are able to effectively prevent their competitors from succeeding. Implementation of this strategy is usually associated with massification of production. Economies of scale are the simplest and often the only way to significantly reduce unit costs. This strategy is beneficial for those who use it skilfully. However, it is connected with high risk. Investment involvement typical of it can bring disaster to a company that loses price competition with another mass producer. Failure to achieve expected sales will not balance the expenditure, threatening the survival of the business. Another threat to this strategy is to change the preferences and purchasing power of customers. Societies that become increasingly richer often turn away from standard and low-cost products to more individualized products. Any change in the trend, style, or technology carries with it the rejection of products that do not fit in these changes. Not noticing such situation or the inability to fund it may result in a disaster.

Prestige advantage strategies (Keller et al. 2011; Kapferer 2012) are denoted in literature by various terms, such as: quality leadership strategy, the advantage of brand and reputation, the strategy of differentiation. The essence of this strategy is the diversity and uniqueness of the company and its products that preferably differentiate the company from all its competitors. In this way the recognition of customers for the product is gained, and consequently his loyalty to the brand of the company is proven. Uniqueness and distinctiveness of a company's market position can be shaped in various ways. The most effective way is to produce high quality products. Their competitive durability and reliability, as well as sophisticated form may be the main ways to create a specific company's prestige. It most involves also a high level of the product's modernity in the field of technology and materials used, as well as its attractive appearance. It should be recognized that not only the product itself determines the prestige of the company, but also the way to promote or distribute it. Hence, so much emphasis is placed on the development of effective forms of marketing and expanding sales and distribution channels. Today's customer is much more demanding in this respect than he was 10–15 years ago. The reputation of the company may also be based on other grounds, for example, on the availability and accuracy of customer service, timely execution of orders, or the efficiency and reliability of service. In practice, usually a lot of the above elements are combined in strategies that fight for the prestige of the company, leading to the creation of a composition that is unique and difficult to copy.

Prestige advantage strategies offer significant benefits with a much more solid basis for other types of strategies. The position of the most reputable manufacturer in the sector allows winners to freely establish margins of profit for their products, thereby achieving high profits even with a reduced production scale. Customers of such a company, unless the product or service does not meet their high standards, are loyal, and the bond with them remains stable. This does not mean, however, that this type of strategy is devoid of risk. Significant threat to the prestige advantage strategy can be encountered in the form of a rather common tendency of customers turning away from brand-name products. Fashion for unbranded products appears especially in those sectors where the producers of standard products effectively improve the quality and level of innovation, and in turn the manufacturers of branded products do not attach importance to their costs. A high price spread loses its justification compared to not so significant difference in quality. Thus, the leading brand strategy is a concept of competitive struggle that does not relieve the producer from watchful observation of trends and changes that occur in the market for both the customers and for producers.

Strategic choices in each of these planes are not separable. There is an obvious link between selecting the area to compete in, the concept of arranging relations with rivals and selecting factors used in competitive activities. They should be arranged in a logically coherent whole, strengthening and complementing each other. Possible combinations of selected solutions out of individual components of competitive strategy can be very diverse, creating a hybrid approach (Claver-Cortés et al. 2012). Each time you should refer them to the specific conditions of the functioning and development of a given company and the characteristics of the competitive market, which will determine the appropriate set of the solutions comprising the right competition strategy.

The basic condition for formulating competitive strategy is to understand the relationship between available resources, capabilities, competitive advantage and its cost effectiveness. It is also very important to understand the mechanisms by which this advantage could be maintained for a long time. This requires such an approach to the strategy development that would enable to the identification and use of the unique features of the enterprise in conducted business, the key competitiveness criteria and to determine their effect on the value of competitive position. This includes taking into account the three basic strategy planes (Fig. 1.4), as well as the key forces of competition which are by M. E. Porter (Fig. 1.5): the intensity of the interaction between competitors, bargaining power of suppliers and buyers, threats of new entrants and substitute products or services.

Strategy development model (Fig. 1.3) is based on the assumption that the primary competitive advantage of the company is accompanied by specific competitive position. The development and implementation of specific strategies affect the position of the company in relation to other market participants. In the long run this would change the competitive advantage, which in turn causes a need to reformulate strategies yet again. This implies the question, in which direction this reformulation should follow in order to maximize the desired effect and minimize the associated risks. Answering this question requires to define the model and to identify the methods supporting the use of this model.

1.3 Model of Competitiveness

The purpose of modelling is to identify those elements which have a decisive impact on the competitiveness of the company and identify the relationships between them. Competitiveness is determined based on, and its effectiveness is measured by, the value of the resulting competitive advantage. The most common and most cited competitive model in competitive literature is Porter's Five Forces Model (Fig. 1.5).

According to M. Porter (2008), there are five main groups of factors that individually and collectively (as a system of internal and external interactions) make up the value of the company's competitive advantage. They are divided into threats and reinforcements of the company's position. The threats to the current position include the impact of competition, the probability of entry of new market participants and the emergence of cheaper alternatives to offered products and services. Reinforcement of the current position is found in customer purchasing power and the supply power of suppliers cooperating with the entrepreneur.

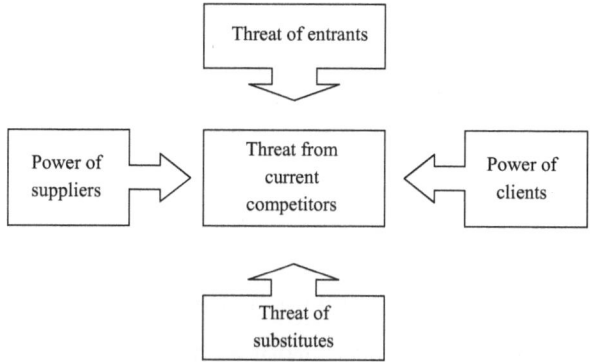

Fig. 1.5 Porter's five competitive forces model [*source*: (Porter 2008)]

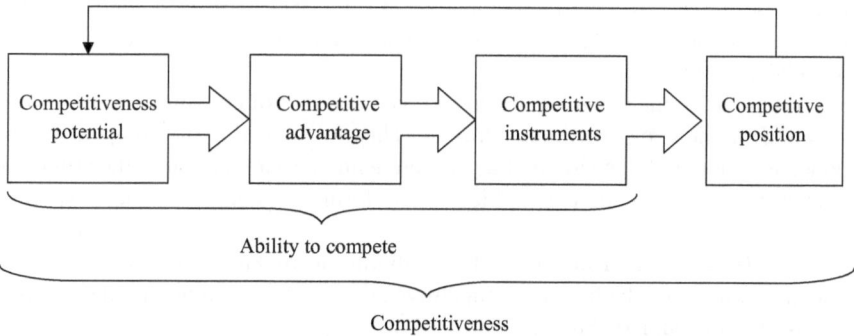

Fig. 1.6 The model of competitiveness development [*source*: (Stankiewicz 2000)]

From the combination of these five elements is created and measured the competitive advantage of the company.

The above-mentioned group of features can be refined by identifying groups of factors that shape competitiveness. One example can be the classification proposed by M.J. Stankiewicz (Stankiewicz 2000), which treats the competitiveness of enterprises as the aggregate of the following four elements (Fig. 1.6): Competitiveness potential, Competitive advantage, Competitive instruments and Competitive position.

Competitiveness potential of the company (Fig. 1.6) denotes the possibility of an efficient operation within the market. It is a system of tangible and intangible resources to enable the enterprise to build competitive advantage.

Gaining *competitive advantage* is the main objective of a company's strategy. Competitive advantage should translate into tangible benefits for the enterprise, such as achieving a greater profit than the average for the industry and to have significant market share.

Competitive instruments are tools and ways to obtain customers and suppliers on terms acceptable to the company, as well as to support the achievement of designated objectives.

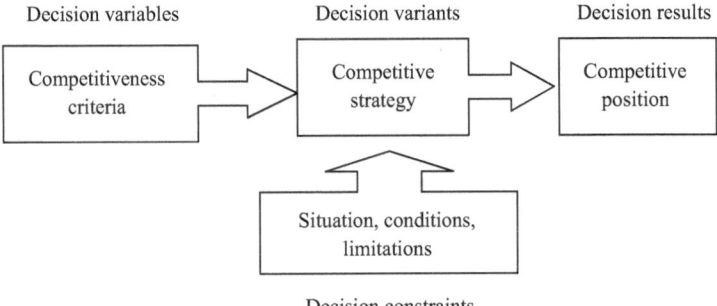

Fig. 1.7 The competitiveness model (*source*: own research)

Competitive position is a result of the assessment by the market (and in particular by the consumers) of what the company can offer. The most basic and synthetic measures of the competitive position of each company is its market share and financial situation.

To summarize the above, it should be noted that part of creating the competitive advantage is the competitiveness strategy. Therefore, treating the competitiveness model as a model of decision-making would define it as a function of the criteria of competitiveness (decision variables) that forms a competitiveness strategy (decision-making capabilities), taking into account the current situation of the company (restrictions decision) and contributing to maximizing the value of the objective function, which is the competitive advantage determined by the competitive position occupied (Fig. 1.7).

This relationship can be included in the form of a decision making model:

$$\text{IF} \quad c_l(z) \leq c \leq c_u(z) \text{ and } v_l(z) \leq v \leq v_u(z) \text{ and } z_l \leq z \leq z_u \tag{1.1}$$
$$\text{THEN} \quad V = f(C, Z)$$

where:

C—a set of decision variables (criteria of competitiveness);
V—decision variants (variants of competitive strategy);
Z—a set of constraints (factors that constrain the variants of competitive strategy);
f—function mapping {C, Z} → V;
l—a lower value;
u—an upper value.

The essence of the model is the right choice for your company's competitive strategy, and the investigation of the relations with a decisive influence on its effectiveness. The establishment of a model requires the definition of criteria for competitiveness (a set of decision variables), the permissible variations decision (selectable variants of competitive strategy) and restrictions affecting the ability to create variants of decision-making.

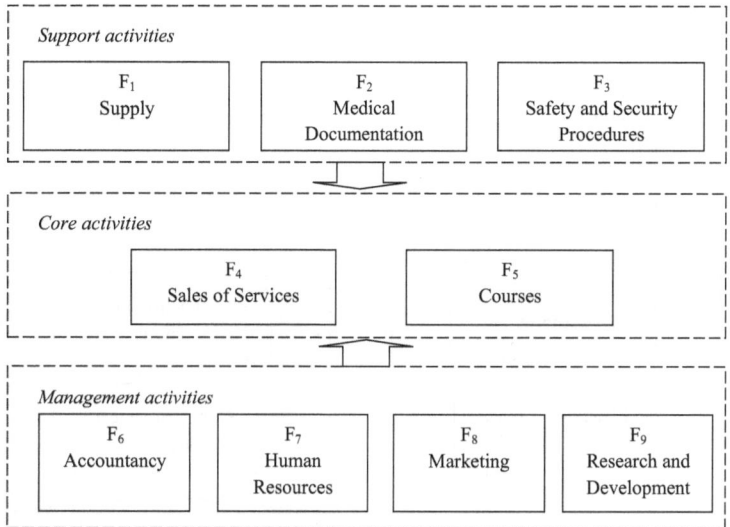

Fig. 1.8 Map of the functional areas at the SME medical industry (*source*: own research)

Proper identification of a set of criteria for competitiveness requires analysing the industry, market and the internal situation of the company. For example, research carried out within the framework of this study, based on analysis of reports on the competitiveness of SMEs (Starczewska-Krzysztoszek 2005, 2006, 2007, 2008a, b, c; Żołnierski and Pyciński 2007; Żołnierski and Zadura-Lichota 2008; Żołnierski 2009; Wilmańska 2010; Walkowska 2010–2011), how Polish medical clinics compete (Mruk 2010) and a detailed analysis of the functioning of the clinics included in the study group (Rostek 2010, 2012, 2014). It should be noted that the clinics analysis was based on the process modelling principles.

The modelling process began in separating functional areas (Fig. 1.8).

For each functional area F_n a characteristic of the set of processes P_{nm} was defined. For example, in area F_1 (*Supply*) the following processes occur:

- P_{11}—*The creation of orders* (for drugs, materials, tools, equipment),
- P_{12}—*The creation of an order* (at the supplier)
- P_{13}—*Realization of delivery.*

The processes are characterized by a set of actions D_{nms}. For example, for the process P_{11} (*The creation of order*) the following actions were highlighted:

- D_{111}—*Collecting the demand for individual products within the group* (drugs, materials, tools, or equipment),
- D_{112}—*Generating aggregate demand* (for drugs, materials, tools, medical equipment).

The degree of completion of each action, and thus the processes are evaluated based on a set of performance indicators W_{nmsw}. For example, the operation of D_{111}

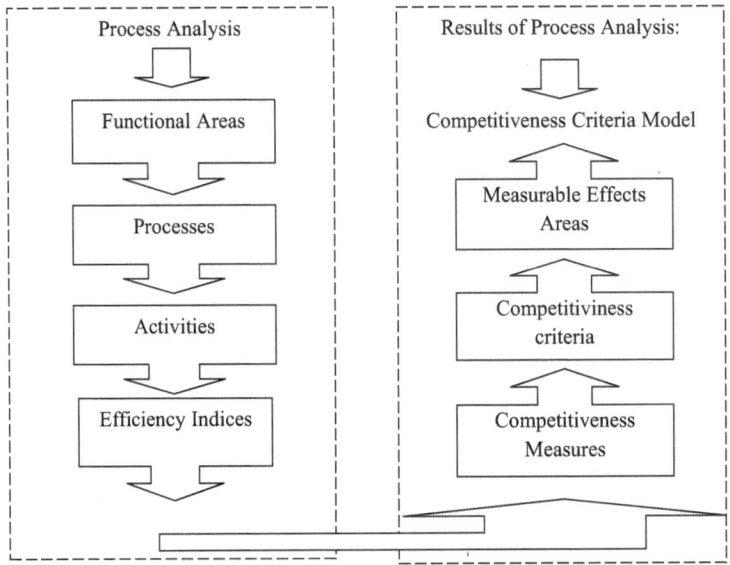

Fig. 1.9 The processes determining method for the structure of competitiveness criteria model (*source*: own research)

(*Collecting the demand for individual products within the group*) is characterized by the following indicators:

– W_{1111}—*Inventory turnover ratio*,
– W_{1112}—*The average size of the demand over a period*,
– W_{1113}—*A prognosis of sales volume of services*.

This creates a reference model of an entity and its analysis allows the identification of areas critical for the competitiveness, processes and activities (competitiveness criteria) and their measures (corresponding to the operation indicators) in accordance with the system presented on Fig. 1.9.

A set of established criteria at different times and with different intensities affect the value of the function to which the competitive position is occupied. Characteristics of this influence, taking into account the interdependencies that exist between the criteria, is used when defining a strategy for competitiveness. Therefore, the deeper understanding of these characteristics generates a greater possibility of a conscious choice for the best strategy of competitiveness. Known and used methods of analysis of competitiveness provide assistance in this matter.

1.4   Methods of Competitive Analysis

Strategic information is a key resource necessary to achieve a competitive advantage (Porter 1985–2011; Kotler 1994). Many researchers point to the need of effective support the SMEs in this field. In their opinion this will condition the possibility of further development for this group in terms of economy internationalisation and globalisation (Ongori and Migiro 2010; Zarębska 2010; Qureshil et al. 2011). The important information for creating a competitive strategy should include:

- competitiveness assessment in relation to other market competitors,
- impact identification and characterization of the factors determining the value of competitive position,
- source areas of competitive advantage potential,
- scenarios to support strategic activities, supporting the achievement and maintaining the expected competitive position.

All the above information is generated in the analytical processing of this data, which is the result of making business and is useful in the development of a competitive strategy. Different methods of competitiveness analysis are used for this purpose. They are carefully selected because of their usefulness in a particular case. The classification of these methods is shown in Fig. 1.10.

Strategic analysis can be defined as identifying current and future developments and trends in the environment of the company and its own potential in order to identify opportunities for its development and future competitive position (Stabryła and Mesjasz 2003). Strategic analysis focuses on the diagnosis of the current situation and projections of future situation. The aim of the diagnosis is to assess the overall situation and the condition of the company and the identification of internal and external conditions that determine the possibility for its development. Projection leads to the definition of feasible options for future strategic solutions. The main objectives of the strategic analysis include mainly (Penc-Pietrzak 2005):

- identification of opportunities and threats generated by the environment in the context of further development of the company,
- detecting malfunctions and their causes,
- self-assessment of the company and the establishment of its place in the market in relation to its main competitors (evaluation of identity and corporate image)
- laying substance and pragmatic foundations to take the necessary measures to boost the company and run the necessary development processes,
- balancing the opportunities and risks inherent in the environment and the strengths and weaknesses of the company in order to define variants of the development strategy and, consequently, management plans and strategies,
- identification of the strengths and weaknesses of the company in terms of the possibility of building a competitive advantage,
- optimisation of the company's portfolio and the overall assessment of the risks associated with different activities,

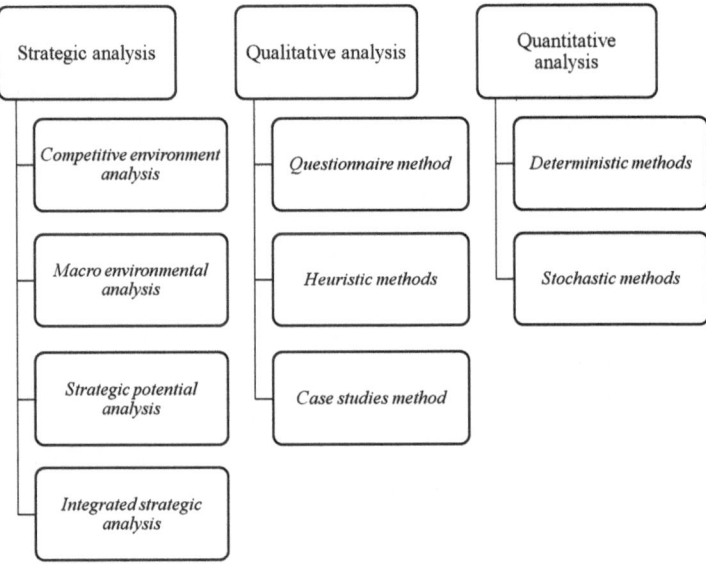

Fig. 1.10 Classification of competitive analysis methods (*source*: own research)

– determining the feasibility of creating added value for customers and other stakeholders.

Strategic analysis covers the three main areas of the company, which are: the macro-environment, the competitive environment and the strategic potential of the company . Thus, strategic analysis uses methods and techniques from the field of these three areas, i.e.:

– *competitive environment analysis* (of the sector): an analysis of Porter's "five strengths", point assessment of the attractiveness of the sector, strategic group map, the curve of experience, benchmarking, strategic segmentation analysis;
– *analysis of the macro-environment*, such as scenario methods, the forecast trend extrapolation, expert evaluation method—the method of Delphi, strategic gap analysis;
– *potential strategic analysis* of the company: analysis of resources, analysis of key success factors, value chain model, product, technology and organisation life cycle, portfolio methods, strategic balance;
– *integrated strategic analysis methods*, which in one research process merge all the problems and solve all the research tasks. These methods are used simultaneously to study macro-environment, the competitive environment and the strategic potential of the company. These methods include: SWOT analysis, ASTRA method, and SPACE analysis.

Qualitative analysis and quantitative analysis are two basic groups of scientific analysis. The difference between the two groups is arbitrary, because although quantitative methods are determined by a positivist reference to the existing facts, whereas qualitative methods by the interpretation of these facts, qualitative interpretation stems from quantitative data analysis and quantitative analysis is pointed by qualitative interpretation of the results. However, this division is maintained, in order to emphasize the dominating importance of either the data analysis, or their contextual interpretation. Instead, their mutual complementary characteristics should be remembered and, therefore, the need for their parallel application in order to obtain results with high business utility.

Qualitative analysis involves a continual interplay between theory and analysis results. In analysing qualitative data it seeks to discover patterns such as dynamic changes over the time or possible causal links between criteria (Patton 2014). Most qualitative research is exploratory, verification or exploratory and verification research. Among these methods are: the questionnaire method, heuristic methods and case studies, among others.

Questionnaire method belongs to a group of prospective survey research methods of heuristic character (Jain et al. 2014). It is used to predict the qualitative and structural processes, including development strategies of companies, sectors and regions. The questionnaire consists of several thematic parts, which form a set of research problems and questions that identify them. It contains closed questions, and is often judged by the respondent according to an adopted scale. It also includes open-ended questions where the respondents, apart from answering, can also express their opinions, make comments and remarks. Questionnaire methodology is often achieved through direct interviews, which should also include CAPI (Computer Assisted Personal Interviewing), used to carry out the tests described in Sect. 3.3.

Heuristic methods are a group of creative thinking methods and creating solutions to the problems of decision-making based on experience and knowledge of experts. These methods use feedback and evaluation of those involved and competent to find the facts and identify the relationships between them, as well as the formulation of judgments and proposed solutions. The heuristic approach to the problem means to awaken the imagination and intuition and focus on the creative elements of the problem currently solved. Dozens of heuristic methods are used. They are classified in the following groups of methods: analytical, based on forced associations, based on free associations, involving the reversal of the point of view, perfect design.

The most popular of the heuristic methods are based on generating collective associations, such as brainstorming (Agarwal et al. 2012) and the Delphi method (Makkonen et al. 2012). They have become the starting point for many other types of methods and techniques, often of hybrid form (e.g. a hybrid method combining SWOT analysis, resource approach and the method of brainstorming (Agarwal et al. 2012)). One of the analytical techniques used widely is the analytical hierarchical process (AHP) developed by an American mathematician T.L. Saaty (Saaty 1996–2001), which combines elements of mathematics and psychology. This technique has been used in the proposed model and the method of analysis of competitiveness, presented in detail in Chap. 3.

Case studies offer an in-depth analysis of the decision problem. It is characterised by rigorous requirements for its realisation, but allows considerable flexibility, especially when it comes to unusual research problems. The science behind the method of the case study is evidenced by objectified, rational, organised, systematic and structured activities, which aim to ensure the reliability of applications (Yin 2014). The most important principle is the triangulation method, in this case understood as extracting data from several independent sources. Using different, independent sources of information should lead to similar (mutually confirming) conclusions. Properly conducted tests on a case study may lead to discoveries that often represent a first step in the process of verification of a theory. The results are also useful in the specification, testing, or creating a new theory (Eisenhardt and Graebner 2007).

Premises leaning to conducting testing on a single case study are the same as in the case of a single experiment. In addition, it is justified when the case is critical from the point of view of the theory, extreme (exceptional), or on the contrary—is typical, visionary, or if the phenomenon is of long-term character (longitudinal). A single case study is desired if the theory on the topic does not exist at all or operates in a specific context, and therefore can be regarded as a pilot study aiming to create an outline of the theory, theoretical assumptions and to prepare the ground for the subsequent examination of a wider range including hypothesis testing (Flyvbjerg 2006).

Developing a theory based on several case studies is considered to be more reliable than on the basis of a single case. The decision to carry out a research by method of multiple case studies should be dictated by the same rationale as the decision to carry out a number of experiments. The other hand, this approach is not used in order to obtain several answers, as in quantitative research. Thus, the scope of the multiple case studies is consistent with the logic of analytical, not statistical, replication. Replication for the needs of a multiple case study can be a literal or theoretical replication. Theoretical replication involves the selection of mutually different cases while a literal selection is based on similar cases. The aim is to provide, respectively—different or very similar conclusions in order to confirm or refute the theory under investigation (Gerring 2007).

Quantitative analysis enables the study of phenomena in an objective and accurate manner based on the analysis of historical data. Therefore, as research shows—quantitative methods are still more prevalent and constitute the majority of published research. Although more and more researchers in this field begin arguing that too much importance attached to the statistical system deprives the researcher of their own imagination and personal responsibility for the presented results and proclaimed theories (Shah and Corley 2006). Quantitative methods are divided into: deterministic and stochastic.

Deterministic methods assume full knowledge of the analysed phenomena and are primarily used in retrospective classification studies. The methods used in this group include: chain substitution, differentiation, rest, cross substitutions, functional, integral (Becker's), logarithmic, partial differences, indicator, or proportional allocation deviations (Kilar's).

Stochastic methods are an essential complement to deterministic methods, because the existence of unpredictable, random factors. By using the achievements of scientific disciplines such as mathematics or statistics, stochastic methods allow for a better understanding of the quantitative relationships in a business process (Gardiner 2009). Among them, the most interesting are the following methods: econometric, taxonomic, additive and discriminatory.

It should be emphasised that qualitative tests are often accompanied by quantitative research, creating a so-called mixed approach, also known as the third paradigm of research (in addition to the quantitative and qualitative paradigm) (Johnson et al. 2008; Teddlie and Tashakkori 2009). Qualitative research preceding quantitative research serves the purpose of easier and more accurate interpretation of the results of quantitative analysis. Quantitative studies assume at the outset any particular theory construct the test on its basis. Thus, prior use of qualitative analysis helps in defining or choosing the correct theory. In turn, qualitative research after quantitative analysis is used to assess the rationality and reliability of the results of this analysis, which increases the security of their future implementation and use.

A multitude of these methods, presented at Fig. 1.10, justifies their aided selection especially for SMEs, which do not have the knowledge, skills and experience in this field. An example aided approach with regards to the choice of competitive analysis is presented in Chaps. 3–5.

1.5 Summarizing: SMEs Significance and Limitations

SMEs are relative terms used to define various small-scale business activities in the formal and informal sectors (Uzor 2011). Therefore there are many definitions that use various quantitative and qualitative criteria.

The quantitative criteria are most commonly used. They define the arbitrary boundaries of small enterprises by showing employment capacity, level of investment capital or sales turnover. The large number of countries set the upper limit of number of employees in the SMEs between 200 and 250, with a few exceptions such as Japan (300 employees) and the USA (500 employees) (OECD 2004). The International Finance Corporation (IFC) classifies SMEs as companies with total assets or sales less than $15 million (IFC 2007). The European Commission (EC) determine a SMEs annual turnover on no more than 50 million euros or an annual balance sheet total on no more than 43 million euros (EC 2005).

The qualitative measures define the functional characteristics of the small enterprises such as the nature of technology, organisation and management skills. The one used by the Bolton Committee regarded firms as small if they satisfied the following three criteria (Bolton Committee 1971):

– they had a relatively small share of their market place;

- they were managed by owners or part-owners in a personalised way and not through a formalised management structure;
- they were independent businesses, in a sense of not forming part of a larger enterprise.

Some other criteria are discusses by Holmes and Gibson (2001):

- management and ownership are rarely separate;
- control over business operations and decisions reside with one or two persons who are usually family members;
- the project's equity is not publicly traded;
- personal security of the owners is required to secure debt acquisition and repayment;
- the level and number of formal contractual relations are kept at a minimum level;
- the personal objectives of the owners guide and influence business decisions directly.

Some institutions and even governments emphasize that standard definitions are useless to them. And this is mainly due to the fact that at the same time they are trying to identify three categories of enterprises (micro, small and medium) with a very large gap in organisation, structure and ways of functioning of the market. Thus, they form other definitions, better adapted and suited to their purposes. One example includes the International Accounting Standards Board's (IASB), which includes to SMEs any company that (IASB 2013):

- has no publicly traded debt or equity;
- does not hold any assets in a fiduciary capacity for other third parties as its main business;
- prepares general purpose financial statements for external users.

Despite the lack of definition and criteria compliance, all researchers agree that SMEs play a key role in transition and developing countries. There is also a growing recognition of the role that SMEs play in sustained global and regional economic recovery (Ayyagari et al. 2007). SMEs typically account for more than 90 % of all firms, constitute a major source of employment and generate significant domestic and export earnings. Empirical studies show that SMEs contribute to over 55 % of GDP and over 65 % of total employment in high-income countries, account for over 60 % of GDP and over 70 % of total employment in low-income countries, while they contribute over 95 % of total employment and about 70 % of GDP in middle-income countries (OECD 2004). It can therefore be assumed that the development of SMEs is one of the most important economic priorities, as evidenced by numerous programs dedicated to regional and international aid.

Despite regular and available support for SMEs in its mass they usually rely for themselves. They must be able to respond quickly and efficiently to market signals to take advantage of trade and investment opportunities and reap the benefits of the trading system. This means they need to be competitive and productive. Effective business support systems are needed to enhance competitiveness and productivity of SMEs (OECD 2004). Wherein conducting research shows that help is needed resulting in long-term and stable change in competitiveness (Ayyagari et al. 2007; Zulkifli-Muhammad et al. 2010; Etuk et al. 2014). The supporting of development competitive strategy leads to such effects.

The effectiveness of competitive strategy, measured by the degree of objectives realisation, depends on the knowledge of the factors determining the competitiveness and the ability to predict the actions undertaken in parallel by the market competitors (Trkman 2010; Zeng et al. 2010). The source of necessary knowledge is the strategic information on the competitiveness assessment of the enterprise and entities from its environment. Obtained through competitive analysis performed on the basis of achieved activities results and compare them to analogical results obtained by competitors. Reaching the information requires access to appropriate financial, organisational, technological and human potential, and the skills to use this potential in the building of competitive strategy. The performed researches show (McAdam and Reid 2001; Kuan and Aspinwall 2005; Salles 2006; Rostek 2010; Bilińska-Reformat 2011; Dziekoński 2011), that SMEs do not have the ability to independently develop the necessary range of strategic information due to lack of:

- knowledge and skills for implementing competitive analysis and using its results to developing a competitive strategy,
- financial, technical, human and organisational resources necessary for the implementation of IT solutions, aiding realization of advanced competitive analysis,
- qualified personnel responsible for handling, maintaining and developing technological solutions, necessary for ensuring the implementation of competitive analysis and the distribution of resulting reports,
- the number of generated and gathered resource of data, which are the powering source for competitive analysis.

Development of a competitiveness strategy in a typical SME company consists of collecting the available results of its performance, preparing them in the form of simple statistical summaries and charts, and on this basis making strategic decisions. This mode of decision-making takes into account only the prospect of the business in question, with a very general knowledge of the market and the actions taken by competitors. Whilst a company's competitiveness is conditioned by this—which products/services and their attributes (like: quality, modernity, diversity, price, availability, delivery time, warranty, specials, discounts) offer in comparison with competitors existing in the common market. This means that the adoption of an appropriate strategy, which guarantees the achievement of competitive advantage, involves the selection of a portfolio of these criteria, within which the company wants and is able to compete.

The answer to the above limitations is competitive cooperation. It is more and more often indicated by the investigator as a useful method to improve the competitiveness of SMEs because it results in (Kirkels and Duysters 2010; Lee et al. 2010):

- increasing competitiveness potential in the range of tangible and intangible resources;
- increasing productivity and innovativeness of enterprises;
- reduction of operating activities costs.

In this context it has been formulated that the main objective of this work as *developing comprehensive approach supporting SMEs in terms of*:

- *identifying the criteria being competitiveness determinants;*
- *prototyping a competitive strategy that will guarantee the achievement of the assumed competitive position;*
- *supporting the implementation of all the above items using modern and the most relevant methods and technologies.*

Realisation of this objective, included in the comprehensive approach— Benchmarking Collaborative Network (BCN), is the contents of the subsequent chapters.

References

Adler, R. W. (2011). Performance management and organizational strategy: How to design systems that meet the needs of confrontation strategy firms. *The British Accounting Review, 43*(4), 251–263.

Agarwal, R., Grassl, W., & Pahl, J. (2012). Meta-SWOT: Introducing a new strategic planning tool. *Journal of Business Strategy, 33*(2), 12–21.

Allred, C. R., Fawcett, S. E., Wallin, C., & Magnan, G. M. (2011). A dynamic collaboration capability as a source of competitive advantage. *Decision Sciences, 42*(1), 129–161.

Anca, H. D. B. (2012). Literature review of the evolution of competitiveness concept. *Annals of the University of Oradea, Economic Science Series, 21*(1), 41–46.

Armentano, D. T. (1982). *Antitrust and monopoly: Anatomy of a policy failure.* New York: John Wiley and Sons.

Ayyagari, M., Beck, T., & Demirguc-Kunt, A. (2007). Small and medium enterprises across the globe. *Small Business Economics, 29*(4), 415–434.

Baarslag, T., Hindriks, K., & Jonker, C. (2011). Towards a quantitative concession-based classification method of negotiation strategies. In D. Kinny, H. J. Yung-Jen, G. Governatori, & A. K. Ghose (Eds.), *Agents in principle, agents in practice* (pp. 143–158). Berlin, Heidelberg: Springer.

Bain, J. (1956). *Barriers to new competition: Their character and consequences in manufacturing.* Cambridge: Harvard University Press.

Barney, J. B. (2001). Resource-based theories of competitive advantage: A ten-year retrospective on the resource-based view. *Journal of Management, 27*(6), 643–650.

Barney, J. B., & Hesterly, W. S. (2011). *Strategic management and competitive advantage* (4th ed.). London: Pearson Education.

Bilińska-Reformat, K. (2011). Marketing audit of a young enterprise. Project as a diagnostic tool of marketing activities of small and medium sized enterprises—Empirical approach. *Research Papers of Wrocław University of Economics, 237*(2011), 315–325.

Bobillo, A. M., López-Iturriaga, F., & Tejerina-Gaite, F. (2010). Firm performance and international diversification: The internal and external competitive advantages. *International Business Review, 19*(6), 607–618.

Bolton Committee. (1971). *Small firms: Report of the Committee of Inquiry on Small Firms.* HMSO, London, Cmnd 4811.

Bork, R. H. (1978). *The antitrust paradox.* New York: Free Press.

Bowden, S. (2003). Kiwi international airlines: Judo strategy and its limits. *Journal of Management & Organization, 9*(2), 1–7.

Cellino, R., & Soci, A. (2002). Pop competitiveness. *BNL Quarterly Review, 55*(220), 71–101.

Chevalier-Roignant, B., & Trigeorgis, L. (2011). *Competitive strategy: Options and games.* Cambridge: MIT Press.

Chikan, A. (2008). National and firm competitiveness: A general research model. *Competitiveness Review, 18*(1/2), 20–28.

Claver-Cortés, E., Pertusa-Ortega, E. M., & Molina-Azorín, J. F. (2012). Characteristics of organizational structure relating to hybrid competitive strategy: Implications for performance. *Journal of Business Research, 65*(7), 993–1002.

D'Aveni, R. (1994). *Hypercompetition.* New York: Free Press.

Demsetz, H. (1973). Industry structure, market rivalry and public policy. *Journal of Law and Economics, 16*(1), 1–9.

Demsetz, H. (1974). Two systems of belief about monopoly. In H. J. Goldschmid, H. M. Mann, & J. F. Weston (Eds.), *Industrial concentration: The new learning* (pp. 164–184). Boston: Little, Brown and Company.

Demsetz, H. (1979). Accounting for advertising as a barrier to entry. *Journal of Business, 52*, 345–360.

Demsetz, H. (1982). *Economic, legal, and political dimensions of competition.* Amsterdam & New York: North Holland.

Dziekoński, K. (2011). Projects in innovative small and medium enterprises. *Economy and Management, 4*(2011), 125–134.

Eisenhardt, K. M., & Graebner, M. E. (2007). Theory building from cases: Opportunities and challenges. *Academy of Management Journal, 50*(1), 25–32.

Etuk, R. U., Etuk, G. R., & Michael, B. (2014). Small and medium scale enterprises (SMEs) and Nigeria's economic development. *Mediterranean Journal of Social Sciences, 5*(7), 656–662.

European Commission. (2005). *The new SME definition. User guide and model declaration. Enterprise and industry publications.* Brussels: European Commission.

Fanelli, J. M. (2003). Micro–macro interactions, competitiveness and sustainability. In A. K. Dutt & J. Ros (Eds.), *Development economics and structuralist macroeconomics.* UK: Edward Elgar Publishing. doi:10.4337/9781781950081.00027.

Flyvbjerg, B. (2006). Five misunderstandings about case-study research. *Qualitative Inquiry, 12* (2), 219–245.

Gardiner, C. (2009). *Stochastic methods. 4th Ed.* A Handbook for the natural and social sciences Series, Vol. 13, Springer Series in Synergetics.

Garelli, S. (2012). The fundamentals and history of competitiveness. *IMD World competitiveness yearbook, 2012*, 492–506.

Gerring, J. (2007). *Case study research. Principles and practices.* Cambridge: Cambridge University Press.

Giachetti, C., & Dagnino, G. B. (2013). Detecting the relationship between competitive intensity and firm product line length: Evidence from the worldwide mobile phone industry. *Strategic Management Journal, 35*, 1398–1409. doi:10.1002/smj.2154.

Gimeno, J. (2004). Playing entrepreneurial Judo: How to compete without a resource advantage. In S. Chowdhury (Ed.), *Next generation business handbook: New strategies from tomorrow's thought leaders.* New York: Wiley.

Gu, Y., Fu, X., & Dou, M. (2012). Research on factors of modern service industry competitiveness in Liaoning province. In *Proceedings of the 2012 3rd International Conference on E-Business and E-Government*-Volume 02, 880–883. IEEE Computer Society.

Gunasekaran, A., Rai, B. K., & Griffin, M. (2011). Resilience and competitiveness of small and medium size enterprises: An empirical research. *International Journal of Production Research, 49*(18), 5489–5509.

Hauptmeir, M., & Greer, I. (2012). Whipsawing: Organizing labor competition in multinational auto companies. In: *International Labor and Employment Relations Association Conference*. 16th World Congress of ILERA, Philadelphia. Url: http://ilera2012.wharton.upenn.edu/ RefereedPapers/ HauptmeierMarco%20IanGreer%20ILERA.pdf.

Herciu, M., & Ogrean, C. (2008). Interrelations between competitiveness and responsibility at macro and micro level. *Management Decision, 46*(8), 1230–1246.

Hitt, M. A., Ireland, R. D., & Hoskisson, R. E. (2012). *Strategic management cases: Competitiveness and globalization* (10th ed.). Mason, OH: Cengage Learning South Western.

Holmes, S., & Gibson, B. (2001). *Definition of small business. Report to the small business coalition.* The University of Newcastle.

Huxham, C., & Vangen, S. (2013). *Managing to collaborate: The theory and practice of collaborative advantage.* London: Routledge.

IASB. (2013). *IFRS for SMEs. A guide for micro-sized entities applying the IFRS for SMEs (2009).* IFRS Foundation.

IFC. (2007). *An integrated annual report.* IFC, World Bank Group.

Jain, B., Adil, G. K., & Ananthakumar, U. (2014). Development of questionnaire to assess manufacturing capability along different decision areas. *The International Journal of Advanced Manufacturing Technology, 71*(9–12), 2091–2105.

Jeppesen, S. (2005). Enhancing competitiveness and securing equitable development: Can small, micro, and medium-sized enterprises (SMEs) do the trick? *Development in Practice, 15*(3–4), 463–474.

Johnson, G., Scholes, K., & Whittington, R. (2008). *Exploring corporate strategy.* Upper Saddle River, NJ: Prentice Hall.

Kapferer, J. N. (2012). *The new strategic brand management: Advanced insights and strategic thinking.* London, UK: Kogan Page Publishers.

Kaplan, R. S., & Norton, D. P. (2008). *The execution premium: Linking strategy to operations for competitive advantage.* Boston, MA: Harvard Business Press.

Kasztelan, A. (2014). A comparative analysis of Lubelskie and Kujawsko-Pomorskie voivodships in the context of environmental competitiveness of regions. *Bulletin of Geography. Socioeconomic Series, 23*, 87–97.

Keller, K. L., Parameswaran, M. G., & Jacob, I. (2011). *Strategic brand management: Building, measuring, and managing brand equity.* Delhi: Pearson Education India.

Kirkels, Y., & Duysters, G. (2010). Brokerage in SME networks. *Research Policy, 39*(3), 375–385.

Kotler, P. (1994). *Marketing management: Analysis, planning, implementation, and control.* Englewood Cliffs: Prentice Hall.

Kriz, A., Voola, R., & Yuksel, U. (2014). The dynamic capability of ambidexterity in hypercompetition: Qualitative insights. *Journal of Strategic Marketing, 22*, 1–13.

Krugman, P. (1994). Competitiveness: A dangerous obsession. *Foreign Affairs, 73*(2), 28–44.

Kuan, Y. W., & Aspinwall, E. (2005). An empirical study of the important factors for knowledge-management adoption in the SME sector. *Journal of Knowledge Management, 9*(3), 64–82.

Lee, C. H., Venkatraman, N., Tanriverdi, H., & Iyer, B. (2010). Complementarity based hypercompetition in the software industry: Theory and empirical test, 1990–2002. *Strategic Management Journal, 31*(13), 1431–1456.

Lee, S., Park, G., Yoon, B., & Park, J. (2010) Open innovation in SMEs—An intermediated network model. *Research Policy, 39*(2), 290–300

Li, Q., Li, X., & Zhou, P. (2010). The strategic choice of core competitiveness in power generating enterprises: Knowledge management. *International Journal of Business and Management, 5*(8), 195–200.

Liu, H. Y., & Hsu, C. W. (2011). Antecedents and consequences of corporate diversification: A dynamic capabilities perspective. *Management Decision, 49*(9), 1510–1534.

Makadok, R. (2010). The interaction effect of rivalry restraint and competitive advantage on profit: Why the whole is less than the sum of the parts. *Management Science, 56*(2), 356–372.

Makkonen, M., Pätäri, S., Jantunen, A., & Viljainen, S. (2012). Competition in the European electricity markets–outcomes of a Delphi study. *Energy Policy, 44*, 431–440.

Mason, E. (1949). The current status of the monopoly problem in the United States. *Harvard Law Review, 62*(8), 1265–1285.

Mason, E. (1957). *Economic concentration and the monopoly problem.* Cambridge: Harvard University Press.

Mathus, T. (1798). An essay on the principle of population. J. Johnson in St. Paul's Church-yard, London.

McAdam, R., & Reid, R. (2001). SME and large organisation perceptions of knowledge management: Comparisons and contrasts. *Journal of knowledge management, 5*(3), 231–241.

Mesquita, L. F., & Lazzarini, S. G. (2010). Horizontal and vertical relationships in developing economies: Implications for SMEs' access to global markets. *New Frontiers in Entrepreneurship, International Studies in Entrepreneurship,* 2010(26) (pp. 31–66). New York: Springer.

Mill, J. S. (1848). *Principles of political economy with some of their applications to social philosophy.* London: Longmans, Green and Co.

Mruk, H. (2010). Sposoby konkurowania gabinetów lekarskich (Ways of compete in medical practices). *Poradnik Stomatologiczny, 10*(3), 106–109.

OECD. (2004). *Promoting SMEs for development.* Proceeding on 2nd OECD conference of ministers responsible for small and medium-sized enterprises (SMEs). Turkey: OECD Publ.

Ongori, H., & Migiro, S. O. (2010). Information and communication technologies adoption in SMEs: Literature review. *Journal of Chinese Entrepreneurship, 2*(1), 93–104.

Patton, M. Q. (2014). *Qualitative research & evaluation methods: Integrating theory and practice* (4th ed.). Thousand Oaks, CA: Sage.

Penc-Pietrzak, I. (2005). The successful strategic planning. *Money and Social Bond, 1*(26), 79–87.

Peng, M. W. (2001). The resource-based view and international business. *Journal of Management, 27*(6), 803–829.

Pierścionek, Z. (2011). *Zarządzanie strategiczne w przedsiębiorstwie (Strategic management in the enterprise).* Warszawa: Wyd Naukowe PWN.

Porter, M. E. (1985). *Competitive advantage: Creating and sustaining superior performance.* London: Collier Macmillan.

Porter, M. E. (1987). From competitive advantage to corporate strategy. *Harvard Business Review, 65*(3).

Porter, M. E. (1998). *Competitive strategy: Techniques for analyzing industries and competitors.* New York: Free Press.

Porter, M. E. (2008). The five competitive forces that shape strategy. *Harvard Business Review, 86* (1), 25–40.

Porter, M. E. (2011). *Competitive advantage of nations: Creating and sustaining superior performance.* New York: Simon and Schuster.

Qureshil, S., Kamal, M., & Wolcott, P. (2011). Information technology interventions for growth and competitiveness in micro-enterprises. *Managing Adaptability, Intervention, and People in Enterprise Information Systems,* 106.

Ricardo, D. (1817). *On the principles of political economy and taxation.* London: John Murray Publ.

Rostek, K. (2010). Business intelligence for SME. In E. Lechman (Ed.), *SMEs and enterpreneurship* (Vol. 2, pp. 164–190). Gdańsk: Gdańsk University of Technology Publishing House.

Rostek, K. (2012). The reference model of competitiveness factors for SME medical sector. *Economic Modelling, 29*(2012), 2039–2048.

Rostek, K. (2014). Modeling commercial potential of innovative projects. *International Review of Management and Business Research, 3*(1), 78–94.

Saaty, T. L. (1996). *The analytic hierarchy process: Planning, priority setting, resource allocation.* Pittsburgh, PA: RWS Publications.

Saaty, T. L. (2001). *Decision making for leaders. The analytic hierarchy process for decisions in a complex world.* Pittsburgh, PA: RWS Publications.

Salles, M. (2006). Decision making in SMEs and information requirements for competitive intelligence. *Production Planning & Control, 17*(3), 229–237.

Shah, S., & Corley, K. (2006). Building better theories by bridging the qualitative-quantitative divide. *Journal of Management Studies, 43*(8), 1821–1835.

Simon, H. (2009). *Hidden champions of the twenty-first century*. Berlin: Springer.

Singh, R. K., Garg, S. K., & Deshmukh, S. G. (2008). Strategy development by SMEs for competitiveness: A review. *Benchmarking: An International Journal, 15*(5), 525–547.

Singh, R. K., Garg, S. K., & Deshmukh, S. G. (2009). The competitiveness of SMEs in a globalized economy: Observations from China and India. *Management Research Review, 33* (1), 54–65.

Smith, A. (1776). *An inquiry into the nature and causes of the Wealth of Nations*. London: Methuen & Co Ltd.

Stabryła, A., & Mesjasz, C. (2003). Principal directions in the evolution of strategic management. *Argumenta Oeconomica Cracoviensia, 2003*(2), 5–26.

Stalk, G., Lachenauer, R., & Butman, J. (2004). *Hardball: Are you playing to play or playing to win?* Boston, MA: Harvard Business Press.

Stankiewicz, M. J. (2000). Istota i sposoby oceny konkurencyjności przedsiębiorstwa. (The essence and methods of assessment of the enterprise competitiveness). *Gospodarka Narodowa, 2000*(7–8), 95–111.

Starczewska-Krzysztoszek, M. (2005). *Badanie konkurencyjności sektora MŚP. Raport z badań*. Warszawa: PKPP Lewiatan.

Starczewska-Krzysztoszek, M. (2006). *Konkurencyjność Małych i Średnich Przedsiębiorstw 2006. Raport z badań*. Warszawa: PKPP Lewiatan.

Starczewska-Krzysztoszek, M. (2007). *Konkurencyjność sektora MŚP. Raport z badań*. Warszawa: PKPP Lewiatan.

Starczewska-Krzysztoszek, M. (2008a). Bariery rozwoju małych i średnich przedsiębiorstw w Polsce. *Zagadnienia Społeczno-Gospodarcze Biura Analiz Sejmowych, 4*(2), Wydawnictwo Indos.

Starczewska-Krzysztoszek, M. (2008b). *Konkurencyjność sektora MŚP 2008. Wyniki badania*. Warszawa: PKPP Lewiatan.

Starczewska-Krzysztoszek, M. (2008c). *Monitoring kondycji sektora MŚP 2008*. Warszawa: PKPP Lewiatan.

Teddlie, C., & Tashakkori, A. (Eds.). (2009). *Foundations of mixed methods research: Integrating quantitative and qualitative approaches in the social and behavioral sciences*. Thousand Oaks, CA: Sage Publications Inc.

Thurow, L. C. (2000). *Building wealth: The new rules for individuals, companies, and nations in a knowledge-based economy*. New York: Harper Collins.

Toh, P. K., & Kim, T. (2013). Why put all your eggs in one basket? A competition-based view of how technological uncertainty affects a firm's technological specialization. *Organization Science, 24*(4), 1214–1236.

Tongzon, J., & Heng, W. (2005). Port privatization, efficiency and competitiveness: Some empirical evidence from container ports (terminals). *Transportation Research Part A: Policy and Practice, 39*(5), 405–424.

Trkman, P. (2010). The critical success factors of business process management. *International Journal of Information Management, 30*(2), 125–134.

Uzor, O. O. (2011). *Clusters, networks, and innovation in small and medium scale enterprises (SMEs): The role of productive investment in the development of SMEs in Nigeria*. Lang, Peter, Internationaler Verlag der Wissenschaften.

Wagner, M., & Schaltegger, S. (2004). The effect of corporate environmental strategy choice and environmental performance on competitiveness and economic performance: An empirical study of EU manufacturing. *European Management Journal, 22*(5), 557–572.

Walkowska, K. (Ed.). (2010). *Działalność przedsiębiorstw niefinansowych w 2008 roku*. Warszawa: Główny Urząd Statystyczny.

Walkowska, K. (Ed.). (2011). *Działalność przedsiębiorstw niefinansowych w 2009 roku*. Warszawa: Główny Urząd Statystyczny.

Wilmańska, A. (2010). *Raport o stanie sektora małych i średnich przedsiębiorstw w Polsce w latach 2008–2009*. Warszawa: PARP.

Yin, R. K. (2014). *Case study research: Design and methods*. Thousand Oaks, CA: Sage.

Yusuf, Y. Y., Gunasekaran, A., Adeleye, E. O., & Sivayoganathan, K. (2004). Agile supply chain capabilities: Determinants of competitive objectives. *European Journal of Operational Research, 159*(2), 379–392.

Zarębska, H. (2010). Information for small and average-size companies SAC in the reality of Unified European Market. *Bibliographical studies, 18*(2010), 183–200.

Zeng, S. X., Xie, X. M., & Tam, C. M. (2010). Relationship between cooperation networks and innovation performance of SMEs. *Technovation, 30*(3), 181–194.

Zulkifli-Muhammad, M., Char, A. K., bin Yasoa, M. R., & Hassan, Z. (2010). Small and medium enterprises (SMEs) competing in the global business environment: A case of Malaysia. *International Business Research, 3*(1), 66–75.

Żołnierski, A. (Ed.). (2009). *Raport o stanie sektora małych i średnich przedsiębiorstw w Polsce w latach 2007–2008*. Warszawa: PARP.

Żołnierski, A., & Pyciński, S. (Eds.). (2007). *Raport o stanie sektora małych i średnich przedsiębiorstw w Polsce w latach 2005–2006*. Warszawa: PARP.

Żołnierski, A., & Zadura-Lichota, P. (Eds.). (2008). *Raport o stanie sektora małych i średnich przedsiębiorstw w Polsce w latach 2006–2007*. Warszawa: PARP.

Chapter 2
New Approaches in Supporting to SMEs Competitiveness

Considering the presented limitations of SMEs, it is obvious that they require support to improve their competitiveness. The Comarch company has given a very accurate response to the question of what would such enterprises need to compete against bigger companies[1] raised at a conference organised for IT producers and suppliers in 2008 (Rostek 2010): *'The same things as large companies, only better, quicker and cheaper.'*

Watching the operation of big and highly competitive companies, we may notice that the power derived from cooperation (Czakon et al. 2014) and mutual trust (Paliszkiewicz and Koohang 2013) is becoming more and more appreciated. These are the grounds for communities that follow the principle of 'paying it forward' (Jones-Kaminski 2009). This principle is to be understood as selfless aid to all those in need in the hope that this aid will return to the donor in an appropriate moment. In effect, this principle contributes to the enhancement of the entire community that follows it. Consortia (Daddi et al. 2012), clusters (Ketels 2011) and strategic networks (Czakon and Klimas 2014) base their might on such foundations.

Cooperation based on trust also create conditions for learning from one another through the application of developed and verified patterns (Rostek 2013b, 2014). Benchmarking defined this way will serve the entire collaborating community and contribute to enhancing its competitiveness. The effectiveness of collaboration in the field of patterns and analyses should be supported by specialised IT technologies such as Business Intelligence (BI) (Akram 2011) or other types of advanced systems of analysis and data reporting (Lai et al. 2011).

The present chapter discusses the aforementioned concepts and related methods and tools. Section 2.1 presents relevant approaches to competitive collaboration, which transforms competitive fight into competitive cooperation, bringing benefits to all stakeholders. In this approach individual entities do not give up on their

---

[1] Comarch—a global powerhouse specialized in the design, implementation and integration of advanced IT services and software (http://www.comarch.co.uk/).

© Springer International Publishing Switzerland 2015   29
K. Rostek, *Benchmarking Collaborative Networks*, Contributions to Management Science, DOI 10.1007/978-3-319-16736-7_2

identity, focus on the achievement of own goals, and run their business in harmony and not in opposition to others. Therefore, various forms of learning from one another are possible with the use of patterns that have been proven and verified by others. This process is supported by the benchmarking method characterised in Sect. 2.2.

Nevertheless, it is also possible to imagine a situation in which a collaborating group established to reinforce its competitiveness does not have enough knowledge and skills even as a sum of entities. A solution to this problem may be information and knowledge brokering presented in Sect. 2.3. It allows for using external knowledge and information reserves to support the achievement of own goals and objectives. Naturally, all of that requires relevant technological support, which is provided by the BI technology described in Sect. 2.4.

The said approach to competition is closely related to the need to trust competitors and business partners because without trust no cooperation is possible. Trust creates the foundations of collaboration and mutual understanding, but may also pose a threat to an entity that does not analyse and rationalise its decisions in this respect. Therefore, Sect. 2.5 presents the basic principles to be followed by an organisation in trust and risk management.

The aforementioned elements are summarised in the BCN concept drafted in Sect. 2.6. Its detailed characteristic is the subject of all the remaining chapters of the present book.

2.1 Collaboration and Coopetition

In strategic management, the paradigm of competition, which interprets it as rivalry between companies (Porter 1985, 1998), is based on constant striving for individual profits (Xavier and Ramachander 2000). The survival of an organisation is in this case determined by measures that reinforce its competitiveness and focus on the creation of individual competitive advantage (Gilpin 2000). Taking into consideration the instability of markets and considerable changes in the economy, aggressive behaviour in line with the rule 'the winner takes it all' predominates in this approach (D'Aveni 1994).

A totally different view on the relations between organisations that ensures their survival on the market prevails in the cooperative perspective. In view of globalisation, intensifying competition and the need to keep up with technological development, cooperation enables business entities to reinforce their own competitive potential. Appropriate use of this potential will translate into effectiveness of the conducted business activity. Therefore, in spite of a natural inclination of companies to compete, numerous forms of cooperation may also be observed (Danik and Lewandowska 2013), which lead to a search for consensus that will bring profit to all parties and not eliminate any of them.

In accordance with the paradigm of cooperation, companies are ordered through the networks of developing interrelations and supported by strategic cooperation

(Thomas and Pollock 1999). Emphasis on the development of cooperation results from the belief that organisations may improve their performance this way. This is possible owing to the fusion of resources, skills and competences, and sometimes even infrastructure. Competitive advantage is achieved through strategic alliances and networks of cooperation (Sroka and Hittmár 2013).

Cooperation between companies defined this way may be viewed from the perspective of horizontal and vertical relations. Vertical cooperation is a natural process because it proceeds along the production—distribution—sale chain between the supplier—producer—distributor—client. This form of cooperation leads to enhancing the innovative potential of participating companies, transfer of knowledge between related entities and above all to a better adaptation to client's needs and expectations, also in terms of the opportunity to shape them. Horizontal cooperation in turn relates above all to enterprises and organisations which traditionally remain market competitors. It is the horizontal interaction that combines two extreme approaches—competitiveness and cooperation.

The concept of competitive collaboration was introduced to management sciences in 1996 by Brandenburger and Nalebuff (Brandenburger and Nalebuff 1996). It is referred to as coopetition, and means simultaneous competition and cooperation between market competitors. Coopetition means that entities are competing and cooperating in a repeatable way, although they remain organisationally separate. Firms can integrate their activities so as to achieve planned mutual benefits, while at the same time acting as rivals in order to pursue their own individual strategic goals (Zakrzewska-Bielawska 2013).

The theoretical basis for coopetition can be found in the game theory (Okura 2007), the theory of transaction costs (Lacoste 2012), the resource based view (Zakrzewska-Bielawska 2013), the theory of social capital (Inkpen and Tsang 2005), and interorganisational dynamics (Tidstrom 2008). By analysing coopetition it is possible to list the main advantages and benefits that a organization may derive from such a strategy as follows (Bigliardi et al. 2011):

- synergistic effect—cooperating companies achieve synergy owing to the exchange of experience and knowledge in the field of management, entrepreneurship, innovativeness, organisational culture, know-how, organisation of manufacturing processes or networks and channels of distribution;
- specialization—coopetition models facilitate access to modern management methods and techniques, marketing capacities, specialist technologies, patents and trademarks;
- advantages of scale—increasing the organisational, economic and technological potential favours achieving market advantage, which may be used to decrease costs or introduce special offers;
- risk reduction—creating networks of cooperation leads to diversifying resources and markets and lowers the risk of the conducted business activity, which in itself often persuades companies to undertake coopetitive measures.

Consequently, different coopetitive solutions involve different proportions of competitiveness and cooperation, as well as resulting benefits. With regard to the

Fig. 2.1 The four partial
coopetition model [*source*:
(Luo 2004)]

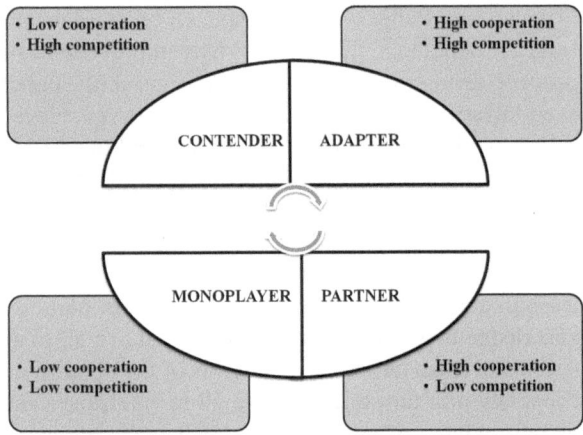

presence of these two factors (competitiveness and cooperation) and their interrelations, the following coopetitive behaviours may be identified ((Luo 2004), Fig. 2.1):

- monoplayer—behaviours that favour individual measures yet are devoid of aggressive competition;
- partner—behaviours that favour teamwork, devoid of aggressive competition;
- adapter—behaviours that favour teamwork but do not reject competitive rivalry;
- contender—behaviours that favour individual measures aimed at competitive rivalry.

The selection of one of these models will depend on three factors that determine the sustainability of cooperation, namely: strategy, culture and organisation, defined as follows (Child et al. 2005):

- a strategic adaptation—in order to clearly identifiable a source of sustainable competitive advantages and develop an increasing level of interdependence;
- a cultural adaptation—in order to provide the right basis for cooperation and a common growth;
- an organizational arrangements—in order to identify the best form of coopetition, to clearly define the responsibilities of each partner and to provide the right mechanisms in order to solve conflicts.

The importance of coopetition seems to be even greater in the context of SMEs. The SMEs need to collaborate with their competitors to be able to create economies of scale, mitigate risk, and leverage resources (Morris et al. 2007). Thanks to coopetition the competitors can to face similar challenges more effective, because possess resources and capabilities that are directly relevant to each other (Gnyawali and Park 2009). It results as consequence, that SMEs could more effectively compete against large players, what has positive impact on their financial performance (Levy et al. 2003). In the Benchmarking Collaborative Network, cooperation between SMEs has been used to create a Benchmarking Collaborative Group, which is described in Chap. 4 *Arranging Benchmarking Collaborative Group*.

2.2   Benchmarking

As shown in the previous sub-chapter, cooperation between SMEs is advisable, and sometimes even crucial, especially if an enterprise strives for long-term and sustainable development. Yet it is also important to determine the scope of cooperation, which should focus on knowledge and experience exchange (Levy et al. 2003), and using the patterns developed by the leaders of the created cooperative groups (Zeng et al. 2010). In effect, this will enable enterprises to develop more effective competitive strategies with more foreseeable results.

The effectiveness of the prepared competitiveness strategy depends on knowledge of the competitive factors and the ability to predict the actions taken by the competitors (Trkman et al. 2010). The source of the necessary knowledge in this area is undoubtedly the experience and skills of managers, which should be supported by information obtained as a result of the pursued competitive analysis. As confirmed by conducted research (Crouch 2011), those economic entities that take into account the results of the competitive analysis and the existing (market and non-market) constraints have the biggest chance of successful entry and effective activities on the market.

The achieved competitive position, understood as a result of the implemented competitive strategy, is constrained not only by business capabilities, but also by the parallel activities carried out by market competitors. So the wider information regarding the operation of the business and its environment, the greater the effectiveness of the prepared strategy for competitiveness. The competitive analysis usually refers to its own results, but expanded to benchmarking, i.e. the process of comparison analysis in many areas of business with other competitors will increase the management efficiency of the competitiveness development strategy (Huggins 2010). An opportunity is the organization of a collaboration group focusing on the use of benchmarking analysis methods.

Benchmarking is an external view of internal activities, functions or operations in order to achieve continuous improvement (Ahmed and Rafi 1998). The essence of benchmarking is the process of identifying the highest standards of excellence for products, services, or processes, and then making the improvements necessary to reach those standards, commonly called best practices (Elmuti and Kathawala 1997). These elements may be compared within an organization or with partners outside the organisation (Ajelabi and Tang 2010). The classification of benchmarking reflect what is compared (i.e. object of comparison, Fig. 2.2) and by what the comparison is being made (i.e. scope of comparison, Fig. 2.2).

The first one involves comparisons of performance, process and strategic benchmarking. Performance benchmarking is the comparison of performance

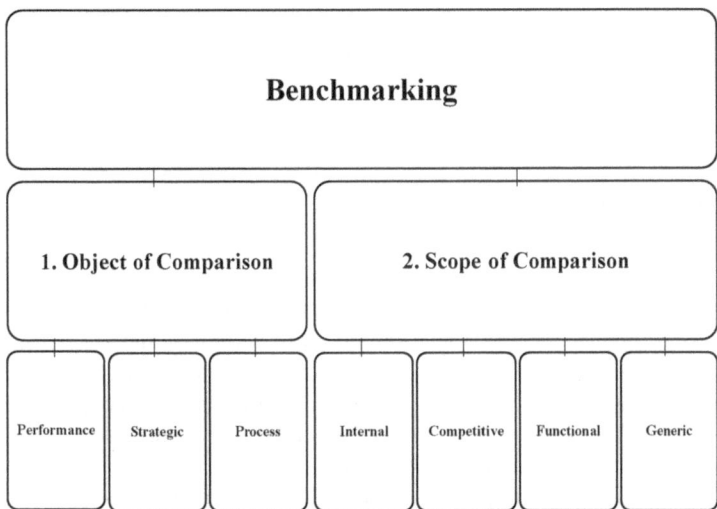

Fig. 2.2 The classification of benchmarking types (*source*: own research)

measures for the purpose of determining how good an organization is in comparison to the others. Process benchmarking compares methods and processes in an effort to improve the processes within an organization. Strategic benchmarking is the comparison of an organisation's strategy with successful strategies from other organizations to help improve capability to deal with a changing external environment.

The second one includes internal, competitive, functional and generic comparisons. Internal benchmarking is the comparisons of performance made between department/divisions of the same organization solely to find and apply best practice information. Competitive benchmarking compares made against the leader in the same market to compare performance and results. Functional benchmarking is comparisons of a particular function in an industry to become the best in this function. Generic benchmarking is the comparison of processes against best process operators regardless of industry.

Due to the presented broad range of applications, benchmarking makes use of various methods of implementation. Yet each of them has to include features that will enable the achievement of the main objective of benchmarking, which is the improvement of efficiency, productivity and/or quality owing to the use of proved patterns, developed and verified by group or market leaders. These features include (Khetrapal and Thakur 2014):

– reliability and credibility of the developed ranking lists and comparisons. All ranking lists have to be accompanied by a detailed method of their development and the obtained results of statistics, which will allow for evaluating and verifying the correctness of the procedure;
– transparency and verifiability of the applied analytical methods, calculations and assumed measurement error. The results of conducted analyses will form

Fig. 2.3 The
benchmarking cycle process
(*source*: own research)

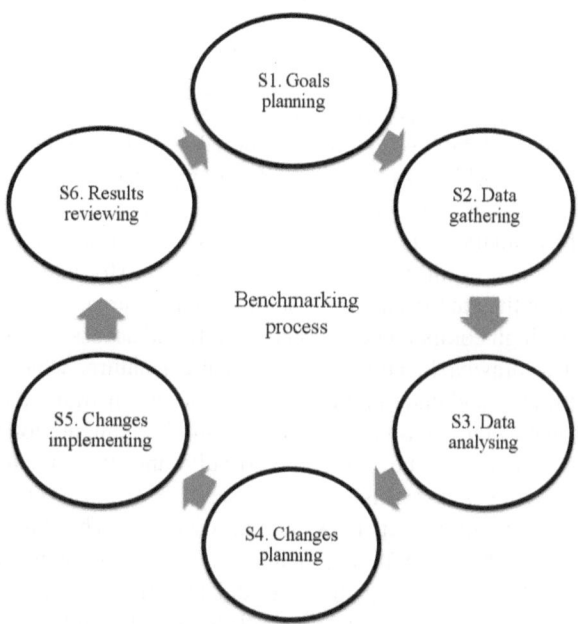

grounds for the ranking lists; therefore, their publication contributes to increasing the creditworthiness of the final outcomes;
– reduction of requirements and obligations resulting from participation in a benchmarking group to those that are really justified and determine the achievement of expected results. Excessive and unjustified requirements may cause reluctance and mistrust of possible group members and limit their number;
– adaptability to various applications and types of compared entities, which allows for generalising the method's applicability and its results;
– compliance with the standards of the economic theory and the use of the most recent developments in economic studies.

Having regard to the above benchmarking appears as a cyclical process comprising six stages shown in Fig. 2.3:

– Stage 1—planning and setting scope, goals and measures of goals in the benchmarking process;
– Stage 2—gathering the adequate data and information for benchmarking analysis;
– Stage 3—analyzing the data, validating and verifying the results;
– Stage 4—planning the changes based on the verified analysis results;
– Stage 5—executing and implementing the defined changes;
– Stage 6—reviewing results, assessing the degree of goals achievement and the need for input to the next process iteration.

Cyclicality of this process is that it doesn't finish after stage 6, but most often returns to the planning phase for the next iteration. Thanks to this the whole process still being subject to improvement and the company achieves next defined goals.

As this stems from Fig. 2.3 benchmarking is performed by analyzing the collected data, so can be considered as a new method of analysis. The adoption of benchmarking as a method for competitive analysis (Raharjo et al. 2010) has resulted in the widening of the scope of its use. The most popular form of benchmarking is an analytical service performed in a defined area of management by the consulting and services companies (for example IBM,[2] Cartesian[3]), which have the data from a specific management area. The strengths of such a service are the high competences of service staff and access to a wide range of necessary data. The drawback, however, is its one-off nature, which is sufficient in the case of projects and undertakings, but becomes a constraint in the case of repetitive actions, such as the continuous projection and implementation of strategies.

There have been attempts to build and disseminate multi-user solutions in the field of benchmarking analysis (Sapio et al. 2007). The strength of these solutions is their durability, openness and accessibility. The drawback, however, is that there are problems with the maintenance, development and flexibility of solutions, upgrades to processing data, and also the interpretation and utility of available results. Hence the new research trend—the knowledge-based benchmarking systems (Lai et al. 2011)—which in a clear, accessible and useful way supports decision-making and the creation of business strategy. The ability to use these solutions entails the need to implement advanced IT technologies such as BI (Completo et al. 2012).

Benchmarking, used as a method of competitive analysis, increases the possibility of traditional analysis, because it not only measures the effects of the strategy, but also identifies causes and points to the possibility of their improvement. Therefore modern benchmarking methods such as the European Benchmarking Procedure (European Commission 2012; Maggetti and Gilardi 2011) or clusters benchmarking (Ketels et al. 2012; Park et al. 2012) show how effectively benchmarking can be used to support a competitive strategy.

In the European Union, benchmarking has become a key instrument in the Open Method of Coordination, supporting the achievement of the competitive advantage in member states in terms of both economic and social objectives (Bruno 2009; European Commission 2012). The method is based on mutual learning through the identification and transfer of best practices at different levels of economy management (i.e. sectoral, national and transnational). On this basis, new benchmarking methodologies are created, taking into account the scope, principles and conditions for their implementation (Dévai et al. 2002; Lilama 2010).

---

[2] http://www-03.ibm.com/systems/services/benchmarkcenter/, date of reading 23-07-2013.

[3] http://www.cartesian.com/technology/technical-services-and-consulting/it-benchmarking, date of reading 23-07-2013.

Also, the benchmarking of clusters, led by the ESCA (*European Secretariat for Cluster Analysis*), is found widely used in the European Union. The ESCA has registered 190 clusters and is currently providing the results of a comparative study in the area of organizational structures, processes, products and services (ESCA 2012). They also make comparisons on a smaller scale, for example for clusters operating in a specific industry (ABC-Network 2007; Inovisa 2012).

The advantage of the presented methods is a wide range of available comparisons and supporting the process of the European institutions. The limitations are the need to involve significant resources and incurring high investment outlays, which require the involvement of government institutions (the European Benchmarking Procedure) or a larger group of cooperating and competing entities (the benchmarking of clusters).

In this context, one can see the need for such an implementation of a benchmarking method, which will be more accessible and flexible for SMEs, which function primarily in the local market, have only a little knowledge and experience in the field of European cooperation and remain outside the existing clusters. The proposed solution is the Collaborative Benchmarking Method, presented in Chap. 4—*Arranging Collaborative Benchmarking Group.*

2.3   Brokering and Crowdsourcing

A significant limitation of SMEs is the lack of knowledge, experience and skills in the proper synthesizing of strategic information. Even if the SMEs collaboration was taken, it will be necessary for the support of a specialist entity in the range of coordinating the activities of SMEs group and being responsible for the quality of provided information. The information broker is such an entity.

The Information broker is a person or a company which provides (for a fee) organised and coordinated access to heterogeneous—structured and semi-structured information sources (Martin et al. 1997). There are four categories of competences information broker needs to master (Denchev and Christozov 2012):

- searching for data and information—to survey, scan and search the heterogeneous sources by exploring all of the components of information environment;
- storing data—to collect and store the obtained information and data;
- analysing of data—to analyse data and information, to visualise results and to send them in a form suitable for the user;
- presenting results—to present matched and analysed results in a suitable and understandable form.

Based on the above requirements the process of information brokering can be established (Christozov and Toleva-Stoimenova 2014):

- selection of the information environment—identifying relevant to the problem domain information sources;

– assessing the sources—viewing the sources from the point of view of relevance
  and accessibility (including economic accessibility);
– collecting information—obtaining information relevant to the defined problem
  and available in matched sources;
– assessing information—from the point of view of relevance, trustfulness, consistency, cause-and-effects relationships, etc.;
– synthesizing information—creating the information product to serve the client
  by formulating the obtained content via creative generalisation and abstraction;
– delivering the information product—i. e. presenting information for the client.

An information broker can be a specialised entity, but can also be a virtual
community, which is called crowdsourcing. As shown, ongoing research into the
transfer of the solving some kind of problems to the online space in some cases
contributes significantly to the rapid finding of solutions and the development of
entities using these solutions (Doan et al. 2011; Poetz and Schreier 2012; Saxton
et al. 2013). As research shows crowdsourcing for enterprises in particular involves
both—harnessing the collective intelligence and workforce (Hetmank 2013).

There is no single accepted definition of crowdsourcing because it is a concept
that is still evolving. However, a synthetic definition of crowdsourcing is proposed
by Estellés-Arolas (Estellés-Arolas and González-Ladrón-de-Guevara 2012) as a
type of participative online activity in which an individual, an institution, an
organisation, or company proposes to a group of individuals the voluntary undertaking of a task. Very important feature of this activity is obtaining the mutual
benefit for task providers and recipients. The providers (crowdsourcers) can receive
economic satisfaction, social recognition, self-esteem, or the development of individual skills. The recipients obtain and utilise for their advantage everything the
crowdsourcers brought to the venture. Crowdsourcing can be applied for a many
purposes such as (Parshotam 2013): production (co-creation), availability of
standby human resources, problem-solving in research and development, project
or venture funding (crowdfunding), forecasting, organisation, tasks performing,
innovation/idea generating, solving problem, classification, decision-making/
support, or propagating information.

Communication in such an approach is realisation via the web platform, here
called a crowdsourcing platform. The crowdsourcing platform is a kind of information broker ensuring providers successfully complete the task requests and the
requestors pay for the charges (Vukovic 2009). It can execute crowdsourcing
requests in a number of different modes, for example: by advertising them on the
marketplace, allowing providers to bid for them or using the form of a competition.
Further use of crowdsourcing platforms can allow requestors and providers to
connect into the work teams.

There are specialised web platforms dedicated to communication with the
community, organisation and individuals under crowdsourcing. Such platforms
categorise the available tools, ordering them according to the range and type of
functionalities. Two basic categories are tools related to (1) resources necessary for

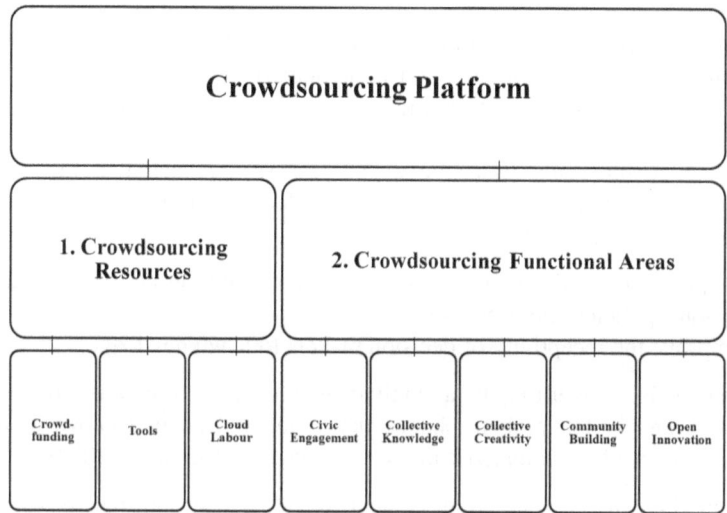

Fig. 2.4 The structure of crowdsourcing web platform (*source*: own research)

undertaking and (2) the specialisation of those carrying out tasks. The detailed division of these tools is presented in (Fig. 2.4):

– crowdsourcing resources:

- crowdfunding—financial contributions from online investors, sponsors or donors to fund crowdsourcing initiatives;
- crowdsourcing tools—applications, platforms and tools supporting collaboration and communication among groups and entities;
- cloud labour—a virtual environment which provides fulfilment of a wide range of tasks on-demand;

– crowdsourcing functional areas:

- civic engagement—a collective actions in public space;
- collective knowledge—knowledge and information resources obtained from contributors;
- collective creativity—obtaining of creative talents for developing original areas of art and science;
- community building—development of communities through connection and engagement of active entities;
- open innovation—use external sources for generating, developing and implementing projects and ideas.

The main condition of usefulness that the information provides via the information broker is its content, quality, scope and form of sharing, which requires having specialist knowledge of organisation, management and technology. In view of foregoing, the information broker should be an expert in the area in which they provide brokering services. These elements provide the direction of brokering services development from information into knowledge brokering (Meyer 2010; Turnhout et al. 2013). This direction is particularly useful for SMEs, where the ability to properly use the acquired information is limited by shortcomings in the area of knowledge.

Knowledge brokering is a strategy or process approach that facilitates the transfer of knowledge between actors. Knowledge brokering serves two purposes (Shaxson and Gwyn 2010):

- to improve the utility of knowledge for a noticeable effect on the quality of decisions, policies and processes;
- to improve the receptivity of decision makers to new knowledge.

A knowledge broker may be an individual, a team or an organization unit. The tasks of a knowledge brokers change depending on the two above mentioned purposes and can be summarized in six different roles (Michaels 2009):

- making-known—disseminating content, targeting decision makers with information, making information easily accessible and digestible; the tools of achieving this role include: factsheets, research synopses, web portals, databases, project seminars;
- link-up—linking expertise to need for a particular research area, helping policymakers address a specific research issue by seeking out the necessary experts; the tools of achieving this role include: project and programme advisory committees, focus groups, linked and specialised websites;
- matchmaking—matching expertise to need across issues and disciplines and helping finding experts with relevant knowledge from another discipline; the tools of achieving this role include: expert advisory committees, research conferences, business and university internships, mapping the specialised databases;
- focused collaboration—constructing formal relationships to focus on a particular issue or contacting people or organizations to provide knowledge on an as needed basis; the tools of achieving this role include: research and development programs, knowledge networks, working and project groups;
- strategic collaboration—lengthening and deepening the collaborative process, strengthening relationships through jointly negotiated methods, tools or/and solutions; the tools of achieving this role include: joint agreements where the emphasis is on equality in the relationships between all actors;
- building sustainable institutions—extending the collaborative relationships to being the one institution; the focus is on co-production of knowledge and joint learning from doing; the arrangements are self sustaining in terms of both funding and function, with all sides contributing resources; the tools of achieving this role include: co-management arrangements, enterprise partnerships, self sustaining consortia.

The above statements have become a premise to propose the project of information technology platform to exchange of strategic information. It is an important tool of knowledge transfer in the range of SMEs competitiveness. Details of this concept are presented in Chap. 5—*Coordinating Collaborative Benchmarking Group*.

2.4   Business Intelligence Technology

Information brokering requires using advanced IT solutions (Honkola et al. 2010; Kim et al. 2011): web, database and analytical applications dedicated for specific uses and types of information. It is also necessary that applied technology can guarantee high quality, confidentiality and security of data and information. Currently the best suited technology for these requirements is BI (Rostek 2013a).

According to Gartner's[4] the definition—BI is an umbrella term that includes the applications, infrastructure and tools, and best practices that enable access to and analysis of information to improve and optimize decisions and performance. BI allows for the extraction and aggregation of any data type coming from technologically different and heterogeneous sources. Provides a wide range of tools for analytical data processing, including OLAP and data mining analysis. Is able to make flexibly reports of analysis results. There are three main approaches in use BI that depends on the goal of usage BI and the required focus (Rouhani et al. 2012):

- managerial approach with focus on improving management decision making;
- technical approach by focusing on tools supporting the processes associated with intelligence in management approach;
- enabling approach by focusing on value-added capabilities in support of information.

The above approaches are consistent with the Gartner Business Analytics Framework (Fig. 2.5), which defines the elements (i.e. people, processes and platforms) need to be integrated and aligned to take a more strategic approach to BI for analytics and performance management initiatives.

Consequently, it is not enough to make the BI technology available to users. A coherent concept of strategic management has to be developed, and the scope of information supporting this management has to be defined. This explains why the application of BI in SMEs is still minor, even though functional solutions suited to their capacities are constantly being developed.

2.4.1   Technological Framework

One of the key characteristic features of the BI technology that determine its usefulness and effectiveness is the fact that since the first tools entered the market 25 years ago, it has undergone systematic changes, both methodological and

---

[4] Gartner Inc. is the world's leading information technology research and advisory company.

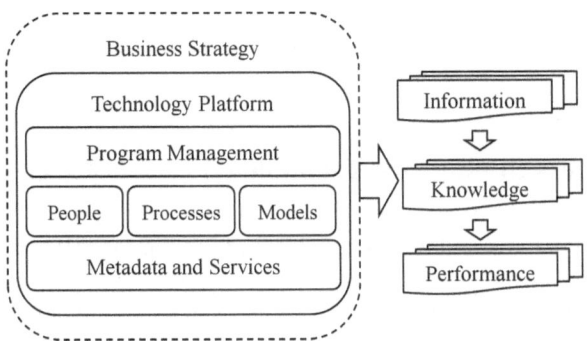

Fig. 2.5 The Gartner business analytics framework [*source*: own research based on (Chandler et al. 2011)]

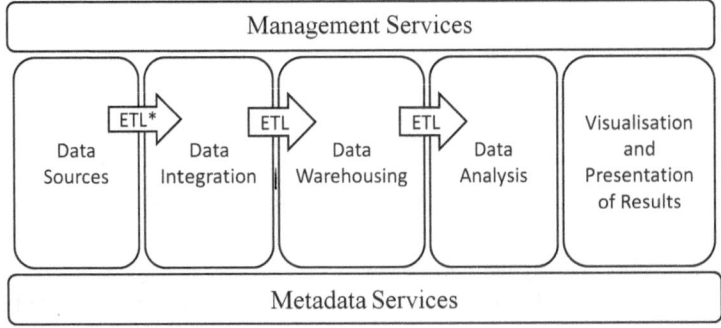

* ETL – Extraction, Transformation, Load

Fig. 2.6 The business intelligence technology framework (*source*: own research)

technological. The architecture of BI technology comprises six layers (Fig. 2.6): (1) the data sources, (2) the data integration, (3) the data warehousing, (4) the data analysis, (5) the visualisation and presentation of results, (6) the management of metadata.

2.4.1.1 The Data Sources Layer

Internet development and the increased network activity of companies influencing the complexity of the source data. The primary internal data sources used, which are usually structured transaction databases, are now supplemented with external data characterised by various degrees of structure (Inmon and Nesavich 2007). In use are heterogeneous data acquired from company's contractors and partners, but also data from text and electronic Internet sources. Data complexity and variety have to be reflected in the process of their integration, whose efficiency determines their utilisation in the system.

2.4.1.2   The Data Integration Layer

An increase in the complexity of the BI system data sources is accompanied by the simultaneous growth in the degree of complexity of the ETL (Extract, Transform and Load Process) technology, which is responsible for the extraction of data from sources and their integration in the system's central repository. This process is also referred to as ETQL (i.e. Extract, Transform, Quality and Load Process) to highlight the significance of data quality in the process of their storage and analysis (Akbar et al. 2013).

2.4.1.3   The Data Warehousing Layer

Data acquired under ETL may be stored in various types of analytical repositories. These may include: enterprises data warehouses (Inmon et al. 2010), data marts (Kimball et al. 2008), operational data stores (Waas et al. 2013) or OLAP cubes (Rivest et al. 2005). Their type depends on the amount, contingency, range and type of stored data. It is also related to the adopted system architecture and method of its implementation and operation. The applied standards are set by various approaches favoured by researches and practitioners (in particular the teams of Bill Inmon (Inmon 2005; Inmon et al. 2010) and Ralph Kimball (Kimball et al. 2008)).

2.4.1.4   The Data Analysis Layer

Data stored in the data warehousing layer are subsequently transferred to the data analysis layer. The scope of analyses to be carried out in the BI system is only limited by the capacities of analytical tools. The most frequently applied analytical methods may be classified into the following groups of analyses: statistical (Ranjan 2009), multidimensional OLAP (Thomas and Datta 2001), data mining (Kantardzic 2011), text mining (Weiss et al. 2005), web mining (Xu et al. 2010), and currently also SNA—Social Networks Analysis (Borgatti et al. 2013).

2.4.1.5   The Visualization and Presentation of Results Layer

Visualisation and presentation of results is particularly important from the user perspective. It is this layer that determines the utility of the tool and its results. It may be supplied in the form of traditional reports and lists, but may also be a data source for a management cockpit (Eckerson 2010) or an information portal (Chan and Chung 2002). It may also be a part of an advisory system that monitors and automatically responds to emerging threats on an ongoing basis (Seufert and Schiefer 2005).

2.4.1.6 The Management of Metadata Layer

Metadata are a logical layer of the BI system. They ensure its correct operation and facilitate system management and administration (Foshay et al. 2014). They also help to recover the system to its condition before a breakdown and to control information security and confidentiality.

The technology framework presented above includes variety solutions used within this technology (as open source BI, BI in memory, cloud BI), which provides the ability to meet the needs and abilities of each type of user, including SMEs.

2.4.2 Business Process Management via Business Intelligence

Business Process Management (BPM) techniques and tools evolve around process models. Process models are used to configure such systems and to analyse "as-is" and "to-be" processes. Unfortunately, these models are often completely disconnected from actual event data. The combination of both process models and event data in BI and BPM integrated system allows for new forms of process-centric analytics (Van der Aalst 2011).

Various types of integration between the BI system and BPM are known, with the most frequently applied one being Business Application Monitoring (Fig. 2.7), in which data from various sources are combined in near-real-time with process-level key performance indicators (KPIs) and visualised via managerial dashboards (Kemper et al. 2013). The role of BI consists in ensuring ongoing process monitoring and enhancement based on the 'Five-R's' cycle, which means (Fig. 2.7): (1) recognition, (2) response, (3) resolution, (4) review to function and (5) delivering ROI (Return On Investment).

The integration of the BI system with BPM at information level ensures (Marjanovic 2010):

– a broader context of process management owing to the possibility to view a single process from the perspective of the interests of the entire organisation,
– making decisions on an ongoing basis without the need to wait e.g. until the end of the month or an even longer reporting period,
– access to complete management information necessary to implement individual stages of the process, which ensures increased safety and accuracy of taken decisions,
– option to easily propagate any information to the recipients at appropriate time,
– option to justify all taken decision owing to a documented source of information.

From the technological perspective, the integration of BI and BPM makes it possible to (Fryman 2007):

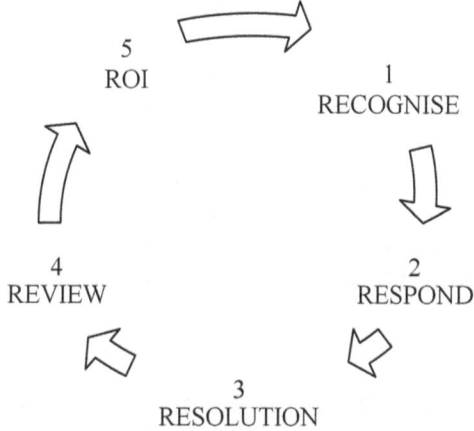

Fig. 2.7 Conception of business application monitoring in the 'Five-R's' cycle (*source*: own research)

- create a joint model of metadata used simultaneously in BI and BPM,
- use state-of-the-art analytical and reporting tools in the management of business processes,
- introduce real-time business process management and make ongoing changes in the course of the process.

2.4.3   In-Memory Analytics

Key difference between conventional BI and in-memory BI is that query data are located in random access memory (RAM) instead at a disk. Normally a query goes to a database and reads the information from multiple tables stored on a hard disk. With an in-memory database all information is initially loaded into memory. From this it follows that accessing data in-memory is more efficient as opposed to accessing that same data from disk. Furthermore the BI architecture needs very little up-front effort and no ETL. That's why it is good proposition for SMEs, tailored to their organisational and financial capabilities.

Another main use for the in-memory approach is to facilitate a more exploratory, visual analysis. Solutions are in this case aimed at supplying advanced graphic data visualisation tools, where the process of creating a report on results is also visualised and operated by a mouse and a cursor.

Benefits arising from the use of in-memory technology include:

- performance improvements—users are querying and interacting with data in-memory which is significantly faster than accessing data from hard disk;
- cost reduces—in-memory approach provides the ability to analyse very large data sets, but is much simpler to set up and administer, because it doesn't need to use data warehouse and ETL tools;

– time reductions—project preparation and system launch are not as time-consuming as in the case of traditional applications due to a lack of a data warehouse and a complex ETL process;
– IT engagement reduces—business users receive self-service access to the right information and possibility of self making reports.

Nevertheless, it is a solution for companies that apart from efficient analyses need to integrate and centralise their data or want to enrich these data through their integration with external sources. That is why the term In-memory Business Intelligence is increasingly often replaced by In-memory Analytics.

2.4.4   Big Data and MapReduce Model

The most common understanding of the concepts of Big Data is such size of dataset which is beyond the ability of typical database software tools to capture, store, manage and analyse (Zicari 2014). But more and more researchers point to the importance of the other features. Patrick Russom (2011) writes that big data must possess the three Vs: Volume (it is a large dataset), Variety (it comes in many formats and can be structured or unstructured), and Velocity (it refers to the speed of generating data). Marissa Mayer (Maltby 2011) suggests that data is defined by the three Ss: Speed (increasing availability of data in real time), Scale (increasing the computing power continues), Sensors (including new types of data, like: social and interactional data or data published by the physical objects—Internet of Things).

Summarising Big Data is not only large volume, but also varied and fast-growing dataset. Such specificity necessitates the use of appropriate technological tools. Thinking about the performance and scalability of classical tools, must pay attention to those that are dedicated to Big Data. These are Map Reduce and Hadoop. MapReduce is a programming model used to handle a large set of data simultaneously. Hadoop is one of the more popular open-source implementations of this model.

The principles MapReduce uses are similar to the distributed grouping and aggregation capabilities that have existed in parallel relational database systems. They are able to scale very well to accommodate for exceptionally large data sets by combining functions of mapping and reducing. The map function transforms each element individually (by grouping and ordering) to an output data element. The reduce function combines input values together (by merging and aggregating), returning a single output value. The final effect of combining these two elements is presenting on Fig. 2.8.

There are many technical and organisational challenges in adopting Big Data technology into the enterprise environment. Concepts of models are created that enable effective and safe implementation of this technology in enterprises. These are often related to the use of cloud computing as a much more scalable environment tailored to the user.

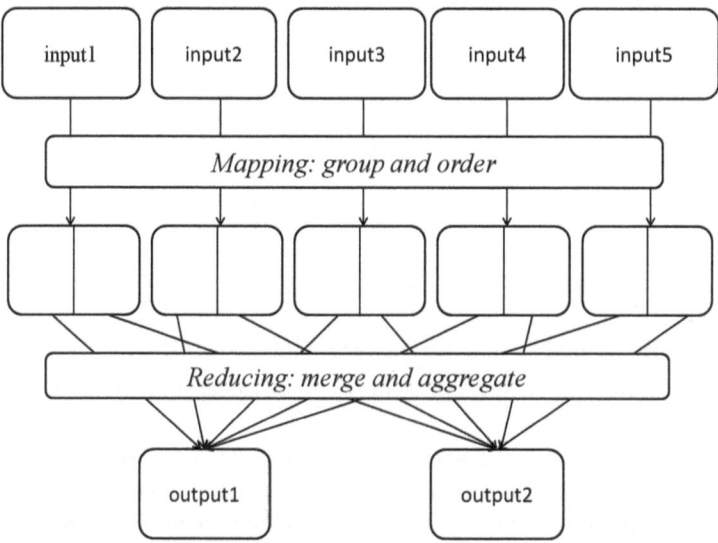

Fig. 2.8 MapReduce model (*source*: own research)

2.4.5 Cloud Computing

Cloud computing (CC) is internet-based and shared resources computing, which are provided on user demand (Ouf and Nasr 2011). CC contains three service models:

- Software as a Service (SaaS)—the consumers use the provider's software applications running on a cloud infrastructure;
- Platform as a Service (PaaS)—the consumers have access to the cloud infrastructure using programming languages and tools supported by the provider;
- Infrastructure as a Service (IaaS)—the consumers have got access to processing, storage, networks, and other fundamental computing resources where are able to implement and run an arbitrary software.

Having regard to the above Cloud Business Intelligence system is used to solve one of three primary customer needs:

- SaaS BI—as an applications package (in the scope of: data visualisations, data analytics and performance management) delivered in time and scope matched to the needs and capabilities of the users;
- PaaS BI—as a scalable applications platform (in the scope of: data warehousing, data integrating, data repository, BI platform hosting) that takes into account individual users' needs which change in time;
- IaaS BI—as a development technological platform (in the scope of: data storage and processing power) that enables embeddable, externally facing applications and sources, needed to solve a specific data analysis problem.

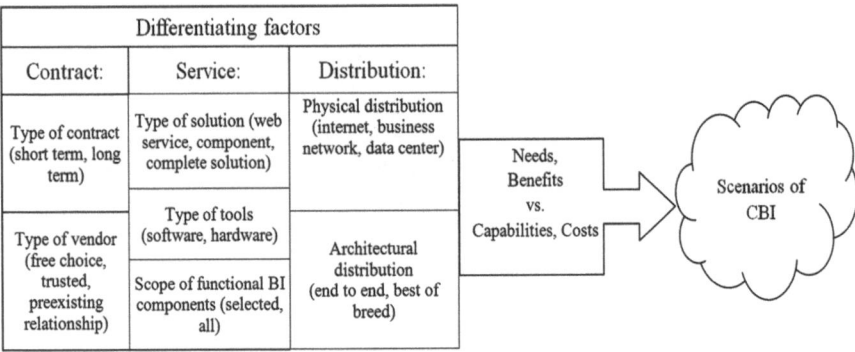

Differentiating factors		
Contract:	Service:	Distribution:
Type of contract (short term, long term)	Type of solution (web service, component, complete solution)	Physical distribution (internet, business network, data center)
Type of vendor (free choice, trusted, preexisting relationship)	Type of tools (software, hardware)	Architectural distribution (end to end, best of breed)
	Scope of functional BI components (selected, all)	

Fig. 2.9 Implementing scenarios for Cloud BI [*source*: (Baars and Kemper 2010)]

Starting from the above characteristics it is possible to propose scenarios variants for implementing BI in CC. The value selection of the three basic elements—(1) contract, (2) service and (3) distribution and their comparison with assessment of costs and benefits (Fig. 2.9) creates suitable scenario schemes.

A significant limitation of using BI in SMEs is the lack of qualified IT personnel, which could take part in its implementation, maintenance of operational capability and actuality. The solution of this problem is moving it to strategic information services provider—i.e. Broker of Strategic Information. The details of a such solution are presented in Chap. 4—*Arranging Collaborative Benchmarking Group*.

2.5 Trust and Risk Management

Given the need to establish cooperation under BCN, the concept of trust has to be considered, without which no cooperation will be effective or even possible. Trust, on which the BCN concept is founded, is consistent with Hosmer's definition (1995). According to this definition, trust is dependency of an individual, an organisation or a group on the freely accepted obligation towards the other party. The objective of trust defined this way is to recognise and protect the rights and interests of entities involved in the joint undertaking and business exchange.

Trust understood as the assumption that one may rely on its partner and that the partner will keep promises and act honestly when given option to do otherwise (Paliszkiewicz 2011) is irrevocably connected with the risk that it will not be so. Henceforth, the definition of trust as the readiness to risk that the other party will act in a way that is significant for the person that places trust (Schoorman et al. 2007). Sztompka (2000) applies an even stricter definition, treating trust as a bet whose object is uncertain future action of others.

Trust is related to uncertainty and risk, but it is a positive concept. It connects social groups, constituting an important element of social capital (Falck and Heblich 2007). It contributes to eliminating anxiety and suspiciousness in an

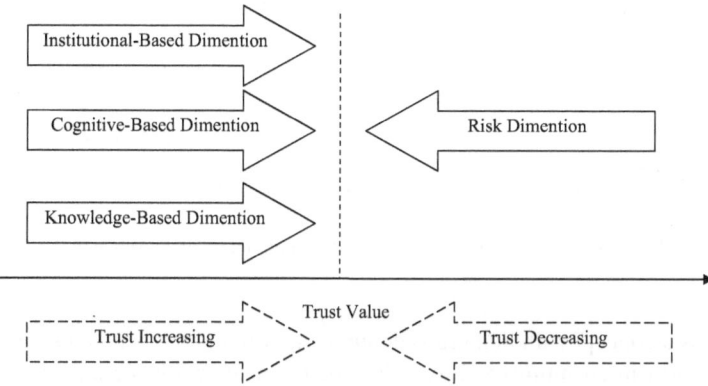

Fig. 2.10 Dimensions of trust value (*source*: own research)

organisation. Owing to this, an organisation becomes more open, aware of its capacities and is ready to face challenges. Trust leads to the achievement of set goals and benefits by all stakeholders, thus having a direct impact on the economic results of an organisation (Grudzewski et al. 2009). This justifies building trust and managing its positive impact on an organisation and its environment.

The trust management model should on the one hand take into account the dimensions of trust that influence its creation and development, and on the other hand consider the risk that is irrevocably combined with the uncertainty of actions related to trust (Fig. 2.10).

The dimensions that shape trust and contribute to its increase include (Fig. 2.10):

– institutional-based dimention:

  • legal—formal and legal regulations that create a safe and ordered space for the establishment of relationships;
  • calculation—trust is based on the calculation of costs and benefits arising from a given relationship, hence on a rational belief that it is beneficial;

– cognitive-based dimension:

  • personality—trust focuses on natural and nurtured personality traits of interacting entities, which guarantee the success of relationship;
  • perceptional—trust results from the perception of others. Since perception is subjective and related to the personality of the perceiver, relationships established on this basis are determined by the personality traits of the perceiver;

– knowledge-based dimension—the most sustainable category of trust based on the gained experiences and skills.

Balance and safety of relationships requires also taking the risk dimension into account (Fig. 2.10). This dimension decreases the final value of trust, but determines holding control over the measures taken on the basis of trust.

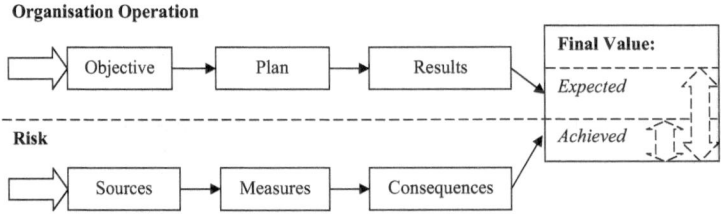

Fig. 2.11 Schema of the risk impact on the activities undertaken in an organization (*source*: own research)

Risk is a concept with numerous definitions, even though people understand and use the term in an intuitive way. It is a function of two basic attributes, i.e. the probability of its occurrence (materialization) and the predicted consequences (profit or loss). A thorough risk analysis allows determination of a more detailed structure. The literature describes the most important elements of this structure (Dionne 2013):

– risk consequences—indicate risk in the form of deviations from the expected value of the intended objective;
– risk sources—highlight the causes (sources) of the risk;
– risk measures—identify the risk with its measures (statistical or probabilistic);
– risk characteristics—accentuate the aspect of uncertainty in the context of the decision-making process.

All of above elements are included in ISO 31000:2009.[5] It is the current gold standard of risk management and presents a schema of risk impact on an organisation's operation (Fig. 2.11).

The activities undertaken in the organisation are determined by the defined objectives, accomplished according to the adopted plan and the effectiveness of their performance is evaluated on the basis of the achieved results. The impact of risk is seen mainly at the stage of comparing those results that have been achieved with those that were expected at the stages of formulating the objective and developing the plan. Reducing the negative impact of risk should take place at the planning stage. During the analysis of risk sources and estimation of its impact, it should be possible to define proper mechanisms for prevention and recovery. The effectiveness of undertaking risk treatment is measured by the difference between expected and achieved results. The organisation should strive for a situation where this difference exhibits a downward trend. An existence of this difference indicates on limitations in abilities of rational planning and predicting the effects of activities and in consequence in abilities in dealing with risk.

The combination of two elements, i.e. trust management and risk management, increases the effectiveness and safety of established collaboration between

---

[5] ISO 31000:2009. *Risk management—Principles and guidelines.*

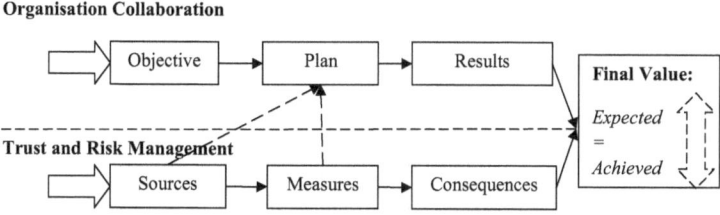

Fig. 2.12 The model of controlled trust (*source*: own research)

organisations in terms of the achievement of defined objectives and completion of tasks (Fig. 2.12).

In accordance with the model presented in Fig. 2.12, each of the constituents (i.e. sources, measures and consequences) has a dual structure—on the one hand it identifies the threats and estimates the related risk, and on the other hand it considers the benefits resulting from the trust that leads to establishing collaboration. Therefore, it is a model that enables the introduction of the so-called controlled trust, which does not hinder collaboration, but rationalises the view of partners and expected benefits.

This model may also be used to identify the elements that are to be included in the collaboration agreement, whose role is to guarantee the safety and usefulness of collaboration for partners. The conditions of creating such an agreement and its structure are described in Chap. 4 (*Arranging Collaborative Benchmarking Group*) and Chap. 5 (*Coordinating Collaborative Benchmarking Group*).

2.6 Summarizing: Concept of Benchmarking Collaborative Network

Integrating the above presented ideas in one common approach leads to concept of Benchmarking Collaborative Network (BCN) presented in Fig. 2.13.

The need to create a BCN is justified by the following claims:

- collaboration between SMEs is necessary to reinforce their competitive potential and will be more efficient than the traditional attitude of competitive fight,
- even though familiarity with the market and factors influencing competitiveness is minor in a single SME, it is much greater in a group,
- competitive collaboration of SMEs requires coordination of measures by an expert with necessary knowledge and skills that SMEs lack.

These result in the concept of BCN, which encompasses (Fig. 2.13) the methods and techniques of competitiveness analysis used to prototype competitive strategies for each member of the collaborating group. The use of the same methods and techniques for a single SME would be inefficient and even impossible.

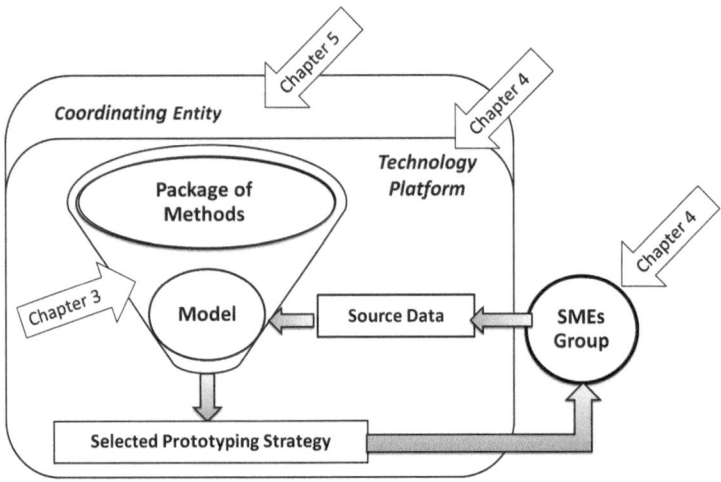

Fig. 2.13 Concept of benchmarking collaborative network (*source*: own research)

Given the shortcomings of SMEs in the area of their skills and knowledge, these measures are carried out by an external coordinating entity. This implies considering the three key elements of BCN's structure, which will be discussed in the subsequent chapters of the present work. These are:

– the method of prototyping competitive strategies for SMEs—Chap. 3,
– the method of organising collaboration within a group of SMEs—Chap. 4,
– the method of coordinating collaboration by an external entity—Chap. 5.

The BCN concept aims to enhance the competitiveness of SMEs to a level that would ensure them more stable operation on a competitive market occupied by small and big business entities.

References

ABC-Network. (2007). *Benchmarking study. Deliverable n. 6. Network of European Agro-Biotech Clusters*. EUROPE INNOVA, European Commission.

Ahmed, P., & Rafi, Q. M. (1998). Integrated benchmarking: A holistic examination of select technics for benchmarking analysis. *Benchmarking for Quality Management and Technology, 5*(3), 1–10.

Ajelabi, I., & Tang, Y. (2010). The adoption of benchmarking principles for project management performance improvement. *International Journal of Managing Public Sector Information and Communication Techniques, 1*(2), 1–8.

Akbar, K., Krishna, S. M., & Reddy, T. V. S. (2013). ETL process modeling in DWH using enhanced quality techniques. *International Journal of Database Theory & Application, 6*(4), 179–197.

Akram, J. K. (2011). The value of Competitive Business Intelligence System (CBIS) to stimulate competitiveness in global market. *International Journal of Business and Social Science, 2*(19), 196–203.

Baars, H., & Kemper, H. (2010). Business intelligence in the cloud? *PACIS 2010 Proceedings. Paper, 145*, 1528–1539.

Bigliardi, B., Dormio, A. I., & Galati, F. (2011). Successful co-opetition strategy: Evidence from an Italian consortium. *International Journal of Business, Management and Social Sciences, 2* (4), 1–8.

Borgatti, S. P., Everett, M. G., & Johnson, J. C. (2013). *Analyzing social networks.* Thousand Oaks, CA: Sage.

Brandenburger, A. M., & Nalebuff, B. J. (1996). *Co-opetition.* New York: Doubleday.

Bruno, I. (2009). The indefinite discipline of competitiveness benchmarking as a neoliberal technology of government. *Minerva, 47*(3), 261–280.

Chan, M. F., & Chung, W. W. (2002). A framework to develop an enterprise information portal for contract manufacturing. *International Journal of Production Economics, 75*(1), 113–126.

Chandler, N., Hostmann, B., Rayner, N., & Herschel, G. (2011). *Gartner's business analytics framework. Gartner Report G00219420.* Stamford, CT: Gartner.

Child, J., Faulkner, D., & Tallman, S. B. (2005). *Cooperative strategy.* Oxford: Oxford University Press.

Christozov, D., & Toleva-Stoimenova, S. (2014). The role of information brokers in knowledge management. *Online Journal of Applied Knowledge Management A Publication of the International Institute for Applied Knowledge Management, 2*(2), 109–119.

Completo, J., Cruz, R. S., Coheur, L., & Delgado, M. (2012). Design and implementation of a Data Warehouse for benchmarking in clinical rehabilitation. *Procedia Technology, 5*, 885–894.

Crouch, G. I. (2011). Destination competitiveness: An analysis of determinant attributes. *Journal of Travel Research, 50*(1), 27–45.

Czakon, W., Fernandez, A. S., & Mina, A. (2014). Editorial—From paradox to practice: The rise of coopetition strategies. *International Journal of Business Environment, 6*(1), 1–10.

Czakon, W., & Klimas, P. (2014). Innovative networks in knowledge-intensive industries: How to make them work? An empirical investigation into the Polish Aviation Valley. In D. Jemielniak (Ed.), *The laws of the knowledge workplace* (pp. 133–158). Farnham: Gower Publishing.

D'Aveni, R. (1994). *Hypercompetition.* New York: Free Press.

Daddi, T., Tessitore, S., & Frey, M. (2012). Eco-innovation and competitiveness in industrial clusters. *International Journal of Technology Management, 58*(1), 49–63.

Danik, L., & Lewandowska, M. S. (2013). Motives and barriers in the field of cooperation between companies. Research outcomes based on the Polish Engineering Industry. *Journal of Economics & Management, 2013*(14), 21–34.

Denchev, S., & Christozov, D. (2012). *Informing and information brokering.* Sofia, Bulgaria: Marin Drinov Publishing House.

Dévai, K., Papanek, G., & Borsi, B. (2002). *A methodology for benchmarking RTD organisations in Central and Eastern Europe.* Budapest: Budapest University of Technology and Economics.

Dionne, G. (2013). Risk management: History, definition, and critique. *Risk Management and Insurance Review. American Risk and Insurance Association, 16*(2), 147–166.

Doan, A., Raghu, R., & Halevy, A. Y. (2011). Crowdsourcing systems on the world-wide web. *Communications of the ACM, 54*(4), 86–96.

Eckerson, W. W. (2010). *Performance dashboards: Measuring, monitoring, and managing your business.* Hoboken, NJ: John Wiley & Sons.

Elmuti, D., & Kathawala, Y. (1997). An overview of benchmarking process: a tool for continuous improvement and competitive advantage. *Benchmarking for Quality Management & Technology, 4*(4), 229–243.

ESCA. (2012). *Benchmarking as a tool of cluster analysis. Cluster excellence makes the difference.* Berlin: European Secretariat of Cluster Analysis.

Estellés-Arolas, E., & González-Ladrón-de-Guevara, F. (2012). Towards an integrated crowdsourcing definition. *Journal of Information science, 38*(2), 189–200.

European Commission. (2012). *Customs 2013 programme benchmarking guide.* Brussels: European Commission.

Falck, O., & Heblich, S. (2007). Corporate social responsibility: Doing well by doing good. *Business Horizons, 50*(3), 247–254.

Foshay, N., Taylor, A., & Mukherjee, A. (2014). A conceptual model of metadata's role in BI success. In W. Yeoh, J. Talburt, & Y. Zhou (Eds.), *Information quality and governance for business intelligence* (pp. 1–19). Hershey, PA: Business Science Reference. doi:10.4018/978-1-4666-4892-0.ch001.

Fryman, H. (2007). The successful path to combining BI and BPM. *Align Journal.* Dallas: TCI Publication.

Gilpin, R. (2000). *The challenge of global capitalism: The world economy in the 21st century.* Princeton, NJ: Princeton University Press.

Gnyawali, D. R., & Park, B. J. R. (2009). Co-opetition and technological innovation in small and medium-sized enterprises: A multilevel conceptual model. *Journal of Small Business Management, 47*(3), 308–330.

Grudzewski, W. M., Hejduk, I. K., & Sankowska, A. (2009). Trust management as a base of new economy management practices. *Economics and Organization of Future Enterprise, 4*(2), 2–8. doi:10.2478/v10061-009-0014-5.

Hetmank, L. (2013). Towards a semantic standard for enterprise crowdsourcing. A scenario-based evaluation of a conceptual prototype. *ECIS 2013 Completed Research. Paper 118.* Url: http://aisel.aisnet.org/ecis2013_cr/118

Honkola J., Laine, H., Brown, R., & Tyrkko, O. (2010). Smart-M3 information sharing platform. In: *IEEE Symposium on Computers and Communications* (ISCC) (pp. 1041–1046), 2010.

Hosmer, L. T. (1995). Trust: The connecting link between organizational theory and philosophical ethics. *Academy of Management Review, 20*(2), 379–403.

Huggins, R. (2010). Regional competitive intelligence: Benchmarking and policy-making. *Regional Studies, 44*(5), 639–658.

Inkpen, A. C., & Tsang, E. (2005). Social capital networks and knowledge transfer. *Academy of Management Review, 30*(1), 146–165.

Inmon, W. H. (2005). *Building the data warehouse* (4th ed.). New York, NY: Wiley.

Inmon, W. H., & Nesavich, A. (2007). *Tapping into unstructured data: Integrating unstructured data and textual analytics into business intelligence.* Upper Saddle River, NJ: Pearson Education.

Inmon, W. H., Strauss, D., & Neushloss, G. (2010). *DW 2.0: The architecture for the next generation of data warehousing: The architecture for the next generation of data warehousing.* San Francisco, CA: Morgan Kaufmann.

Inovisa. (2012). *International benchmarking study of competitiveness poles and clusters and identification of best practices.* Ribatejo, Portugal: The Cluster Agro-Industrial.

Jones-Kaminski, S. (2009). *I'm at a networking event–Now what?* Silicon Valley: HappyAbout. Info.

Kantardzic, M. (2011). *Data mining: Concepts, models, methods, and algorithms* (2nd ed.). Hoboken, NJ: John Wiley & Sons.

Kemper, H. G., Baars, H., & Lasi, H. (2013). An integrated business intelligence framework. Closing the gap between IT support for management and for production. In P. Rausch, A. F. Sheta, & A. Ayesh (Eds.), *Business intelligence and performance management theory, systems and industrial applications* (pp. 13–26). New York: Springer.

Ketels, C. (2011). Clusters and competitiveness: Porter's contribution. In: R., Huggins, & H., Izushi (eds.) *Competition, competitive advantage and clusters: The ideas of Michael Porter* (pp. 173–191). Oxford: Oxford University Press.

Ketels, C., Lindqvist, G., & Sölvell, Ö. (2012). *Strengthening clusters and competitiveness in Europe.* Stocholm: Stocholm School of Economics.

Khetrapal, P., & Thakur, T. (2014). A review of benchmarking approaches for productivity and efficiency measurement in electricity distribution sector. *International Journal of Electronics and Electrical Engineering, 2*(3), 214–221. Doi: 10.12720/ijeee.2.3.214-221.

Kim, S., Suh, E., & Jun, Y. (2011). Building a knowledge brokering system using social network analysis: A case study of the Korean financial industry. *Expert Systems with Applications, 38* (12), 14633–14649.

Kimball, R., Ross, M., Thorthwaite, W., Becker, B., & Mundy, J. (2008). *The data warehouse lifecycle toolkit.* Indianapolis, IN: John Wiley & Sons.

Lacoste, S. (2012). Vertical coopetition: The key account perspective. *Industrial Marketing Management, 41*(4), 649–658.

Lai, M. C., Huang, H. C., & Wang, W. K. (2011). Designing a knowledge-based system for benchmarking: A DEA approach. *Knowledge-Based Systems, 24*(5), 662–671.

Levy, M., Loebbecke, C., & Powell, P. (2003). SMEs, coopetition and knowledge sharing: The role of information systems. *European Journal of Information Systems, 12*(1), 3–17.

Lilama. (2010). *Observatory of good practices. Benchmarking method guide.* The Lilama Network, European Commission.

Luo, Y. (2004). A coopetition perspective of MNC-host government relations. *Journal of International Management, 10*(4), 431–445.

Maggetti, M., & Gilardi, F. (2011). The policy-making structure of European regulatory networks and the domestic adoption of standards. *Journal of European Public Policy, 18*(6), 830–847.

Maltby, D. (2011). Big data analytics. *Proceeding of Association for Information Science and Technology 2011,* 74th Annual Meeting, New Orleans.

Marjanovic, O. (2010). The importance of process thinking in business intelligence. *International Journal of Business Intelligence Research, 1*(4), 29–46.

Martin D., Oohama H., Moran D., & Cheyer A. (1997). Information brokering in an agent architecture. In: *Proceedings of the Second International Conference on the practical application of intelligent agents and multi-agent technology,* (pp. 467–489).

Meyer, M. (2010). The rise of the knowledge broker. *Science Communication, 32*(1), 118–127.

Michaels, S. (2009). Matching knowledge brokering strategies to environmental policy problems and settings. *Environmental Science and Policy, 12*(2009), 994–1011.

Morris, M. H., Kocak, A., & Özer, A. (2007). Coopetition as a small business strategy: Implications for performance. *Journal of Small Business Strategy, 18*(1), 35–55.

Okura, M. (2007). Coopetitive strategies of Japanese Insurance firms—A game theory approach. *International Studies of Management and Organization, 37*(2), 53–69.

Ouf, S., & Nasr, M. (2011). Business intelligence in the cloud. In *Communication Software and Networks (ICCSN), 2011 I.E. 3rd International Conference on* (pp. 650–655). IEEE.

Paliszkiewicz, J. (2011). Trust management: Literature review. *Management, 6*(4), 315–331.

Paliszkiewicz, J., & Koohang, A. (2013). Organizational trust as a foundation for knowledge sharing and its influence on organizational performance. *Online Journal of Applied Knowledge Management, 1*(2), 116–127.

Park, Y. W., Amano, T., & Moon, G. (2012). Benchmarking open and cluster innovation: Case of Korea. *Benchmarking: An International Journal, 19*(4/5), 517–531.

Parshotam, K. (2013). Crowd computing: a literature review and definition. In *Proceedings of the South African Institute for Computer Scientists and Information Technologists Conference* (pp. 121–130). ACM.

Poetz, M. K., & Schreier, M. (2012). The value of crowdsourcing: Can users really compete with professionals in generating new product ideas? *Journal of Product Innovation Management, 29* (2), 245–256.

Porter, M. E. (1985). *Competitive advantage: Creating and sustaining superior performance.* London: Collier Macmillan.

Porter, M. E. (1998). *Competitive strategy: Techniques for analyzing industries and competitors.* New York: Free Press.

Raharjo, H., Chai, K. H., Xie, M., & Brombacher, A. C. (2010). Dynamic benchmarking methodology for quality function deployment. *Benchmarking: An International Journal, 17*(1), 27–43.

Ranjan, J. (2009). Business intelligence: Concepts, components, techniques and benefits. *Journal of Theoretical and Applied Information Technology, 9*(1), 60–70.

Rivest, S., Bédard, Y., Proulx, M. J., Nadeau, M., Hubert, F., & Pastor, J. (2005). SOLAP technology: Merging business intelligence with geospatial technology for interactive spatio-temporal exploration and analysis of data. *ISPRS Journal of Photogrammetry and Remote Sensing, 60*(1), 17–33.

Rostek, K. (2010). Business intelligence for SME. In E. Lechman (Ed.), *SMEs and enterpreneurship* (Vol. 2, pp. 164–190). Gdańsk: Gdańsk University of Technology Publishing House.

Rostek, K. (2013a). Dedicated business intelligence system for SMEs consortium. *African Journal of Business Management, 7*(13), 999–1014.

Rostek, K. (2013b). The mutual benchmarking method for SMEs' competitive strategy development. *Foundations of Management, International Journal, 5*(2), 81–96.

Rostek, K. (2014). The paradigm of mutual benchmarking in the context of SMEs' competitiveness development. *International Journal of Business and Management Research, 2*(1), 66–89.

Rouhani, S., Asgari, S., & Mirhosseini, S. (2012). Review study: Business intelligence concepts and approaches. *American Journal of Scientific Research, 50*, 62–75.

Russom, P. (2011). *Big data analytics. TDWI best practices report.* Renton: The Data Warehouse Institute.

Sapio, B., Palombini, I., & Cioffi, S. (2007). IBIS: International benchmarking of the information society. *Observatorio (OBS*) Journal, 1*(2007), 225–233.

Saxton, G. D., Onook, O., & Kishore, R. (2013). Rules of crowdsourcing: Models, issues, and systems of control. *Information Systems Management, 30*(1), 2–20.

Schoorman, F. D., Mayer, R. C., & Davis, J. H. (2007). An integrative model of organizational trust: Past, present, and future. *Academy of Management Review, 32*(2), 344–354.

Seufert, A., & Schiefer, J. (2005). *Enhanced business intelligence: Supporting business processes with real-time business analytics.* In: Database and Expert Systems Applications, 2005. Proceedings. Sixteenth International Workshop on IEEE, (pp. 919–925).

Shaxson L., & Gwyn, E. (2010). *Developing a strategy for knowledge translation and brokering in public policymaking.* In: The knowledge translation and brokering, the Special Workshop on 2010, Montreal, Canada.

Sroka, W., & Hittmár, Š. (2013). *Management of alliance networks: Formation, functionality, and post operational strategies.* Berlin: Springer.

Sztompka, P. (2000). *Trust: A sociological theory.* Cambridge: Cambridge University Press.

Thomas, H., & Datta, A. (2001). A conceptual model and algebra for on-line analytical processing in decision support databases. *Information Systems Research, 12*(1), 83–102.

Thomas, H., & Pollock, T. (1999). From I-O economics' S-C-P paradigm through strategic groups to competence-based competition: Reflections on the puzzle of competitive strategy. *British Journal of Management, 10*(2), 127–140.

Tidstrom, A. (2008). Perspectives on coopetition on actor and operational levels. *Management Research, 6*(3), 207–218.

Trkman, P., McCormack, K., De Oliveira, M. P. V., & Ladeira, M. B. (2010). The impact of business analytics on supply chain performance. *Decision Support Systems, 49*(3), 318–327.

Turnhout, E., Stuiver, M., Klostermann, J., Harms, B., & Leeuwis, C. (2013). New roles of science in society: Different repertoires of knowledge brokering. *Science and Public Policy, 40*(3), 354–365.

Van der Aalst, W. M. (2011). Using process mining to bridge the gap between BI and BPM. *IEEE Computer, 44*(12), 77–80.

Vukovic, M. (2009). Crowdsourcing for enterprises. *Services-I, 2009 World Conference on*, IEEE, 686–692. DOI: 10.1109/SERVICES-I.2009.56

Waas, F., Wrembel, R., Freudenreich, T., Thiele, M., Koncilia, C., & Furtado, P. (2013). On-demand ETL architecture for right-time BI: Extending the vision. *International Journal of Data Warehousing and Mining, 9*(2), 21–38.

Weiss, S. M., Indurkhya, N., Zhang, T., & Damerau, F. (2005). *Text mining: Predictive methods for analyzing unstructured information.* New York: Springer.

Xavier, M. J., & Ramachander, S. (2000). The pursuit of immortality: A new approach beyond the competitiveness paradigm. *Management Decision, 38*(7), 480–490.

Xu, G., Zhang, Y., & Li, L. (2010). *Web mining and social networking: Techniques and applications* (Vol. 6). Berlin: Springer Science & Business Media.

Zakrzewska-Bielawşka, A. (2013). Coopetition in high-technology firms: Resource-based determinants. In: A. Zaharim, R. G. Rodrigues (eds.), *Recent advances in management, marketing and finances* (pp. 51–56). Business and Economic Series (4). Cambridge: WSEAS Press.

Zeng, S. X., Xie, X. M., & Tam, C. M. (2010). Relationship between cooperation networks and innovation performance of SMEs. *Technovation, 30*(3), 181–194.

Zicari, R. V. (2014). Big data: Challenges and opportunities. In R. Akerkar (Ed.), *Big data computing* (pp. 103–128). Boca Raton, FL: CRC Press.

Chapter 3
Prototyping Competitive Strategy

A competitive strategy is a complex process that enables developing and maintaining positive relationships between the company's objectives, its resources and the changing environment (Zakrzewska-Bielawska 2012). It consists of a set of guidelines for decisions and measures to be taken by decision-makers at a specific time, within specific areas and in relation to specific resources (Williamson et al. 2004; Romanowska and Gierszewska 2009). Small companies usually apply strategies that limit their activity to the closest environment and ensure safe operation without the need to confront their competition. For this reason, the strategies of small companies focus above all on:

- overcoming weaknesses and reinforcing natural advantages—focusing on striving for excellence and company's development (Matejun 2008; Seidel et al. 2009);
- exploring opportunities and market niches—locating the company and its business activity in the most favourable conditions (Pierścionek 2006; Obłój 2013);
- evaluating and adjusting strengths to emerging opportunities—intensifying the use of the existing advantages of the company and avoiding emerging threats (Pierścionek 2011; Verbano and Venturini 2013).

The definition formulated by K. Obłój (Obłój 2013) states that *strategy is a coherent concept of operation based on a few key complementing choices that allow for developing competitive advantage and ensure the achievement of above-average results*, and refers to three key areas indicating:

- where a company is at a given stage of development;
- where it would like to be in the future;
- how it intends to achieve the desired position.

That is why the adopted methods and techniques supporting competitive strategy should correspond to the indicated decision-making areas. Taking the above guidelines into consideration, a method is sought that would make it possible to:

© Springer International Publishing Switzerland 2015
K. Rostek, *Benchmarking Collaborative Networks*, Contributions to Management Science, DOI 10.1007/978-3-319-16736-7_3

- identify the current competitive position of the company;
- specify possible strategies that would lead to achieving the defined objective;
- indicate which of the specified strategies will most probably enable achieving this objective in a specified time.

The applied method has to take into account the SMEs' knowledge and experience shortages in the development of competitive strategy, and limited access to expert knowledge. Therefore, it should use techniques that are based on the company's performance and automate the process of analysis and drawing conclusions by prototyping alternative strategies. Moreover, it is crucial for the selection and choice of competitive strategies to be individualised, namely to consider the company's characteristics—its strengths and weaknesses, as well as the nature of its operation in the market environment.

It was for this purpose that the HRPM method (*Hierarchical-Regression Prototyping Method*) was developed as a process which uses the results from analysis of historical data (the company's performance) to support the decision-making process in terms of specifying competitive strategies. It is proposed in two versions:

- crisp (Sect. 3.2), which requires accurate data for analysis;
- fuzzy (Sect. 3.4), which provides for inaccuracy of processed data and resulting fuzziness of outcomes.

The effectiveness of the proposed method was presented with the example of a group of SMEs from the health care sector (in the crisp version—Sect. 3.3, in the fuzzy version—Sect. 3.5).

The HRPM method serves the HMDP model (*Hierarchical Model of Decision Problem*), which defines the relations between the objective of the strategy, alternative ways of achieving it (alternative strategies) and factors determining the achievement of this objective (competitiveness criteria). This conception is illustrated at Fig. 3.1.

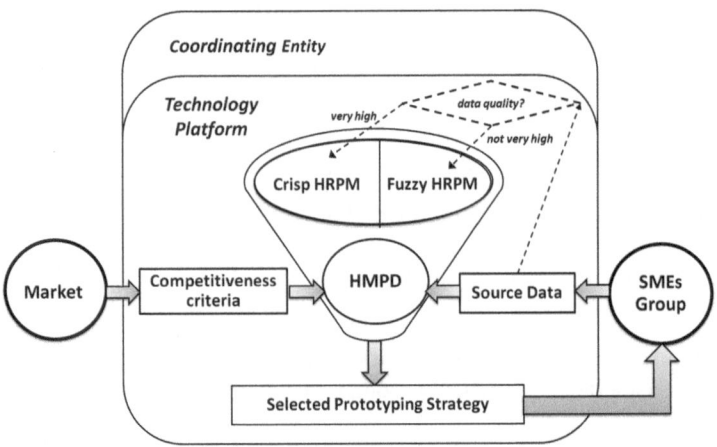

Fig. 3.1 The conception of supporting the competitive strategy (*source*: own research)

Therefore, the presentation of the HRPM method will begin with the presentation of the HMDP model's structure (Sect. 3.1).

3.1 Hierarchical Model of Decision Problem

The decision problem model using the HRPM method defines hierarchical relations between the main goal, intermediate goals, the criteria of evaluation and alternative solutions. This concept is known and used in the AHP method (Analytic Hierarchy Process).

AHP, developed by Thomas L. Saaty in the 1990s (Saaty 1990–2001), is a commonly accepted and used tool for making complex decisions based on any number of criteria. AHP hierarchically decomposes the criteria of problem evaluation and its alternative solutions. The structure of the hierarchy of importance in the AHP method is pre-defined (Fig. 3.2).

The hierarchy's main elements are the main goal of the decision process (G_s—main goal) and alternative solutions ($V_1, \ldots, V_m$—decision variants), which will be more or less successful in achieving this goal. The selection of the best alternative is based on a set of determined criteria ($C_1, \ldots, C_n$—criteria).

In the classic AHP, the decision-maker has a significant impact on the results, which makes this method expert-based. The expert decision-maker evaluates possible alternatives and their impact on reaching the goal in terms of the impact of individual criteria, in accordance with his/her knowledge and discretion resulting from experience. In the HRPM, the role of the expert is limited due to the limited knowledge and experience of its users in SMEs and lack of access to external experts.

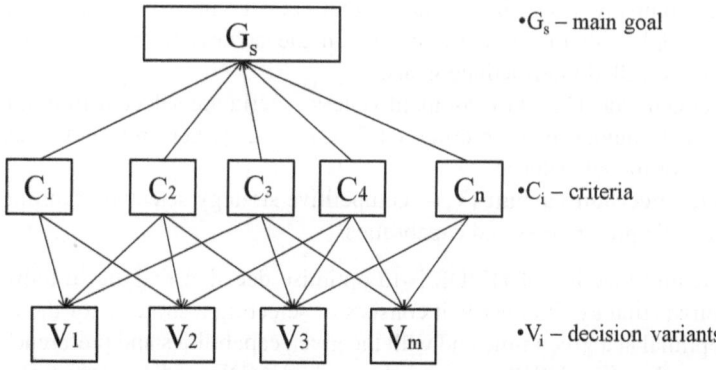

Fig. 3.2 Structure of analytic hierarchy process [*source*: (Saaty 1990–2001)]

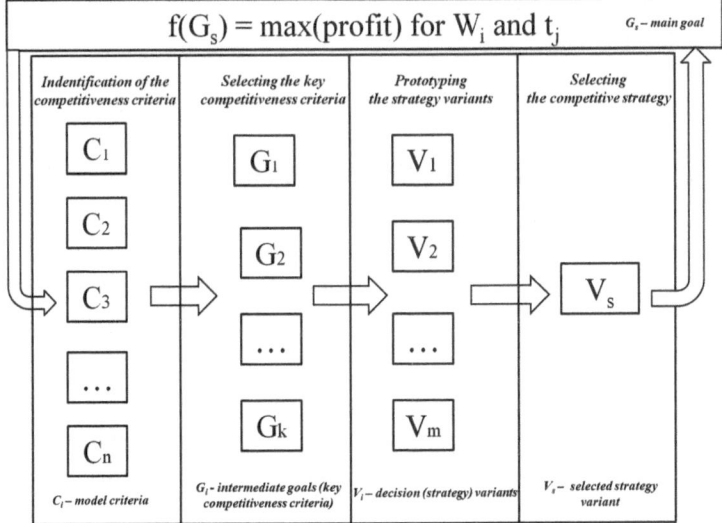

Fig. 3.3 Hierarchical model of decision problem (*source*: own research)

HRPM draws on the Hierarchical Model of Decision Problem (HMDP, Fig. 3.3).
It is also based on the AHP model, and consists of the following elements (Fig. 3.3):

- **main goal (G_s)**—adopted objective (goal) function $f(G)$ envisages efforts
  towards maximising the profit of the company W_i in the time t_i;
- **alternative decision variants (V_i)**—the main goal is reached by means of
  implementing one of the prototyped alternative competitive strategies $\{V_1,
  V_2, \ldots, V_m\}$; the effectiveness of individual alternative competitive strategies
  may change for various companies at different time;
- **intermediate goals (G_i)**—the selection of the best competitive strategy for a
  given company takes into consideration key competitiveness criteria $\{G_1,
  G_2, \ldots, G_k\}$ with the greatest impact on the achievement of the main goal,
  which are called intermediate goals;
- **model criteria (C_i)**—key competitiveness criteria are selected from among all
  identified competitiveness criteria $\{C_1, C_2, \ldots, C_n\}$, here referred to as partial
  criteria or model criteria;
- **selected decision variant (V_s)**—competitive strategy selected according to the
  company's preferences and capabilities.

The main objective of HMDP is to optimise decision making in terms of the
competitive strategy. It consists it consists of selecting a strategy for the company
that is optimal at a given time and with the given capabilities and preferences of the
decision-maker. The HRPM method serves the HMDP model in terms of:

- identifying model criteria—specifying known competitiveness criteria for a given group of companies, taking into account the type and form of business activity, their size, location and the market characteristic;
- selecting key competitiveness criteria—selecting from among all identified model criteria those with the greatest impact on the main goal, which is the amount of generated profit;
- prototyping alternative competitive strategies—specifying acceptable solutions with a comparable level of predicted profit;
- selecting alternative strategies—selecting from among the acceptable alternative strategies the one that will most probably and most effectively ensure the envisaged main goal.

The use of the HMDP model offers broad support for companies, consisting in the use of analytical capacity of data to overcome knowledge and experience shortages. However, its effectiveness is conditioned by the cardinality and quality of source data provided to the model, as well as capabilities of the IT technology supporting its service.

3.2 Hierarchical-Regression Prototyping Method

HRPM method has been developed while considering the following assumptions:

- the measure of the company's competitive position is the size of the profit achieved in stipulated time;
- improvement of competitive position is equivalent to an increase of generated profits;
- effectiveness of competitive strategy depends on the knowledge of the value and the impact of the key competitiveness criteria on the position occupied by the company;
- there are alternative strategies resulting in a similar level of competitiveness, but showing a diverse efficacy in relation to the various companies.

Considering the above was defined within the HRPM method (Fig. 3.4), and serves to provide possible variations to competitive strategy, and helps to identify the one that is most beneficial for a particular company at the current time.

3.2.1 PM1: Identification of the Competitiveness Criteria

The HRPM implementation starts from identification of the competitiveness criteria which is characteristic in the analyzed group of companies. As indicated by literature research there is a great diversity both among the criteria and objectives of competitiveness, which justifies the need for their individual selection.

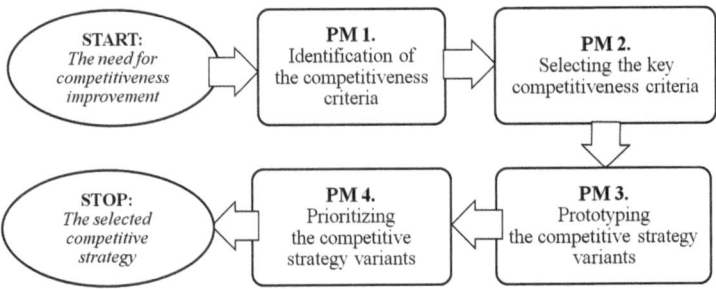

Fig. 3.4 Hierarchical-Regression Prototyping Method (*source*: own research)

For example, M. E. Porter believed that successful competing requires the application of the cost leadership strategy and distinguishing oneself from the competition through offer differentiation (Porter 1998). According to K. Ohmae, successful approaches consist in measures aimed at adjusting the offer to the needs of recipients and in efforts to change the value of key success factors (Ohmae 1982). Hamel and Prahalad noticed that a sole analysis of current benefits and current competitive potential in relation to competitors will not ensure maintaining current advantage in the future (Prahalad and Hamel 1989). A prognostic approach to the development of competitive strategies, predicting and reaping emerging benefits and avoiding imminent threats are crucial (Prahalad and Hamel 1990). D'Aveni suggested that in order to achieve sustainable competitive advantages, one should not focus on its current sources, but keep developing new ones (D'Aveni 1994).

In response to this diversity, a number of research projects are carried out to identify local competitiveness factors related to a specific industry (Crouch 2011; Zheng and Qi 2011), market or country (Porter 2011), or even the size and level of company's internationalisation (Rugman et al. 2012; Lanvin and Evans 2013). The impact of the most frequent competitiveness factors is also identified (Barge-Gil and Modrego 2011), and the factors are evaluated with reference to the competitive position (Rostek 2012).

Scientists highlight the dynamics of the process of competitive strategy development (Shay and Rothaermel 1999; Warren 2008) and the resulting need for a relevant selection of methods, models and supporting tools (Eden and Ackermann 2013). They also stress the need for a detailed definition of a group of companies for which criteria determining competitiveness will be identified (Blažek et al. 2011), which enables the application of a common approach to competitiveness evaluation.

The competing is a dynamically changing process with a broad variety of criteria determining the final result. Therefore, studying competitiveness criteria and their impact on the effectiveness of a defined group of companies is not a trivial matter. Provided that group leaders have developed effective procedures, the analysis of their operations and their effects should provide knowledge on the effectiveness of various alternative competitive strategies within this group. This assumption is the basis of the approach presented below.

3.2.2 PM2: Selecting the Key Competitiveness Criteria

At this stage the key criteria shall be identified from the whole criteria set. The need to limit the number of criteria is justified by prototyping competitive strategies at the next stage of the method. Without a doubt, a company will not be able to effectively use recommendations concerning several dozen competitiveness factors identified in the specified decision-making areas (Rostek 2012). Therefore, it is justified to select only those that will have the greatest impact on the value of the objective function, and to use them to develop a competitive strategy.

The basis for identification of key criterion is the strength of its impact on the value of the objective function. For this purpose the regression method of analysis is used because it allows examination of all the criteria's impact on the goal function and selecting the key competitiveness criteria on this basis. A similar use of the regression method as the supplementation of the classical AHP analysis as regards the specification of preference estimations may be found in the works of (Sugihara et al. 2004; Priya and Venkatesh 2012).

Regression analysis makes it possible to study the strength, direction and value of the impact of explanatory (independent) variables on the response (dependent) variables, which is the purpose of the conducted study. The method is able to specify the characteristics of an average population. Therefore, it is often used as preliminary analysis in the process of solving complex analytical problems.

It consists of the estimation of parameters within a theoretical equation in order to reflect the value and strength of the impact as accurately as possible. The value of a multiple linear regression function is derived from the following formula (Kleinbaum 2007):

$$Y = \beta_1 X_1 + \beta_2 X_2 + \ldots + \beta_n X_n + \beta_0 + \varepsilon \qquad (3.1)$$

where:

Y—the response variable (dependent variable);
X_i—the ith explanatory variable (independent variable);
β_i—the ith coefficient of the regression model;
ε—the random component of the regression model, which cannot be explained with explanatory variables.

The random component represents random disturbances of functional connection between the values of the response variable and the values of the explanatory variable ε. It includes all factors which influence the response variable y other than the explanatory variable x. It is related to the lack of a perfect match between the analytical form of the regression function and the actual relations between the analysed variables. It can be expressed by the following formula (Kleinbaum 2007):

$$\varepsilon_i = y_i - \hat{y}_i \tag{3.2}$$

where:

y_i—the estimated value of the response variable from the ith observation from a sample;
$\hat{y}_i$—the actual value of the response variable from the ith observation from a sample.

The criterion of estimating unknown regression parameters may be formulated on this basis as (Kleinbaum 2007):

$$f(\varepsilon) = \sum_{i=1}^{n} \varepsilon_i^2 = \sum_{i=1}^{n} (y_i - \hat{y}_i)^2 = \min \tag{3.3}$$

β_i coefficients values of the regression model are unknown. Their values are estimated on the basis of the analysed research sample of observations (x_i, y_i) for $i = 1, 2, \ldots, n$. The values of parameters in the regression equation are estimated by means of the least squares method, where the objective is to minimise the sum of squared vertical distances between the observed responses in the dataset and the responses predicted by the linear approximation. Hence, the values of regression coefficients may be expressed by the following formulas (Kleinbaum 2007):

$$\beta_0 = \bar{y} - \sum_{i=1}^{n} \beta_i \bar{x} \tag{3.4}$$

$$\beta_i = \frac{\sum_{i=1}^{n} (x_i - \bar{x})(y_i - \bar{y})}{\sum_{i=1}^{n} (x_i - \bar{x})^2} \tag{3.5}$$

where:

$\bar{y}$—the mean value of the response variable for the sample;
$\bar{x}$—the mean value of the explanatory variable for the sample.

Assuming that some independent variables do not have a significant impact on the regression value, it is justified to eliminate them. Explanatory variables are selected stepwise. The approach may take the form of (Hegyi and Garamszegi 2011; Zhou et al. 2012):

- forward selection—subsequent adding of explanatory variables that have the most significant impact on the response variable;
- backward elimination—from the initial set of all explanatory variables, the ones with the smallest impact on the response variable are removed;
- bi-directional elimination (called as stepwise regression)—the combination of the forward and the backward approach. In the previous two cases, each

explanatory variable was taken into account only once. In the bidirectional procedure, explanatory variables are subject to analysis all at once, but the analysis takes place a number of times, in various configurations that should maximise the impact on the response variable and minimise inter-correlations.

In the presented study, a backward elimination of explanatory variables was applied, which in the first step requires an estimation of the regression equation with the maximum number of explanatory variables. Next, an independent variable is eliminated where the value of Student's T-test statistic, which proves the significance of model regression coefficients, is the smallest and is located in the admissible region for null hypothesis H_0. This entails individual testing of hypotheses on the significance of individual variables (Sen and Srivastava 1990):

$$H_0^i : \beta_i = 0 \quad \text{vs.} \quad H_1^i : \beta_i \neq 0 \tag{3.6}$$

If H_0 is true, then the value of Student's T-test statistic takes the form of the following formula (Sen and Srivastava 1990):

$$T_i = \frac{\hat{\beta}_i}{SE_{\hat{\beta}_i}} \tag{3.7}$$

where:

$\hat{\beta}_i$—the theoretical value of the ith regression coefficient;
SE—the mean square error;
TS_i—the Student's T-test statistic of the ith regression coefficient.

On this basis, the level of significance of each ith explanatory variable (p-value) is determined (Sen and Srivastava 1990):

$$p_i = p(|TS_i| < |TS_\lambda|) \tag{3.8}$$

where:

p_i—p-value for ith explanatory variable;
λ—level of significance.

Thus variables are rejected where the value of p_i is maximum and higher than the adopted level of significance λ. The procedure is repeated until all the remaining p-values are lower than λ. Hence all remaining variables are significant, which means that their empirical value on the Student's T-test statistic is located in the critical region of H_0.

3.2.3   PM3: Prototyping the Competitive Strategy Variants

The selected variables, cited as key competitiveness criteria, become the basis for the definition of variants of competitive strategy prototyping through the use of decision trees method. The decision trees method allows for the generation and evaluation of particular variants of strategy in the perspective of their effect, i.e. possible to achieve, forecasted value of the goal.

A similar approach of combining AHP and decision tree methods of analysis was proposed in the work of (Dey 2002). In this study, the AHP was used to evaluate criteria determining the selection of alternative solutions, and the decision trees were used to select these alternatives on the basis of their impact on the achievement of the desired goal. In the HRPM, decision trees are used to prototype alternative strategies by means of key competitiveness factors selected at the previous stage (by means of regression analysis).

Decision trees are a graphic method supporting the decision-making process preferred by analysts and recipients of analyses owing to their transparency and ease of understanding for people without analytical knowledge. Decision trees make it possible to identify sub-sets of observations that significantly diverge from the mean population. Therefore, they are often coupled with regression analysis, making it more complete and adding detail.

The decision tree is a hierarchical structure with nodes and edges that connect them. Each node implements a test that splits space according to the attribute's value, and each obtained outcome corresponds to one branch outgoing from the node. In general, this test takes the form of the following inequality (Zhai 2011):

$$TT_{ij} = \begin{cases} 0, & \text{where } o_{ij} \leq \delta_j \\ 1, & \text{where } o_{ij} > \delta_j \end{cases} \tag{3.9}$$

where:

TT_{ij}—the test splitting the set of the ith observation in the jth tree node;
δ_j—the threshold value in the jth tree node that the test is based on;
o_{ij}—the value of the ith observation in the jth tree node.

The type of test depends on the attribute that determines the split of the set. The following categories of tests are distinguished (Rokach and Maimon 2005):

- identification tests—identifying the test with the attribute, applied in the case of nominal or ordinal attributes;
- equality tests—they check equality with the value of the attribute, applied in the case of nominal or ordinal attributes;
- membership tests—they determine whether the attribute's value belongs to a set, applied in the case of any type of attributes;
- division tests—they check whether an attribute belongs to sub-sets created by the split of the attribute's co domain, applied in the case of any type of attributes;

– inequality tests—they determine inequality for the value of the attribute, applied in the case of ordinal and continuous attributes.

The method of test selection determines the level of complexity of a decision tree; therefore, it is reasonable to aim at constructing the simplest possible tree in the choice of tests. This increases its ease of understanding and limits the risk of over adaptation. In order to achieve this, subsequently selected tests should, as quickly as possible, lead to the creation of a leaf node, which represents a class label and is not subject to further divisions.

In order to select the best type of test, numeric functions assessing increases in information are used. The most frequently used function is entropy (Krishnan and McCalley 2013). Entropy is defined as the average amount of information contained in each message received from a source of information characterised by the probability distribution of samples drawn from it. The value of entropy is derived from the following formula (Gray 2011):

$$EN_j = \sum\nolimits_{i=1}^{n} p(o_{ij}) \log_r \frac{1}{p(o_{ij})} = -\sum\nolimits_{i=1}^{n} p(o_{ij}) \log_r p(o_{ij}) \tag{3.10}$$

where:

$p(o_{ij})$—the occurrence probability of the ith observation in the jth node;
r—the adopted base of the logarithm used (in the information theory r usually equals $\{2; 10; e\}$).

In the conducted study, due to the interval nature of the response variable, variance was chosen as the test searching for and assessing the competing decision rules, which minimises the mean square error of the value of attributes in each node (Heath et al. 1993):

$$SE_j = \sum\nolimits_{i=1}^{n} \left(o_{ij} - \overline{o_J}\right)^2 = min \tag{3.11}$$

where:

SE_j—the mean square error of observations' value in the jth node;
$\overline{o_J}$—the mean of observations' value in the jth node.

The graphical illustration of the decision tree results allows for their simple interpretation (Fig. 3.5). The rule generated on the basis of the decision tree results includes the one complete path—from the initial node (called a root node) to the final node (called a leaf node).

The marked rule (Fig. 3.5) is as follows:

IF $c_7 < 10$ AND $c_{12} <= 37$ THEN $Profit_{avg} = 283.11$

where:

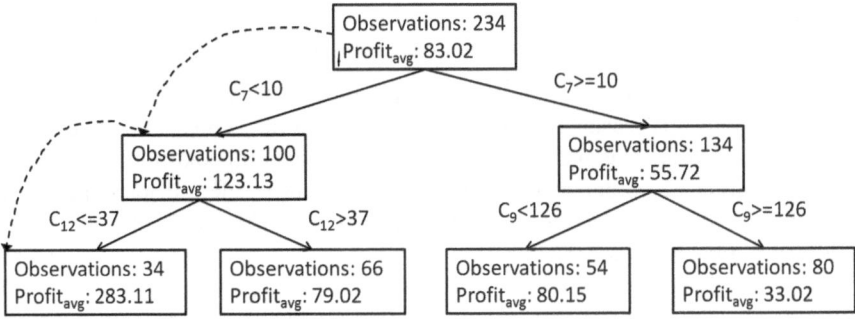

Fig. 3.5 The interpretation of decision tree results (*source*: own research)

c_i—the value of the ith competitiveness criteria;
$Profit_{avg}$—the average profit value (the main goal of compete).

The above rule should be interpreted as follows: *If the value of the competitiveness criteria* $C_7 < 10$, *and the value of the competitiveness criteria* $C_{12} <= 37$, *then the predicted value of the average profit is 283.11.*

Thus generated rules form sets of competitiveness criteria which also are prototyping competitive strategies with predicted efficiency of their implementation.

3.2.4 PM4: Prioritizing the Competitive Strategy Variants

The emergence of alternative strategies, resulting in a similar value of the aim, initiates the questions—which option is the best for the particular entity. The selection of the best approach is implemented by hybrid AHP, wherein expert coefficients and validity priorities have been replaced by the parameters obtained in stages PM2 (from regression analysis) and PM3 (from decision trees analysis). This way of using the AHP method is a new approach.

AHP envisages a decomposition of the examined phenomenon by creating a hierarchical model of its structure (Fig. 3.2). A broad scope of application of AHP in decision support processes proves its utility. Below, we present example studies that used this method to:

- improve the effectiveness of strategic planning (Arbel and Orgier 1990);
- select the contractor in the project management process (Al-Harbi 2001);
- choose the provider of a long-term service (Tam and Tummala 2001);
- select alternative schedules for warehouse supplies (Farooq 2007);
- optimise the choice of location of a service point (Wu et al. 2007);
- support a group decision on a choice of a development solution (Lai et al. 2002);
- choose the best manufacturing strategy in manufacturing companies (Hofmann and Knébel 2013).

In AHP individual elements of the hierarchy are pair wise compared in order to determine the degree of their relative importance, which leads to the development of a judgment matrix (Saaty 1990; Sipahi and Timor 2010):

$$A_k = \{a_k(i, j)\} \tag{3.12}$$

where:

A_k—the kth judgment matrix;
$a_k(i, j)$—the degree of importance of the ith element in the relation to the jth element in terms of their impact on the kth element.

On the basis of the judgment matrix values, priorities are derived representing the distribution of importance of each element in the hierarchy. We assume that matrix A_k is consistent, i.e. (Saaty 2001):

$$a(i, j) = \frac{1}{a(j,i)} \text{ and } a(i,i) = 1 \text{ and } a(i,1)*a(1, j) = a(i, j), \tag{3.13}$$

What follows is that the vector of priorities' distribution SS_k is derived from the sum of judgment matrices A_k standardised to 1 (Saaty 1994):

$$NV_k(i) = \sum\nolimits_{j=1}^{n} a_k(i, j) \tag{3.14}$$

$$SV_k(i) = \frac{NV_k(i)}{\sum\nolimits_{j=1}^{n} NV_k(j)} \tag{3.15}$$

where:

NV_k—the non-standardised value of the kth judgment vector;
SV_k—the standardised value of the kth judgment vector.

Decision making consists in finding a solution among defined options (the decision variants at Fig. 3.2) with the highest aggregate priority calculated along the vertical structure of the hierarchy. Deriving this priority requires determining the weight of each of the vertical hierarchy structures (Saaty 1996):

$$w_k(i) = \sum\nolimits_{j=1}^{n} SV_k(j)*w_j(i) \tag{3.16}$$

where:

w_k—the weight of the ith element is calculated in relation to kth element.

Creating a ranking list and selecting the best possible decision variant V_s in a specific case is achieved by assigning priorities to individual alternative decisions V_i, basing on the global weights w_k (Saaty 2001):

$$\text{IF } w_k(V_i) \text{ is max THEN } V_s = V_i \qquad (3.17)$$

where:

V—the set of possible alternative decisions $V \in \{V_1, V_2, \ldots V_m\}$;
V_s—the best selected decision with the maximum of the global weight value w_k.

3.2.5 Summarizing the HRPM Method

AHP is not an expert-based method in which the judgment matrix is based on expert opinions (Schmoldt 2001; Wu et al. 2007). However, if such an approach is applied in a SME, it is very likely that the knowledge and experience of the decision-maker will not be sufficient to objectively judge the importance of competitiveness criteria and alternative competitive strategies.

In the present work, a hybrid version of this method is suggested, in which the judgment matrix is based on results obtained from regression analysis and decision trees. Such modification is justified by the fact that SMEs do not have access to expert knowledge which allows for independent, objective and reliable comparison of the significance of individual elements of a hierarchic decision problem. The suggested method does not require expert participation, and is useful even in the absence of an expert, which has been proven at the stage of its verification.

3.3 Crisp Method: Case Study and Utilities Verification

A two-step research plan was developed in this group, which contained a quantitative research and a research experiment, in order to verify the usefulness of HRPM.

3.3.1 Step 1: Quantitative Research

Quantitative research was carried out by means of a personal interview with the use of a CAPI (Computer Assisted Personal Interviewing) electronic form. The research sample was selected with a purposely random method among all private dental practices belonging to SMEs, of which, in 2009, there were 3,693 (Walkowska 2010–2011). The purposefulness of selection was based on the fact that all the clinics were located in large Polish cities, had computers and belonged to SMEs. The required sample size for this set was determined by the following assumptions:

- confidence level $(1 - \alpha) = 95\%$;
- confidence interval $\gamma = 1.96$;
- estimation of the population fraction possessing the analyzed characteristic η $= 50\%$;
- estimation of the population fraction not possessing the analyzed characteristic $(1 - \eta) = 50\%$;
- the maximum permissible error of measurement d $= 80\%$.

After considering all this, the minimum sample size was set at 150 clinics:

$$n = \frac{\gamma^2 \eta (1 - \eta)}{d^2} = \frac{1.96^2 * 0.5 * 0.5}{0.08^2} = 150.0625 \tag{3.18}$$

The results of quantitative research[1] determined factors significant in the analysis of the competitiveness of the Polish private dental clinics belonging to SMEs. The analysis of these factors enabled the clinics to determine the competitive position they occupied within the study group, and thus better adapt their strategic activities to the diagnosed inside and outside situation.

3.3.2   Step 2: Research Experiment

The research experiment was used with research groups from 10 dental clinics, selected from the starting group (150 dental clinics). Selection criteria included the clinic's location in Warsaw and consent to take part in a 6-month experiment. We invited 20 clinics to the study, of which 14 expressed their consent, but before the start of collaboration 2 of them declared bankruptcy and 2 others were acquired and assumed by large medical clinics. Therefore, eventually ten clinics took part in the experiment. This situation points to a high economic and organisational liability of SMEs and the resulting need to cope better with the risk of conducted activity.

In the research experiment, the HMDP model and the HRPM method were applied. The experiment showed the usefulness of the proposed method within a predicted range of probable value of objective function, and selection appropriate strategic activities resulting in the assumed value of objective function. The outcomes of the experiment will be demonstrated in stages presented in Fig. 3.4.

3.3.3   The HMDP Model

The structure of the HMDP model was defined according to the scheme presented in Fig. 3.3. It was decided that the maximisation of generated profit will serve as the

---

[1] The detailed results of the quantitative research are shown in Annex 1.

objective function. The value of this function is determined primarily by the values of key competitiveness criteria achieved by a company. It is common knowledge that generating the same or similar level of profit is possible with various configurations of values of individual criteria. The model is used to search for alternative ways of obtaining a similar profit, and to select the one that is best suited to company's needs and capabilities. This can be achieved with the use of HRPM in the configuration presented in Fig. 3.4.

3.3.4   PM1: Identification of the Competitiveness Criteria

In the presented case of a group of Polish dental clinics, results of quantitative research (a survey in a group of 150 clinics) and desk studies (reports of PKPP Lewiatan[2] (Starczewska-Krzysztoszek 2005–2008a, b, c) and PARP were used[3] (Żołnierski 2007–2009; Wilmańska 2010)). They allowed for the selection of 24 competitiveness criteria significant for the analysed study group (Table 3.1).

3.3.5   PM2: Selecting the Key Competitiveness Criteria

The criteria with key impact on the generated profit were selected from the complete set of criteria. In order to select criteria, backward stepwise regression was used,[4] with minimisation of the error of validation of analysis results as the criterion of selection of the final solution. The model turned out to be significant (the F-test statistic[5] $F = 37.63$; p-value statistic[6] $p < 0.0001$) and useful—predictors explained 92 % of the response variable (the R-squared statistic[7] $R^2 = 0.9180$) in total. From among 24 explanatory variables (Table 3.1), the 11 most significant ones were selected in terms of the type and strength of their impact on the change in the value of the response variable (i.e. the generated profit). The strength and type (positive–favourable/negative–unfavourable) of this impact are presented by means of the following equation:

---

[2] PKPP Lewiatan—Polish Confederation Lewiatan.

[3] PARP—Polish Agency for Enterprise Development.

[4] In the first iteration of backward stepwise regression analysis, all explanatory variables are introduced. In subsequent iterations, they are gradually eliminated to obtain an equation with the highest determination coefficient and preserved significance of parameters.

[5] F-test—a statistic has an F-distribution under the null hypothesis.

[6] p-value—a statistic used for quantify the statistical significance of evidence of the null hypothesis.

[7] R-squared statistic—a statistical measure of how close the data are to the fitted regression line.

Table 3.1 Competitiveness criteria for Polish dental clinics

Criterion	Description
C_1	Value of sold innovative medical services as % of the value of sold services
C_2	Investment and development expenditures as % of the value of sold services
C_3	Number of complaints as % of the number of provided medical services
C_4	Value of complaints as % of the value of sold services
C_5	Number of registered patients per one employed medical staff member
C_6	Average time of waiting for a visit
C_7	Average duration of a visit
C_8	Number of patients repeatedly resorting to company's services as % of the total number of patients
C_9	Number of loyal patients resorting to company's services as % of the total number of patients
C_{10}	Number of visiting patients resorting to company's services as % of the total number of patients
C_{11}	Number of foreign patients resorting to company's services as % of the total number of patients
C_{12}	Number of sold services per one employed member of medical staff
C_{13}	Value of sold medical services per one employed member of medical staff
C_{14}	Sales profitability
C_{15}	Average wage of the medical staff
C_{16}	Average wage of the administrative staff
C_{17}	Labour cost of the administrative staff as % of the labour cost of medical staff
C_{18}	Labour cost of the administrative staff as % of the value of sold services
C_{19}	Promotion and marketing costs as % of the value of sold services
C_{20}	Total value of fixed assets as % of the value of sold services
C_{21}	Value of medical equipment as % of the value of sold services
C_{22}	Value of medical equipment per one employed member of medical staff
C_{23}	Profit per man-hour of a member of medical staff
C_{24}	% of employees under any type of training

Source: own research

$$
\begin{aligned}
\text{Profit}_{avg} = {} & 89.2236\ C_{17} + 76.3225\ C_{21} + 22.5100\ C_8 + 9.2250\ C_{23} \\
& + 5.5109\ C_{15} + 0.1917\ C_{13} + 0.1115\ C_{12} - 0.0021\ C_{22} \qquad (3.19) \\
& - 2.5075\ C_{16} - 10.8349\ C_7 - 42.2789\ C_{24} - 51.3335
\end{aligned}
$$

The significance of individual explanatory variables in the equation above should be interpreted as follows: a change in the value of each of them by one unit results in a change in the value of the response variable (profit) by a value indicated by the coefficient accompanying this variable. The absolute term in the equation corrects the error arising from the estimation of equation coefficients. The existence of such an error and its consequences for the predicted result of estimation were taken into account in the fuzzy version of the HRPM.

3.3.6 PM3: Prototyping the Competitive Strategy Variants

Variables defined as key competitiveness criteria became the basis for prototyping alternative competitive strategies identified with the use of decision trees. Since the response variable (profit) was of the interval type, variance was selected as the search criterion and method of evaluation of rules splitting the decision tree.

Each explanatory variable (from the set of key competitiveness criteria) could be used to split the tree only once. It was assumed that a maximum of three tree splits at each level, up to six subsequent generations in the hierarchy and at least five observations in each node are allowed. This way, a set of rules was obtained (Fig. 3.6) which indicates alternative paths towards the achievement of similar profits. These paths, i.e. admissible and possible alternative competitive strategies, are defined by rules generated in each leaf node of the decision tree.

All generated rules (Fig. 3.6) are ordered according to the value of the predicted profit. Next, those with comparable profit values were identified. For example, there are two alternative rules (strategies) for the expected profit of PLN 90,000–100,000:

$$S_{99} : \text{IF } C_{23} \in [9.5833;\ 17.4154) \text{ and } C_{13} >= 83.6538 \text{ THEN Profit}_{avg} = \text{PLN } 99,600$$

$$(3.20)$$

$$S_{93} : \text{IF } C_{23} < 9.5833 \text{ and } C_7 < 25 \text{ THEN Profit}_{avg} = \text{PLN } 93,000 \qquad (3.21)$$

And in the case of expected profit of PLN 40,000–50,000, the rules are:

$$S_{52} : \text{IF } C_{23} \in [9.5833; 17.4154) \text{ and } C_{13} < 83.6538 \text{ THEN Profit}_{avg} = \text{PLN } 51,720$$

$$(3.22)$$

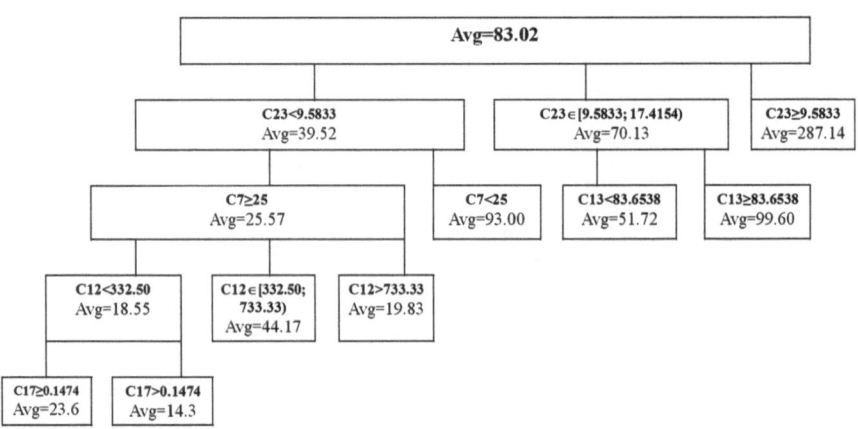

Fig. 3.6 The results of prototyping alternative strategies with the use of decision trees (*source*: own research)

$$S_{44} : \text{IF } C_{23} < 9.5833 \text{ and } C_7 >= 25 \text{ and } C_{12} \in [332.5; 733.33)$$
$$\text{THEN Profit}_{avg} = \text{PLN } 44,170 \tag{3.23}$$

The existence of alternative strategies (S_{99}/S_{93} and S_{52}/S_{44}) raised the question of which alternative was better/worse in each individual case. The approach that was best suited to the needs and capabilities of a given clinic was chosen with the use of the hybrid AHP method.

3.3.7 PM4: Prioritizing the Competitive Strategy Variants

The hybrid AHP procedure started with determining the vector of preference for all criteria present in the rules of compared strategies:

- for strategies S_{99}/S_{93} these were criteria: C_7, C_{13} and C_{23},
- for strategies S_{52}/S_{44} these were criteria: C_7, C_{12}, C_{13} and C_{23}.

The vector of criteria preference was derived from the matrix that considered the strength and value of impact of individual criteria (expressed by the regression coefficients) and the values of criteria achieved by a given clinic (indicating its potential and capabilities). An example vector for clinic W06[8] in relation to alternative strategies S_{99}/S_{93} is presented in Table 3.2.

Next, considered alternative strategies S_{99}/S_{93} were compared in relation to each criterion involved in the associated rule (formulas 3.20 and 3.21). The example matrix of preferences for alternative strategies S_{99}/S_{93} in relation to criterion C_7 for clinic W06 is presented in Table 3.3.

The value of the profit which is feasible in view of the value of the comparison criterion was adopted according to the rule associated with a specific alternative strategy (Table 3.3). If the criterion was not present in the definition of a considered rule, the actual value of clinic's profit was adopted.

Finally, preferences of implementation of each of the compared alternative strategies for a given clinic were specified (Table 3.4).

On the basis of the obtained results, it can be concluded that in the examined case it would be more beneficial and effective for clinic W06 to implement strategy S_{93}. This judgment is based on the assumption that clinic W06 wants to achieve profit ranging from PLN 90,000 to 100,000. The assessment considered coefficients derived from the regression equation, defining the impact of key competitiveness factors on the value of generated profit and rules generated by the decision tree defining alternative strategies with predicted profit values.

Hence, the use of the HRPM enabled clinic W06 to acquire the following information and knowledge:

---

[8] The detailed results of the analysis for the clinic W06 are presented in Annex 2.

Table 3.2 Matrix of criteria preferences defining alternative strategies

Regression coefficients:		0.0922943	0.1917	9.225	
Criterion value achieved by a clinic:		C_7	C_{13}	C_{23}	Weight of criterion preference in strategy evaluation
20.000000	C_7	216.698000	104.329700	2.168021680	0.33713693
38.461538	C_{13}	416.726900	200.634000	4.169272462	0.64834025
0.861538	C_{23}	9.334683	4.494202	0.093391703	0.01452282
Σ					1.00000000

Source: own research

Table 3.3 Matrix of preferences of alternative strategies in relation to their defining criterion

Criterion C_7	Profit value:	56	93	
Profit value:	Strategy:	S_{99}	S_{93}	Weight of strategy preference in relation to the criterion
56	S_{99}	1.000000	0.602151	0.375838926
93	S_{93}	1.660714	1.000000	0.624161074
Σ				1.000000000

Source: own research

Table 3.4 Matrix of preferences of alternative strategies for clinics

Weight of criterion preference:	0.337137	0.648340	0.014522822	Strategy preference for a clinic
Weight of strategy preference in relation to criterion:	C_7	C_{13}	C_{23}	
S_{99}	0.375839	0.480134	0.500000000	0.445
S_{93}	*0.624161*	*0.519866*	*0.500000000*	*0.555*
Σ				1.000

Source: own research

- which competitiveness criteria among all considered ones determine competitiveness measured with the value of generated profit;
- what alternatives of competitiveness improvement are available and what rules determine the success of implementation of each of them;
- which of the considered alternative strategies, taking the existing competitiveness criteria and those considered in the HMPD into account, is most likely to be successfully implemented by a clinic.

Thus, the application of the HRPM enabled the achievement of the goal specified in the introduction to the method and provided answers to the questions formulated there, which were the essence of support of competitive strategies in a SME.

3.3.8   Verification of HRPM's Utility

The verification of HRPM's utility demonstrated that the predicted results prove correct both in the event of achieving and not achieving expected profit. In order to document this statement, examples of two clinics using the HRPM—W03 and W09—are presented. At first, both clinics made profits that did not match their expectations and needs. Both showed development potential and willingness to introduce changes in accordance with the recommendations of the best-suited competitive strategy. Clinic W09 declared the need to increase its profit to PLN 90,000–100,000; therefore, the S_{99}/S_{93} strategies were considered in this case. Clinic W03 decided that it was realistic for it to increase profits to PLN 40,000–50,000, which entailed the assessment of strategies S_{52}/S_{44}.

3.3.9   Example 1: The Case of Clinic W09

Matrix of preferences prepared for clinic W09[9] showed a definite advantage of strategy S_{99} over that of strategy S_{93} (Table 3.5).

In accordance with formula 3.20 the strategy's most important elements included ensuring high value of sold services (C_{13}) and profitability of services provided by the medical staff (C_{23}):

$$S_{99} : \text{IF } C_{23} \in [9.5833; 17.4154) \text{ and } C_{13} >= 83.6538 \text{ THEN Profit}_{avg}$$
$$= \text{PLN } 99,600$$

A competitiveness development strategy for the clinic was adjusted to these recommendations, which resulted in a change in the level of generated profit from PLN 43,000 to PLN 130,000 (Table 3.6, the bold line indicates the time of S_{99} strategy implementation).

Table 3.5   Matrix of strategy preferences for clinic W09

Weight of criterion preference:	0.182413	0.797474275	0.020112254	Strategy preference for a clinic
Weight of strategy preference in relation to criterion:	C_7	C_{13}	C_{23}	
S_{99}	0.627096	0.698457223	0.5	0.681
S_{93}	0.372904	0.301542777	0.5	0.319
Σ				1.000

Source: own research

---

[9] The detailed results of the analysis for the clinic W09 are presented in Annex 2.

Table 3.6 Results of key competitiveness criteria achieved by clinic W09

Period	C_7	C_8	C_{12}	C_{13}	C_{15}	C_{16}	C_{17}	C_{21}	C_{22}	C_{23}	C_{24}	Profit
2008 I–VI	30.00	1.77	1,124.00	103.26	36.35	17.09	0.40	0.38	40.06	1.66	0.12	25.00
2008 VII–XII	30.00	1.78	1,122.06	103.33	34.51	16.42	0.41	0.39	40.53	1.00	0.12	15.00
2009 I–VI	30.00	1.58	1,700.15	128.61	37.71	21.62	0.48	0.37	48.07	1.38	0.19	18.00
2009 VII–XII	30.00	1.58	1,700.23	131.15	40.30	22.30	0.46	0.37	48.76	3.30	0.19	43.00
2010 I–II	30.00	2.53	1,000.00	92.30	43.00	22.30	0.46	0.52	48.76	10.00	0.00	88.00
2010 III–IV	30.00	2.53	1,000.00	92.30	43.00	22.30	0.46	0.52	48.76	10.00	0.00	100.00
2010 V–VI	30.00	2.75	923.07	92.30	43.00	22.30	0.46	0.52	48.76	10.00	0.00	130.00

Source: own research

Having analysed the values of criteria C_{13} and C_{23}, which are crucial for this strategy, it can be concluded that clinic W09 kept the value of sold services (C_{13}) at the level required by formula 3.20 and significantly increased their profitability (C_{23}). This led to achieving the expected profit increase. Hence, in the case of fulfilling the requirements of the rule associated with a given alternative strategy, the reliability and utility of the recommended method was proven.

3.3.10   Example 2: The Case of Clinic W03

Another matrix of preferences, this time prepared for clinic W03,[10] indicated strong preference for the implementation of strategy S_{44} (Table 3.7).

In accordance with formula 3.23 the strategy's most important elements included increasing the number (C_{12}) and profitability of provided services (C_{23}) and decreasing the time of waiting for a visit to a selected physician (C_7):

$$S_{44} : \text{IF } C_{23} < 9.5833 \text{ and } C_7 >= 25 \text{ and } C_{12} \in [332.5; 733.33) \text{ THEN}$$
$$\text{Profit}_{avg} = \text{PLN } 44,170$$

The competitiveness development strategy for the clinic was adjusted to these recommendations, yet its implementation did not bring the expected results (Table 3.8, the bold line indicates the time of implementation of strategy S_{44}).

Having analysed criteria C_7, C_{12} and C_{23} defined in formula 3.23, it needs to be concluded that clinic W03 failed to meet the requirements determining the success of this alternative strategy. The number of sold medical services (C_{12}), which is crucial for the success of this strategy and which was a strong asset of this clinic in 2008–2009, fell in 2010 below the level required in formula 3.23. The presented

Table 3.7 Matrix of preferences of alternative strategies for clinic W03

Weight of criterion preference:	0.034816	0.928433	0.030947776	0.005802708	
Weight of strategy preference in relation to criterion:	C_7	C_{12}	C_{13}	C_{23}	Strategy preference for a clinic
S_{52}	0.369731	0.447761	0.775179856	0.5	0.455
S_{44}	0.630269	0.552239	0.224820144	0.5	0.545
Σ					1.000

Source: own research

---

[10] The detailed results of the analysis for the clinic W03 are presented in Annex 2.

Table 3.8 The results of key competitiveness criteria achieved by clinic W03

Period	C_7	C_8	C_{12}	C_{13}	C_{15}	C_{16}	C_{17}	C_{21}	C_{22}	C_{23}	C_{24}	Profit
2008 I–VI	30.00	0.50	1,000.00	50.00	50.00	30.00	0.12	0.60	30.00	5.00	0.33	10.00
2008 VII–XII	30.00	0.50	1,000.00	50.00	50.00	30.00	0.12	0.60	30.00	7.50	0.33	15.00
2009 I–VI	30.00	0.45	800.00	26.66	50.00	30.00	0.10	0.81	21.66	6.66	0.37	20.00
2009 VII–XII	30.00	0.45	800.00	26.66	50.00	30.00	0.10	0.81	21.66	5.00	0.37	15.00
2010 I–II	30.00	1.14	320.00	20.00	50.00	30.00	0.10	1.08	21.66	3.33	0.25	10.00
2010 III–IV	30.00	1.14	240.00	15.00	50.00	30.00	0.10	1.08	16.25	2.50	0.00	10.00
2010 V–VI	30.00	1.06	257.50	15.00	50.00	30.00	0.10	2.75	41.25	2.50	0.11	10.00

Source: own research

Table 3.9 Comparison of predicted and actual profit of clinics W06 and W09

Clinic	Predicted profit [PLN 1,000]	Generated profit [PLN 1,000]	Difference [PLN 1,000]	Difference [%]
W06	93.00	150.00	57.00	61
W09	99.60	130.00	30.40	31

Source: own research

example shows that the success of the HRPM depends on the fulfilment of all requirements specified in the rule determining the competitive strategy.

3.4   Summarizing

Both presented examples confirm the utility of the HRPM and prove that expert opinion may be successfully replaced by an analysis based on results provided by the HMDP.

While analysing the obtained results, we need to notice that the results predicted by rules and expressed as average profit differ significantly from the actually obtained values. The results achieved by the already presented clinics W06 and W09 may serve as an example (Table 3.9).

Although in the described cases the generated profit considerably exceeded the predicted profit (Table 3.9), such situation also indicates that it is possible for the actual profit to be lower than the predicted profit (in spite of fulfilling all requirements prescribed by the adequate rule). A similar situation will always give rise to the discussion of utility, reliability and safety of use of this method. Therefore, it would be advisable to offer such a version of it that would predict profit expressed in intervals instead of exact values. Such an option is possible in the fuzzy version of the HRPM method—the Fuzzy Hierarchical-Regression Prototyping Method (FHRPM).

3.5   Fuzzy Hierarchical-Regression Prototyping Method

The proper implementation of the HRPM method requires the delivery of good quality, correct and complete source data, which are the results of business activity conducted by entities of the cooperating group. It is assumed that the coefficients of the regression equation and the parameters of decision trees analysis are certain values, when in reality they are flawed, dependent on the quantity and quality of source data introduced to the HMDP model. Thus, the suggested method should also take into consideration data inaccuracy through a fuzzy, instead of an exact presentation of analysis results.

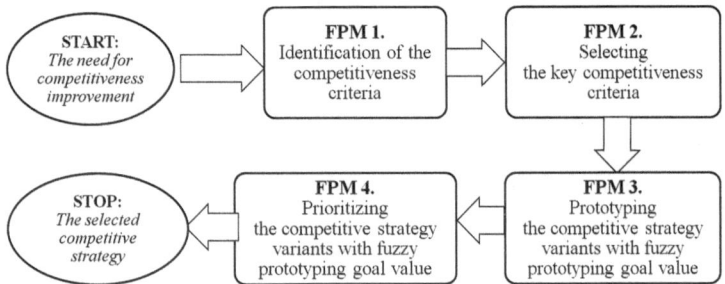

Fig. 3.7 The Fuzzy hierarchical-regression prototyping method (*source*: own research)

As follows from literature research, classical methods are being combined with fuzzy number theories in various areas of decision support processes. Fuzzy variants of neuron networks are used to predict and specify competitiveness assessment models (Lee et al. 2012; Pousinho et al. 2012). Also expert methods are integrated in the fuzzy approach, such as AHP (Yumei 2010; Xue-Liang and Chang-Li 2011; Ohnishi et al. 2011) or Promethee (Senvar et al. 2014). A fuzzy approach is also taken in the case of methods with smaller knowledge and data requirements, such as decision trees (Evans et al. 2013) or linear regression (Chen 2013).

In the case of the FHRPM, the objective was to shift from absolute values, which may be misleading in some cases, to interval-fuzzy results that take source data inaccuracy into consideration. The augmentation of the FHRPM concerns stages FPM3 and FPM4 (Fig. 3.7).

3.5.1   FPM3: Prototyping the Competitive Strategy Variants with Fuzzy Prototyping Goal Value

Defining alternative strategies has been automated with the use of decision trees. An approach combining AHP and decision tree methods of analysis (yet only in the exact version) was proposed in the work of (Dey 2002). In this study, AHP was used to evaluate criteria determining the selection of alternative solutions, and the decision tree was used to select these alternatives due to their impact on the achievement of the desired goal.

In FHRPM, hybrid AHP was combined with fuzzy decision trees. Fuzzy decision trees were used to prototype feasible alternative strategies, while taking into account the results of selection of key competitiveness factors derived from regression analysis (FPM2 stage of FHRPM).

The structure of a decision tree with fuzzy nodes is the same as the tree structure in the basic version. Yet the value of the split test is determined differently. In fuzzy decision trees, each node contains a test that assigns the assessed observation not to one child node, but to all of them to a certain degree expressed by a percentage membership function. Therefore, the split test is expressed by the following inequality (Zhai 2011):

$$TT_{ij} = \begin{cases} \mu_0(o_{ij}), \text{jeżeli } o_{ij} \leq \delta_j \\ \mu_1(o_{ij}), \text{jeżeli } o_{ij} > \delta_j \end{cases} \tag{3.24}$$

where:

TT_{ij}—the test splitting the set of the ith observation in the jth tree node;
o_{ij}—the value of the ith observation in the jth tree node;
δ_j—the threshold value in the jth tree node that the test is based on;
$\mu(o_{ij})$—the membership function specifying observation's affiliation to a child node.

For example, a rule expressed by formula 3.24 inequality takes the following form (Matiaško et al. 2006):

$$\text{IF } O_{1j} = o_{1j} \text{ and } O_{2j} \text{ is } o_{2j} \text{ and} \ldots \text{and } O_{nj} \text{ is } o_{nj} \text{ THEN } V_k \text{ is } v_k \text{ with } f_k \tag{3.25}$$

where:

O_{ij}—the ith observation in the jth tree node;
V_k—the kth decision variant;
f_k—the certainty degree of the kth decision variant.

What distinguishes exact and fuzzy rules is the value of the membership function which is expressed by the degree of certainty of the rule's conclusion. Such a solution informs us that a rule derived from predicting is likely to come true to a certain extent, which resolves the problem of predicting inaccuracy and distribution of the final result.

3.5.2 FPM4: Prioritizing the Competitive Strategy Variants with Fuzzy Prototyping Goal Value

A defined set of alternative strategies is selected by means of a hybrid-fuzzy AHP method. A fuzzy version of AHP uses a triangular membership function instead of a classical valuation by means of pair wise comparisons to create judgment matrices (Rostamy et al. 2013):

$$\hat{A}_k = \{\hat{a}_k(l, m, u)\} \tag{3.26}$$

where:

$\hat{A}_k$—the kth fuzzy judgment matrix;

$\hat{a}_k(l, m, u)$—l is the lower limit, u is the upper limit and m is the most likely value of importance of the kth element.

When operations on fuzzy numbers are performed (Bhushan and Kanwal 2004):

$$\text{IF } \hat{A}_1 = (l_1, m_1, u_1) \text{ and } \hat{A}_2 = (l_2, m_2, u_2) \text{THEN :}$$

$$\hat{A}_1 + \hat{A}_2 = (l_1 + l_2, m_1 + m_2, u_1 + u_2) \tag{3.27}$$

$$\hat{A}_1 * \hat{A}_2 = (l_1 * l_2, m_1 * m_2, u_1 * u_2) \tag{3.28}$$

$$\frac{1}{\hat{A}_1} = \frac{1}{l_1} + \frac{1}{m_1} + \frac{1}{u_1} \tag{3.29}$$

Fuzzy values of judgment and priority vectors are calculated with preserved relationships presented in formulas 3.27–3.29:

$$\hat{R}_k(i) = \sum_{j=1}^{n} \hat{A}_k(i, j) \tag{3.30}$$

$$\hat{r}_k(i) = \frac{\hat{r}_k(i)}{\sum_{j=1}^{n} \hat{r}_k(j)} \tag{3.31}$$

$$\hat{w}_k(i) = \sum_{j=1}^{n} \hat{r}_k(j) * \hat{w}_j(i) \tag{3.32}$$

where:

$\hat{R}_k$—the kth fuzzy priority vector;
$\hat{r}_k$—the value of the kth fuzzy priority vector;
$\hat{w}_k$—the fuzzy weight is calculated in relation to kth element.

The choice of the best possible decision variant requires defuzzification of the fuzzy values of alternatives' priorities. Several methods are known and used for this purpose, such as: Middle of Maxima, First of Maxima, Last of Maxima, Centre of Gravity, Centre of Sum or the Height Method. The simplest and most frequently used method is The Average Method (Chang and Wang 2009).

The application of FHRPM explains the issue of inaccuracy of the predicted objective function results, which is due to the inaccuracy of source data and errors of estimated predicted results. In this version, the value of the predicted objective function is presented in the form of a class (corresponding to a specified range of values), and not an exact value. Additionally, each predicted value is associated with a degree of certainty that informs us about the likelihood of it coming true.

3.6 Fuzzy Method: Case Study and Utilities Verification

3.6.1 FPM1: Identification of the Competitiveness Criteria

This stage does not differ in any way from the HRPM method.

3.6.2 FPM2: Selecting the Key Competitiveness Criteria

Backward stepwise regression with minimisation of the erroneous validation of analysis results as the criterion of selection of the final solution was once again used to select model criteria in order to define the ones with key impact on the value of generated profit. Yet this time, the absolute term was omitted during modelling since the error of result estimation was taken into account by means of making its value fuzzy.

The model turned out to be significant (the F-test statistic $F = 93.10$; p-value statistic $p < 0.0001$) and useful—predictors explained in total over 94 % of the response variable (the R-squared statistic $R^2 = 0.9455$). From among 24 explanatory variables (Table 3.1) the 11 most significant ones were selected in terms of the value of their impact on the change in the value of the response variable (i.e. the generated profit). The type and strength of their impact are described with the following equation:

$$
\begin{aligned}
\text{Profit}_{avg} = {} & 154.50 \ C_{17} + 71.36 \ C_{18} + 37.21 \ C_{12} + 13.20 \ C_9 \\
& + 9.03 \ C_{23} + 3.97 \ C_{15} + 0.08 \ C_{12} - 0.38 \ C_{22} - 3.20 \ C_{16} \\
& - 9.14 \ C_7 - 59.21 \ C_{24}
\end{aligned}
\tag{3.33}
$$

In this case, the absolute term was omitted since it was decided that the inaccuracy of estimation would be reflected on stages FPM3 and FPM4.

3.6.3 FPM3: Prototyping the Competitive Strategy Variants with Fuzzy Prototyping Goal Value

Variables defined as key competitiveness criteria became the basis for prototyping alternative competitive strategies identified with the use of decision trees. Since the source data for the model was often estimated and not calculated, it was decided that the results of prototyping should also take this inaccuracy into account. Therefore, a shift was made from prototyping exact profit values to prototyping interval values expressed by means of classes. It was decided that a four-grade quartile scale would be used for this purpose, which informed that an entity belonged to:

– Q1—first quartile (0–25 %)—low profit values that cover 25 % of observed results with the lowest values,
– Q2—second quartile (25–50 %)—medium-low profit values, higher than Q1 (25 % of observed results with the lowest values) and lower than Q3 and Q4 (50 % of observed results with the highest values),
– Q3—third quartile (50–75 %)—medium-high profit values; higher values are only achieved by group Q4 (25 % of observed results with the highest values), and lower by groups Q1 and Q2 (50 % of observed results with the lowest values),
– Q4—fourth quartile (75–100 %)—high profit values that cover 25 % of observed results with the highest values.

In order to transform exact values into interval values (profit classes), the distribution of profit generated by individual companies was analysed and broken down into a four-grade quartile scale (Fig. 3.8).

The scale was later used to make a shift from exact profit values to interval values, which, as can be seen in Fig. 3.9, are fuzzy intervals. Their fuzziness is expressed by an ambiguous membership of certain profit values in specific intervals. As results in Fig. 3.9 show, there are profit values that belong to a certain extent to two neighbouring profit intervals. The function of membership μ is used to determine the level of belonging to the appropriate quartile. For example, the profit value bolded at Fig. 3.9 (profit = 35) belongs both to the quartile Q1 ($\mu = 28$ %) and to the quartile Q2 ($\mu = 72$ %). This means that a profit value is PLN 35,000 is sufficient for placing in the quartile Q2 at 72 %, but may also be sufficient only for the lowest quartile at 28 %.

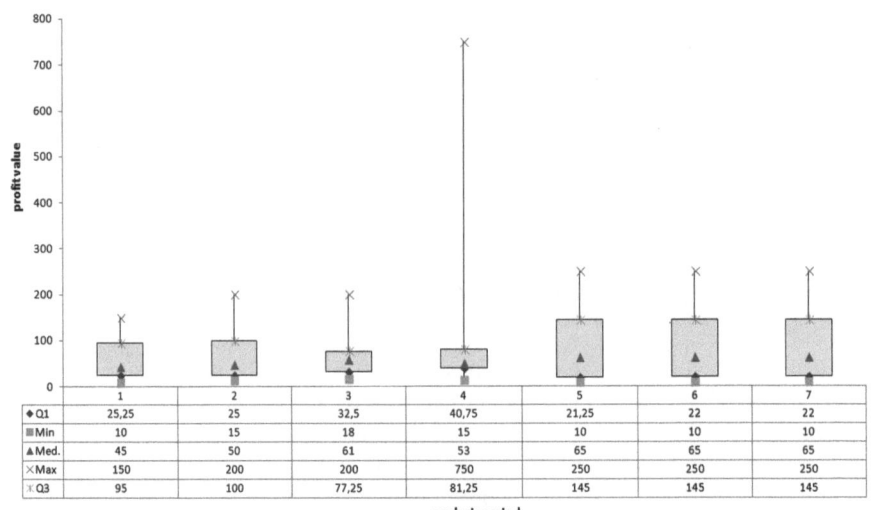

	1	2	3	4	5	6	7
♦ Q1	25,25	25	32,5	40,75	21,25	22	22
▬ Min	10	15	18	15	10	10	10
▲ Med.	45	50	61	53	65	65	65
× Max	150	200	200	750	250	250	250
⊞ Q3	95	100	77,25	81,25	145	145	145

analysis period

Fig. 3.8 Quartile distribution of profit values (*source*: own research)

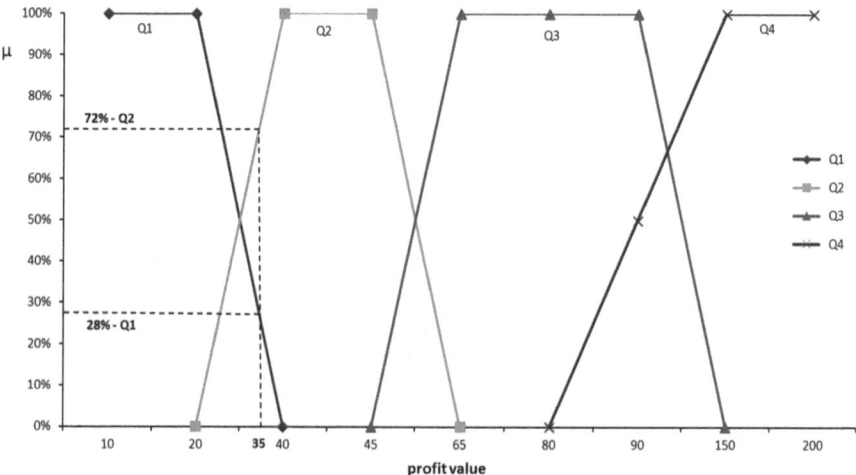

Fig. 3.9 Fuzzy intervals of profit values (*source*: own research)

Quartile intervals define a trapezoid function showing how prototyping results become fuzzy, and the four-grade quartile scale replace exact results of decision trees' analysis:

$$\text{Class\_Profit} = \begin{cases} Q1, & \text{for profit} \leq \text{PLN } 40,000 \\ Q2, & \text{for profit} \leq \text{PLN } 65,000 \text{ and profit} \geq \text{PLN } 20,000 \\ Q3, & \text{for profit} \leq \text{PLN } 150,000 \text{ and profit} \geq \text{PLN } 45,000 \\ Q4, & \text{for profit} \geq \text{PLN } 80,000 \end{cases}$$

$$(3.34)$$

As results from the reasoning presented above indicate, a shift into the interval variable Class profit from exact variable Profit requires an analysis of results achieved by examined entities in specified time. This means that the limits of specified intervals are changeable and depend on the group structure and level of competitiveness achieved by individual entities in the group. The analysis of interval values in Fig. 3.9 and formula 3.34 makes it possible to assess the degree of the group's diversity in terms of the level of competitiveness.

Since the response variable (Class_Profit) has become a nominal variable, entropy with 5 % significance level was chosen as the criterion for searching and assessing decision tree split rules. Each explanatory variable (from the set of key competitiveness criteria) could be used to split the tree only once. It was assumed that the maximum of three tree splits at each level, up to six subsequent generations in the hierarchy and at least five observations in each node are allowed. This way, a set of rules were obtained (Fig. 3.10) which indicate alternative paths (competitive strategies) towards the achievement of similar profits, e.g.

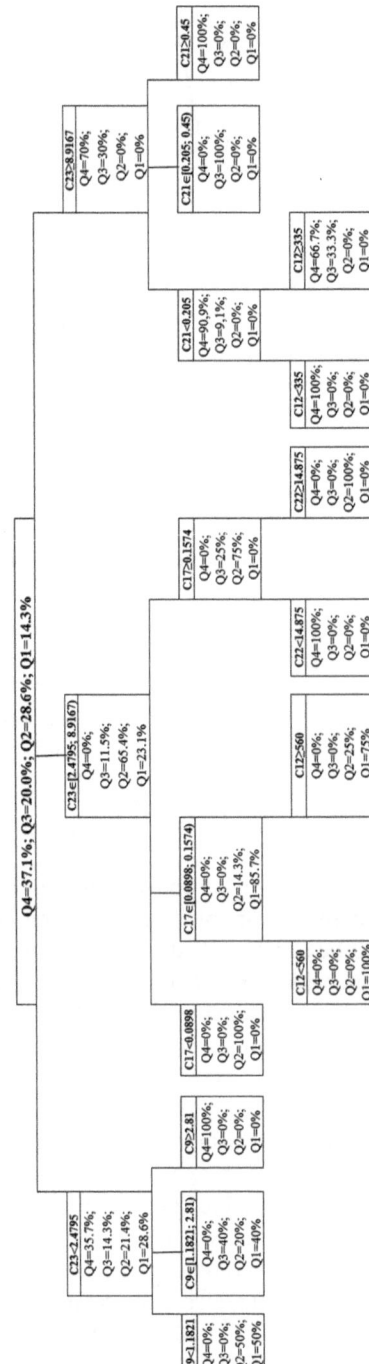

Fig. 3.10 The results of predicting with the fuzzy tree method (*source*: own research)

S_{4a} : IF $C_{23} < 2.48$ and $C_9 >= 2.81$ THEN Predicted Class_Profit : Q4
$\quad = 1.00$ \hfill (3.35)

S_{4b} : IF $C_{23} >= 8.917$ and $C_{21} >= 0.45$ THEN Predicted Class_Profit
$\quad$: Q4 = 1.00 \hfill (3.36)

$S_{4/3}$: IF $C_{23} >= 8.917$ and $C_{21} < 0.205$ and $C_{12} >= 335$
$\quad\quad$ THEN Predicted Class_Profit : Q4 = 0.67, Q3 = 0.33 \hfill (3.37)

S_3 : IF $C_{23} >= 8.917$ and $C_{21} >= 0.205$ and $C_{21} < 0.45$
$\quad\quad$ THEN Predicted Class_Profit : Q3 = 1.00 \hfill (3.38)

Rules obtained this way inform us which profit class may be achieved and how likely it is that the rule will come true. The existence of alternative strategies (S_{4a}/S_{4b}/$S_{4/3}$/S_3) raised the question of which alternative was better/worse in each individual case. The best suited approach was selected with the use of the hybrid AHP method (stage FPM4).

3.6.4   FPM4: Prioritizing the Competitive Strategy Variants with Fuzzy Prototyping Goal Value

The hybrid AHP procedure began with determining the vector of preference for all criteria present in the rules of compared strategies. For example, in the case of strategy S_{4a}/S_{4b}/$S_{4/3}$/S_3 these included: C_9, C_{12}, C_{21} and C_{23}. The vector of criteria preference was derived for the matrix that considered the type (positive/negative) and strength (value) of impact by individual criteria (expressed by the regression coefficients) and the values of criteria achieved by a given clinic (indicating its potential and capabilities). An example vector for clinic W09[11] in relation to alternative strategies S_{4a}/S_{4b}/$S_{4/3}$/S_3 is presented in Table 3.10.

Next, considered alternative strategies S_{4a}/S_{4b}/$S_{4/3}$/S_3 were compared in relation to each criterion involved in the associated rule (formulas 3.35–3.38). Example matrix of preferences for alternative strategies S_{4a}/S_{4b}/$S_{4/3}$/S_3, in relation to criterion C_9 for the selected example is presented in Table 3.11.

The profit class which is feasible in view of the value of the comparison criterion was adopted according to the rule associated with a specific alternative strategy (Table 3.11). If the criterion was not present in the rule definition, the actual class of profit generated by the clinic was adopted.

Finally, preferences of implementation of each of the compared alternative strategies for a given clinic were specified (Table 3.12).

The alternative with the highest preference value has the greatest chance of coming true in the examined clinic. Therefore, in the presented case, it would be

---

[11] The detailed results of the analysis for the clinic W09 are presented in Annex 2.

Table 3.10 Matrix of criteria preferences for clinic W09

Regression coefficients:		13.20	0.08	37.21	9.03	
Criterion value achieved by clinic W09:		C_9	C_{12}	C_{21}	C_{23}	Weight of criterion preference
0.905	C_9	0.069	11.158	0.024	0.100	0.00053
1,700.154	C_{12}	128.761	20,963.673	45.688	188.362	0.99844
0.374	C_{21}	0.028	4.609	0.010	0.041	0.00022
1.385	C_{23}	0.105	17.073	0.037	0.153	0.00081
Σ						1.00000

Source: own research

Table 3.11 Matrix of preferences for alternative strategies in relation to criterion C_9

Criterion C_9	Profit class:	4	1	1	1	
Profit class:	Strategy	S_{4a}	S_{4b}	$S_{4/3}$	S_3	Weight of strategy preference
4	S_{4a}	1.000	4.000	4.000	4.000	0.571
1	S_{4b}	0.250	1.000	1.000	1.000	0.143
1	$S_{4/3}$	0.250	1.000	1.000	1.000	0.143
1	S_3	0.250	1.000	1.000	1.000	0.143
Σ						1.000

Source: own research

Table 3.12 Matrix of preferences of alternative strategies for clinic W09

Weight of criterion preference:	0.00053	0.99844	0.00022	0.00081	Strategy preference for a clinic
Weight of strategy preference in relation to criterion:	C_9	C_{12}	C_{21}	C_{23}	
S_{4a}	0.571	0.150	0.086	0.273	0.150
S_{4b}	0.143	0.150	0.343	0.273	0.150
$S_{4/3}$	*0.143*	*0.550*	*0.314*	*0.250*	*0.550*
S_3	0.143	0.150	0.257	0.204	0.150
Σ					1.000

Source: own research

advisable to implement strategy $S_{4/3}$, which predicts profit ranging from PLN 80,000 to 150,000 (Fig. 3.9) and 67 % likelihood of entering the sub-set of 25 % richest clinics in the group (formula 3.37):

$S_{4/3}$: IF C_{23} >= 8.917 and C_{21} < 0.205 and C_{12} >= 335 THEN
Predicted Class_Profit :   Q4 = 0.67,   Q3 = 0.33.

The prediction for the same W09 clinic in the exact version of the method indicated likely profit of PLN 99,600. Yet as a result of introduced changes, the clinic achieved the profit of PLN 130,000. In the fuzzy method, a profit of PLN

130,000 falls within the predicted interval of PLN 80,000–150,000. As results from the above, although the precision of the result has been lost, it has contributed to an increased consistency of the prediction with the facts.

Similarly to the HRPM, the use of the FHRPM enabled clinic W09 to obtain information on which competitiveness criteria (from all criteria considered as part of current operations) determine its competitiveness measured with the value of generated profit. The clinic also found out which alternatives of competitiveness improvement are available and what rules determine the success of implementation of each of them. It determined which of the considered alternative strategies, taking the existing competitiveness criteria and those considered in the HMPD into account, is most likely to be successfully implemented by the clinic. Thus, the application of the FHRPM makes it possible to achieve the defined objective and provides answers to the questions formulated in the introduction.

3.7   Summarizing: How to Effectively Implement Analytical Method?

An enterprise wanting to compete effectively in the market must have knowledge about competitiveness criteria, their value and impact on the competitive position. Also it must know how to apply this knowledge in workable variants of competitive strategy. The search for the best strategy to compete is an issue of multi-criteria decision analysis, where dealt are different approaches leading to similar result, but in different ways tailored to the capabilities and preferences of a particular enterprise and its market situation.

Such is the problem of developing the competitive strategy points to the desirability of using multi-criteria decision analysis methods. Considering that the decision problem consists of choosing best variant of strategy with known conditions of its implementation, defined by a set of competitiveness criteria, the right solution is the Analytic Hierarchy Process, called the AHP method.

However in the case of uses such an approach in SMEs has a high probability that both the knowledge and the experience of the decision maker will not be sufficient for an objective assessment of the validity of the competitiveness criteria and variants of competitive strategy. Therefore, here is proposed a hybrid version of the AHP method, for which the assessment of the significance as competitiveness criteria are calculated from the regression equation. In addition the assessed significance of various strategy variants is obtained from rules generated by decision trees models. Thus the Hierarchical-Regression Prototyping Method was created, allowing use even in the case of expert knowledge shortage, which is the typical situation in SMEs.

Although the proposed method is useful, as has been proven in the examples, it still cannot be used by an average SME. Above all, its utility is measured with the information potential provided by the group, which submits its data (results of

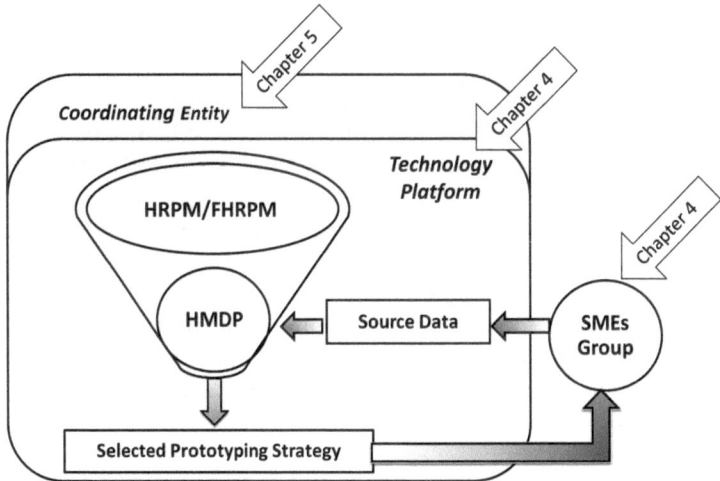

Fig. 3.11 Elements to ensure the use of the HRPM/FHRPM method by SMEs (*source*: own research)

business operations) and acquires information in the areas specified in the introduction to this chapter, i.e.:

– where exactly is my company against the background of achievements of others in the group?
– where would it like to be in the future?
– how can it achieve this goal in the specified time?

In other words, there must be a group of entities applying the HRPM in order to acquire information and knowledge in the expected areas (Fig. 3.11). Since these entities will have to make their data available and share the results of analyses, it is crucial to specify in detail the principles and organisation of their cooperation.

Consequently, the HRPM should be supplemented by the organisation of cooperation within a group of SMEs that use a common HMDP, but compete in the same market. The terms of organisation and coordination of this group presented in the form of procedures will be described in Chap. 4 (Fig. 3.11).

References

Al-Harbi, K. M. (2001). Application of the AHP in project management. *International journal of project management, 19*(1), 19–27.

Arbel, A., & Orgier, Y. E. (1990). An application of the AHP to bank strategic planning. *European Journal of Operational Research, 48*(1990), 27–37.

Barge-Gil, A., & Modrego, A. (2011). The impact of research and technology organizations on firm competitiveness. Measurement and determinants. *The Journal of Technology Transfer, 36* (1), 61–83.

Bhushan, N., & Kanwal, R. (2004). *Strategic decision making: applying the analytic hierarchy process*. London: Springer.

Blažek, L., Pudil, P., & Špalek, J. (2011). The factors affecting competitiveness of companies: Contribution and limits of the statistical pattern recognition methods. *Acta Universitatis Agriculturae et Silviculturae Mendelianae Brunensis, 7*(2011), 69–80.

Chang, T. H., & Wang, T. C. (2009). Using the fuzzy multi-criteria decision making approach for measuring the possibility of successful knowledge management. *Information Sciences, 179*, 355–370.

Chen, T. (2013). A flexible way of modeling the long-term cost competitiveness of a semiconductor product. *Robotics and Computer-Integrated Manufacturing, 29*(3), 31–40.

Crouch, G. I. (2011). Destination competitiveness: An analysis of determinant attributes. *Journal of Travel Research, 50*(1), 27–45.

D'Aveni, R. (1994). *Hypercompetition*. New York: Free Press.

Dey, P. K. (2002). Project risk management: A combined analytic hierarchy process and decision tree approach. *Cost Engineering, 44*(3), 13–27.

Eden, C., & Ackermann, F. (2013). *Making strategy: The journey of strategic management*. London: Sage.

Evans, L., Lohse, N., & Summers, M. (2013). A fuzzy-decision-tree approach for manufacturing technology selection exploiting experience-based information. *Expert Systems with Applications, 40*(16), 6412–6426.

Farooq, S. (2007). *Manufacturing technology selection: A supply chain perspective* (Doctoral dissertation, University of Nottingham, Nottingham).

Gray, R. M. (2011). *Entropy and information theory* (Vol. 1). New York: Springer.

Heath, D., Kasif, S., & Salzberg, S. (1993). Learning oblique decision trees. In R. Bajcsy (Ed.), *Proceedings of the 13th International Joint Conference on Artificial Intelligence* (pp. 1002–1007). Burlington, MA: Morgan Kaufmann.

Hegyi, G., & Garamszegi, L. Z. (2011). Using information theory as a substitute for stepwise regression in ecology and behavior. *Behavioral Ecology and Sociobiology, 65*(1), 69–76.

Hofmann, E., & Knébel, S. (2013). Alignment of manufacturing strategies to customer requirements using analytical hierarchy process. *Production & Manufacturing Research, 1*(1), 19–43.

Kleinbaum, D. G. (2007). *Applied regression analysis and multivariable methods*. Belmont: Thompson Higher Education.

Krishnan, V., & McCalley, J. D. (2013). Progressive entropy based contingency grouping for deriving decision trees for multiple contingencies. *International Journal of Electrical Power & Energy Systems, 45*(1), 35–41.

Lai, V. S., Wong, B. K., & Cheungk, W. (2002). Group decision making in a multiple criteria environment: A case using the AHP in software selection. *European Journal of Operational Research, 137*(1), 134–144.

Lanvin, B., & Evans, P. (2013). *The global talent competitiveness index: 2013*. Singapore: Novus Media Solutions Pte Ltd. ISBN 978-2-9522210-4-7.

Lee, W. I., Shih, B. Y., & Chen, C. Y. (2012). A hybrid artificial intelligence sales forecasting system in the convenience store industry. *Human Factors and Ergonomics in Manufacturing & Service Industries, 22*(3), 188–196.

Matejun, M. (2008). *Barriers to development of high-technology small and medium-sized enterprises*. Lodz: Lodz University of Technology Press.

Matiaško, K., Boháčik, J., Levashenko, V., & Kovalík, Š. (2006). Learning fuzzy rules from fuzzy decision trees. *Journal of Information, Control and Management Systems, 4*(2), 143–154.

Obłój, K. (2013). *Passion and discipline of strategy*. London: Palgrave. ISBN 978-1137334930.

Ohmae, K. (1982). *The mind of the strategist: The art of Japanese business*. New York: McGraw-Hill.

Ohnishi, S., Yamanoi, T., & Imai, H. (2011). A fuzzy representation for non-additive weights of AHP. *Fuzzy Systems (FUZZ), 2011 IEEE International Conference on*, (pp. 672–675), DOI: 10.1109/FUZZY.2011.6007440

Pierścionek, Z. (2006). *Strategie konkurencji i rozwoju przedsiębiorstwa (Competitive strategies and development of the enterprise)*. Warszawa: PWN. ISBN 978-83-01-14085-4.

Pierścionek, Z. (2011). *Zarządzanie strategiczne w przedsiębiorstwie (Strategic management in the enterprise)*. Warszawa: Wyd Naukowe PWN.

Porter, M. E. (1998). *Competitive strategy: Techniques for analyzing industries and competitors*. New York: Free Press.

Porter, M. E. (2011). *Competitive advantage of nations: Creating and sustaining superior performance*. New York: Simon and Schuster.

Pousinho, H. M. I., Mendes, V. M. F., & Catalão, J. P. S. (2012). Short-term electricity prices forecasting in a competitive market by a hybrid PSO–ANFIS approach. *International Journal of Electrical Power & Energy Systems, 39*(1), 29–35.

Prahalad, C. K., & Hamel, G. (1989). Strategic intent. *Harvard Business Review, 69* (1989).

Prahalad, C. K., & Hamel, G. (1990). The core competence of the corporation. *Harvard Business Review, 79–91* (1990).

Priya, P., & Venkatesh, A. (2012). Integration of analytic hierarchy process with regression analysis to identify attractive locations for market expansion. *Journal of Multi-Criteria Decision Analysis, 19*(3–4), 143–153.

Rokach, L., & Maimon, O. (2005). Top-down induction of decision trees classifiers-a survey. *IEEE Transactions on Systems, Man, and Cybernetics, Part C: Applications and Reviews, 35* (4), 476–487.

Romanowska, M., & Gierszewska, G. (2009). *Analiza strategiczna przedsiębiorstwa (Strategic analysis of the enterprise)*. Warszawa: PWE. ISBN 978-83-208-1824-6.

Rostamy, A. A., Shaverdi, M., & Ramezani, I. (2013). Green supply chain management evaluation in publishing industry based on Fuzzy AHP approach. *Journal of Logistics Management, 2*(1), 9–14.

Rostek, K. (2012). The reference model of competitiveness factors for SME medical sector. *Economic Modelling, 29*(2012), 2039–2048.

Rugman, A. M., Oh, C. H., & Lim, D. S. (2012). The regional and global competitiveness of multinational firms. *Journal of the Academy of Marketing Science, 40*(2), 218–235.

Saaty, T. L. (1990). How to make a decision: The analytic hierarchy process. *European Journal of Operational Research, 48*, 9–26.

Saaty, T. L. (1994). *Fundamentals of decision making and priority theory with the analytic hierarchy process*. Pittsburgh, PA: RWS Publications.

Saaty, T. L. (1996). *The analytic hierarchy process: Planning, priority setting, resource allocation*. Pittsburgh, PA: RWS Publications.

Saaty, T. L. (2001). *Decision making for leaders. The analytic hierarchy process for decisions in a complex world*. Pittsburgh, PA: RWS Publications.

Schmoldt, D. L. (Ed.). (2001). *The analytic hierarchy process in natural resource and environmental decision making*. The Netherlands: Kluwer Academic Publishers.

Seidel, M., Seidel, R., Tedford, D., Cross, R., Wait, L., & Hämmerle, E. (2009). Overcoming barriers to implementing environmentally benign manufacturing practices: Strategic tools for SMEs. *Environmental Quality Management, 18*(3), 37–55.

Sen, A., & Srivastava, M. S. (1990). *Regression analysis: Theory, methods, and applications*. Berlin: Springer.

Senvar, O., Gülfem, T., & Cengiz, K. (2014). Multi criteria supplier selection using fuzzy PROMETHEE method. In: *Supply Chain Management Under Fuzziness* (pp. 21–34). Berlin, Heidelberg: Springer.

Shay, J. P., & Rothaermel, F. T. (1999). Dynamic competitive strategy: Towards a multi-perspective conceptual framework. *Long Range Planning, 32*(6), 559–572.

Sipahi, S., & Timor, M. (2010). The analytic hierarchy process and analytic network process: An overview of applications. *Management Decision, 48*(5), 775–808.

Starczewska-Krzysztoszek, M. (2005). *Badanie konkurencyjności sektora MŚP. Raport z badań*. Warszawa: PKPP Lewiatan.

Starczewska-Krzysztoszek, M. (2006). *Konkurencyjność Małych i Średnich Przedsiębiorstw 2006. Raport z badań*. Warszawa: PKPP Lewiatan.

Starczewska-Krzysztoszek, M. (2007). *Konkurencyjność sektora MŚP. Raport z badań*. Warszawa: PKPP Lewiatan.

Starczewska-Krzysztoszek, M. (2008a). Bariery rozwoju małych i średnich przedsiębiorstw w Polsce. *Zagadnienia Społeczno-Gospodarcze Biura Analiz Sejmowych, 4*(2), Wydawnictwo Indos.

Starczewska-Krzysztoszek, M. (2008b). *Konkurencyjność sektora MŚP 2008. Wyniki badania*. Warszawa: PKPP Lewiatan.

Starczewska-Krzysztoszek, M. (2008c). *Monitoring kondycji sektora MŚP 2008*. Warszawa: PKPP Lewiatan.

Sugihara, K., Ishii, H., & Tanaka, H. (2004). Interval priorities in AHP by interval regression analysis. *European Journal of Operational Research, 158*(3), 745–754.

Tam, M. C., & Tummala, V. M. (2001). An application of the AHP in vendor selection of a telecommunications system. *Omega, 29*(2), 171–182.

Verbano, C., & Venturini, K. (2013). Managing risks in SMEs: A literature review and research agenda. *Journal of Technology Management & Innovation, 8*(3), 186–197.

Walkowska, K. (Ed.). (2010). *Działalność przedsiębiorstw niefinansowych w 2008 roku*. Warszawa: Główny Urząd Statystyczny.

Walkowska, K. (Ed.). (2011). *Działalność przedsiębiorstw niefinansowych w 2009 roku*. Warszawa: Główny Urząd Statystyczny.

Warren, K. (2008). *Competitive strategy dynamics*. New York: John Wiley & Sons.

Williamson, D., Cooke, P., Jenkins, W., & Moreton, K. M. (2004). *Strategic management and business analysis*. Oxford: Elsevier Ltd. ISBN 9780750642958.

Wilmańska, A. (2010). *Raport o stanie sektora małych i średnich przedsiębiorstw w Polsce w latach 2008–2009*. Warszawa: PARP.

Wu, C. R., Lin, C. T., & Chen, H. C. (2007). Optimal selection of location for Taiwanese hospitals to ensure a competitive advantage by using the analytic hierarchy process and sensitivity analysis. *Building and Environment, 42*(3), 1431–1444.

Xue-Liang, L., & Chang-Li, W. (2011). The study of fuzzy mathematics and AHP used in performance evaluation. *Machine Learning and Cybernetics (ICMLC) 2011 International Conference on, 1*, 302–306. DOI: 10.1109/ICMLC.2011.6016721.

Yumei, C. (2010). Fuzzy AHP-based method for project risk assessment. *2010 Seventh International Conference on Fuzzy Systems and Knowledge Discovery (FSKD)* (vol 3, pp. 1249–1253). DOI: 10.1109/FSKD.2010.5569128.

Zakrzewska-Bielawska, A. (2012). The strategic dilemmas of innovative enterprises: Proposals for high-technology sectors. *R&D Management, 42*(4), 303–314.

Zhai, J. H. (2011). Fuzzy decision tree based on fuzzy-rough technique. *Soft Computing, 15*(6), 1087–1096.

Zheng, Y. J., & Qi, Z. Y. (2011). Variation analysis of energy industrial structure, competitiveness disparities and total factor productivity: Based on the empirical research of china's province data from 2000 to 2009. *AISS: Advances in Information Sciences and Service Sciences, 3*(9), 347–359.

Zhou, N., Pierre, J. W., & Trudnowski, D. (2012). A stepwise regression method for estimating dominant electromechanical modes. *IEEE Transactions on Power Systems, 27*(2), 1051–1059.

Żołnierski, A., & Pyciński, S. (Eds.). (2007). *Raport o stanie sektora małych i średnich przedsiębiorstw w Polsce w latach 2005–2006*. Warszawa: PARP.

Żołnierski, A., & Zadura-Lichota, P. (Eds.). (2008). *Raport o stanie sektora małych i średnich przedsiębiorstw w Polsce w latach 2006–2007*. Warszawa: PARP.

Żołnierski, A. (Ed.). (2009). *Raport o stanie sektora małych i średnich przedsiębiorstw w Polsce w latach 2007–2008*. Warszawa: PARP.

Chapter 4
Arranging Benchmarking Collaborative Group

The development of an appropriate strategy requires access to information on the needs and expectations of the customer market and the possibility of competitors (manufacturer market), as well as support due to the timing of the decisions and the size of the processed data. Attaining the information from the environment and effective (competitive) support tools is usually beyond the reach of a single SME company. Therefore collaboration remains, resulting in synergies, enabling access to more complete and efficient (than would be possible individually) information, more accurate choice of strategy and aids in making management decisions.

This collaboration may take various forms and have varied scope, as was presented in Sect. 2.1. The aim of collaboration is to increase the competitiveness of individual companies without aggressive competition. The "all or nothing" principle applied to date is replaced by the search for consensus from which each of the involved entities will benefit, while agreeing that other cooperating entities will gain access as well. In relation to the HRPM/FHRPM, a form of collaboration is sought that will ensure a group of SMEs access to shared competitiveness analysis. The use of the proposed method depends on providing data documenting a group's performance to the HMDP and preparing a technological platform dedicated to the use of the method and its users. These conditions give rise to questions regarding:

- security and confidentiality of data processed in the HMDP;
- organisation, maintenance and proper exploitation of the technological platform dedicated to the HRPM/FHRPM method;
- ethical principles concerning the use of the outcomes of analyses obtained as result of cooperation.

Answers to the questions above are provided in the present chapter. The purpose and scope of cooperation is presented in Sect. 4.1. The principles of cooperation organisation are discussed in Sect. 4.2. In Sect. 4.3, the suggested approach is verified in the study group characterised in Sect. 3.3. The approach is summarised

© Springer International Publishing Switzerland 2015
K. Rostek, *Benchmarking Collaborative Networks*, Contributions to Management
Science, DOI 10.1007/978-3-319-16736-7_4

in Sect. 4.4 by means of presenting subsequent questions determining the success of proposed collaboration.

4.1 Benchmarking Collaborative Paradigm

The preparation for a competitiveness strategy in a typical SME company consists of collecting the available results of its performance, preparing them in the form of simple statistical summaries and charts, and on this basis making strategic decisions. This mode of decision-making takes into account only the prospect of their own business, with a very general knowledge of the market and the actions taken by competitors. Whilst a company's competitiveness is conditioned by this—which products/services and what their attributes (like: quality, modernity, diversity, price, availability, delivery time, warranty, specials, discounts) offer in comparison with competitors existing in the common market. This means that the adoption of an appropriate strategy, which guarantees the achievement of competitive advantage, involves the selection of a portfolio of these criteria, within which the company wants to compete. On this basis, the HRPM/FHRPM method was proposed in Chap. 4, which draws on the analysis of SME group's performance, predicts and selects alternative competitive strategies. Thus, the usability of the method depends on the formation of a group of collaborating SMEs.

The suggested type of cooperation is coopetition consisting of the common benchmarking of results of conducted business activity. Its aim is to reinforce the analytical potential of data submitted to the HMDP model in order for the resulting information to be useful for group members. It is assumed that although a single entity only contributes data limited to their own company's performance, aggregate data illustrates the functioning and conditions of the relevant market. Therefore, the main benefit gained by a company from cooperation is the access to data that illustrates the condition of its competitive environment. And the price that it has to pay for it is the submission of data to report its performance at a time and in accordance with the schedule specified in the collaboration agreement. The approach is expressed by a Benchmarking Collaborative Paradigm illustrated in Fig. 4.1.

Benchmarking Collaborative Paradigm
The organization of the Benchmarking Collaborative Network leads to a creation of specialization in individual entities. The Benchmarking Collaborative Network provides the entities market activity in more stable way and much longer period than could happen if they act on their own.

Thus, a the Benchmarking Collaborative Network is a new approach to improve companies' competitiveness. The BCN is specifically dedicated to SMEs, for which

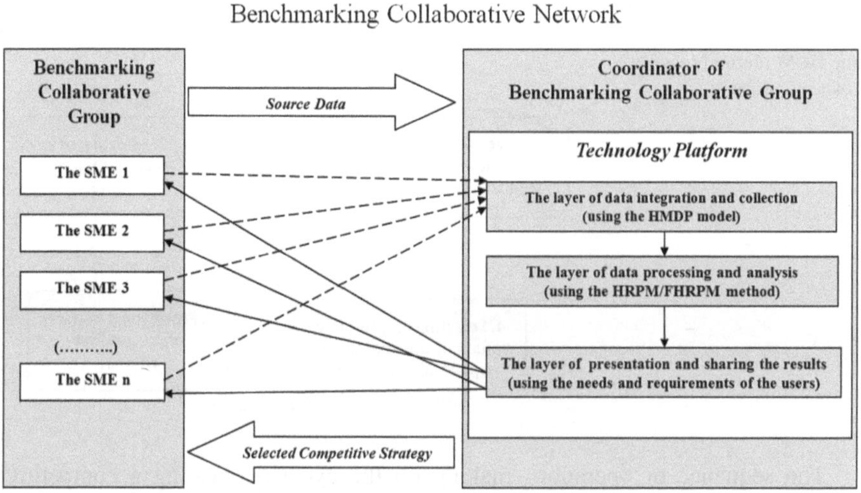

Benchmarking Collaborative Network

Fig. 4.1 Benchmarking Collaborative Paradigm (*source*: own research)

data shortages and limited access to knowledge and technologies, as well as limited financing capacities, are considerable barriers to sustainable development of competitiveness. This does not, however, exclude the option and appropriateness of the use of this approach by companies other than SMEs.

The organization of the BCN leads to implementing shared competitive analysis. It results in every group member receiving information about the possibilities of effective ways to compete in this market area, which has been designated by the data set provided by the network members. Thus the BCN guarantees preserving individuality by each network member (individual selection of a competitive strategy), but makes use of synergy concerning the submitted and integrated data sets for the HMDP (data set subject to analysis is the sum of data provided by individual network members).

4.2 Benchmarking Collaborative Method

The organization of the Benchmarking Collaborative Network, defined in the Benchmarking Collaborative Paradigm, is demonstrated in using the Benchmarking Collaborative Method (BCM). The BCM guarantees the proper organization of companies' collaboration and creation of prototyping competitive strategy. It is necessary to use the most suitable analytical methods, models, tools, technology and data sources in order to build the most useful analysis-reporting solution. This will ensure its correct functioning and continuous development throughout the whole cycle—from the beginning to the end of the collaboration.

Fig. 4.2 The life cycle of
the competitive strategy in
the BCM method (*source*:
own research)

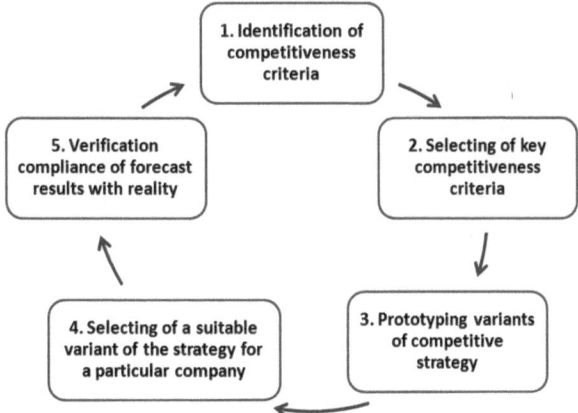

The sequence of operations making up the cycle of creating a competitive strategy is presented in Fig. 4.2. This cycle is compatible with the HRPM/FHRPM method, supporting the process of data analysis and reporting results.

Taking the above into consideration, the BCM has to ensure:

- the organisation of a Benchmarking Collaborative Group;
- the launch of a technological platform dedicated to data collection and analysis;
- the implementation of the HMDP and the HRPM/FHRPM on the prepared technological platform;
- the organisational and technical operation of the technological platform and an analytical-reporting application throughout the term of the collaborative benchmarking of the group.

The above elements were taken into consideration in the BCM presented in Fig. 4.3.

4.2.1 AM1: Creating the Benchmarking Collaborative Group

This stage of the method is crucial for its utility for future users. A group of companies is organised, which are comparable[1] and:

- are interested in taking measures to increase their market competitiveness;
- accept the form of collaborative benchmarking;
- are willing to provide data which documents their performance in the amount, area and according to the schedule specified in the agreement;

---

[1] Their comparability should relate to: the same industry, employment rate, form of conducted activity, location, sales offer and market area on which a company competes.

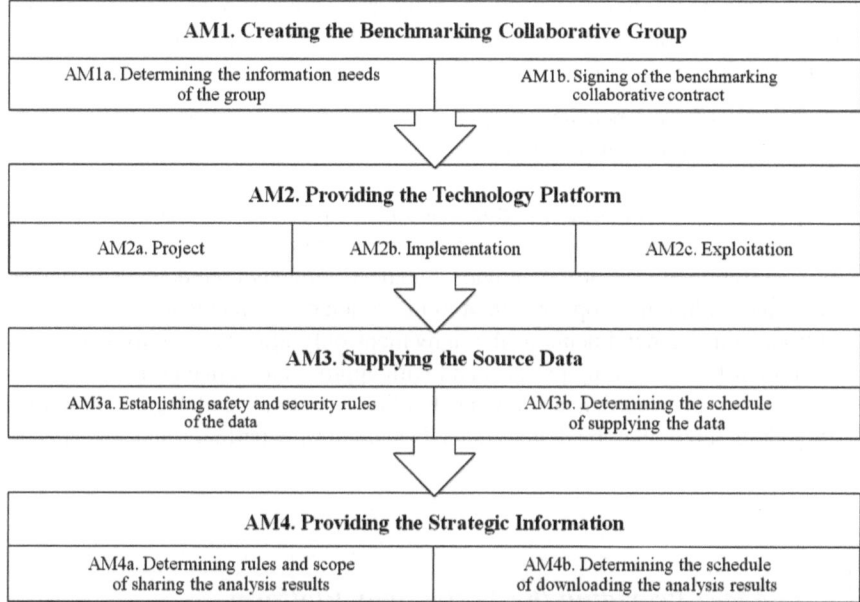

Fig. 4.3 Benchmarking Collaborative Method (*source*: own research)

- declare to be honest and observe business ethics with respect to the veracity and completeness of submitted source data, as well as the use of acquired strategic data.

The group will be referred to as the Benchmarking Collaborative Group (BCG).

Security and continuity of cooperation between companies under the BCG should be ensured by the drawn agreement (stage AM1b). The agreement facilitates accurate registration of shared information and specifies the time, place and entities taking part in the project. Any possible disputes are settled on the basis of its provisions. That is why it is important for the agreement to be accurate with respect to:

- the adopted terms and binding legal provisions regulating cooperation during the term of agreement;
- the appointment of a coordinator and the scope of assistance provided by this person;
- commitments made in relation to individual group members;
- financial arrangements;
- identification of data and information that will be shared;
- the purposes for which obtained information may be used;
- dates of planned audits;
- terms and conditions of terminating/withdrawing from the agreement;
- terms of repairing damage and paying damages in the event of a breach of agreement.

The terms and conditions adopted in the agreement should comply with the applicable Benchmarking Code of Conduct (APQC 2010; GBN 2012), according to which participants should:

- be prepared for the benchmarking procedure and duly meet own commitments;
- not use the acquired information in a way that is unethical or non-compliant with the adopted arrangements;
- respect their benchmarking partners and never purposefully act to their disadvantage, in particular if they are direct market competitors;
- always keep data, information and mutual agreements confidential during the time and within the scope specified in the concluded agreement;
- introduce any amendments to the agreement only after having arranged them with their benchmarking partners and with appropriate notice period;
- always act in accordance with the binding standards and legal regulations, including those that bind individual benchmarking partners and are specific to them.

4.2.2   AM2: Providing the Technology Platform

The scope of analyses envisaged under the HRPM/FHRPM makes it necessary to prepare a technological platform that will provide an automated form of the method's operation. The IT tool has to be developed (stage AM2a) and implemented (stage AM2b) in accordance with the needs and requirements of the group that is going to use it (stage AM2c). The structure of the tool has to ensure the implementation of the cycle presented in Fig. 4.2 and the implementation of the HMDP that will specify the group's competitiveness characteristics. Therefore, the BI technology is the most suitable one.

In spite of undoubted advantages of the BI in the context of the suggested application, its usage in SMEs is still not common enough. According to the conducted studies (Rostek 2010), a typical SME limits itself to the use of an Excel sheet, rarely supporting it with more advanced analytical applications, in spite of a considerable stress on the development of BI tools dedicated to SMEs (Grabova et al. 2010; Guarda et al. 2013; Rostek 2013), also including crowdsourcing (Dresner 2013). Constraints concerning the application of BI technologies result from the lack of (Rostek 2013):

- knowledge of which specialist technological and analytic tools may effectively support the decision process;
- conviction that these tools will prove to be successful and will enhance the efficiency of the decision-making process;
- organisational, economic, technical and personnel capacities to implement and operate specialist IT tools.

Therefore, it is obvious that the functioning of a collaborative benchmarking group will not be possible without the support of an outside coordinating entity that will be responsible for providing a technological platform with a dedicated BI tool. The functioning of a coordinator in the BCN organisation is presented in Chap. 5.

4.2.3 AM3: Supplying the Source Data

Companies that enter into benchmarking cooperation commit in the concluded agreement to cyclically submit data to the HMDP model (Fig. 4.4). On the basis of this data, the values of defined competitiveness criteria characterising the examined collaborative group and the market in which this group operates are derived.

The submitted data also includes confidential data, which is valuable for the analysis but dangerous in the hands of competitors since they can identify a rival company's strengths and weaknesses (e.g. sales structure and profitability, personnel productivity, effectiveness of fixed assets or customers' structure). On the other hand, lack of this data will make it impossible to use the HRPM/FHRPM method effectively. Therefore, detailed agreements on the confidentiality and security of using data under the established cooperation are needed (stage AM3a).

Ensuring the appropriate level of security for collected data is impossible without an IT system. Security management in an IT system should be in line with the guidelines of a series of international standards ISO/IEC 27000: *Information technology—Security techniques—Information security management systems—Overview and vocabulary*. ISO/IEC 27002, entitled *Information*

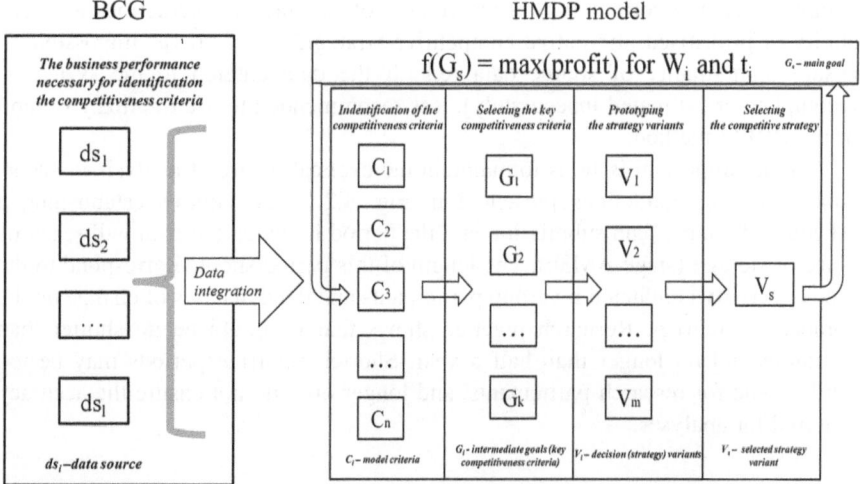

Fig. 4.4 Supplying the source data into the HMPD model (*source*: own research)

technology—Security techniques—Code of practice for information security management is of particular importance. It provides recommendations of the best practices in information management for people responsible for initiating, implementing and maintaining information security management systems. Information security is specified in the standard with a triad of three qualities C-I-A (ISO/IEC 27002):

- C—confidentiality—providing access to data and information only to authorised entities;
- I—integrity—ensuring accuracy and completeness of information and methods of its processing;
- A—availability—providing access to information and related assets to all authorised entities at the time when they require it.

C-I-A refer to three areas of management: (1) infrastructure and the environment, (2) human resources and (3) access control. Each of those areas implies the generation of specific threats, and in each preventive measures should be taken, appropriate to the estimated level of risk. This way, protection covers data collected in the system and information derived from data analysis and processing. The adopted data confidentiality and security principles have to be observed unconditionally by group participants, or else the cooperation agreement shall be terminated.

Next to the need to maintain data confidentiality and ensure data security, a common data standard has to be agreed upon with respect to nomenclature and definitions, scope of information, uniform methods of measurement and level of detail. This will ensure comparability of collected resources and the options to aggregate them in different ways in order to derive the values of individual competitiveness criteria used in the HMDP. It is important at this stage to make BCG participants aware of the significance of data quality (i.e. their veracity, completeness and correctness) in the context of accuracy of predictions and reliability of prioritised alternative competitive strategies. If it proves impossible to ensure high quality of source data (e.g. if the data entered to the system is incomplete or estimated inaccurately), it is recommended to use the fuzzy version of the HRPM method.

Another important issue is to maintain the cyclical nature of analysis in accordance with the guidelines presented in Fig. 4.2. This requires establishing a schedule of source data submission and the period in which the data will reach its place of storage (stage AM3b). The length of this period should correspond to the type of activity conducted by group participants and the dynamics of change on the competitive market. Research practice shows that it should be no shorter than 2 months and no longer than half a year. Shorter reporting periods may be too burdensome for research participants, and longer ones do not ensure the accuracy required for analyses.

4.2.4 AM4: Providing the Strategic Information

While it is crucial to ensure the security of data collection and use in the stage AM3, it is equally important to publish processed information in a way that ensures anonymity and confidentiality in relation to the entities participating in the BCG (stage AM4a). It is inadmissible for the collaborating companies to acquire information in a way that may be used against specific entities from the group. The essence of benchmarking cooperation within the framework of the BCM is coopetition that results in deriving benefits by all group participants, and not aggressive rivalry and fighting competition.

Therefore, also at this stage it is justified to use the ISO/IEC 27000 standards. Moreover, the application of methods and procedures known in the IT system implementation practice is recommended. One such method consists of replacing the names of companies with code labels (e.g. W01, W02, ... Wn, Fig. 4.5). With a sufficiently big the BCG it allows for the publishing of detailed data. Security is ensured by an inability to identify a company on the basis of the assigned code label.

A different option is to present detailed performance results of a company only in reference to the group's aggregate statistics (Table 4.1). In such a case, a company does not learn about the value of detailed data from other research participants, but may relate its own performance to the group's aggregate summaries.

Regardless of which method is applied, it is crucial for the arrangements concerning the method of results presentation to be provided in the concluded agreement and to be unconditionally observed, or else the agreement shall be cancelled and cooperation terminated.

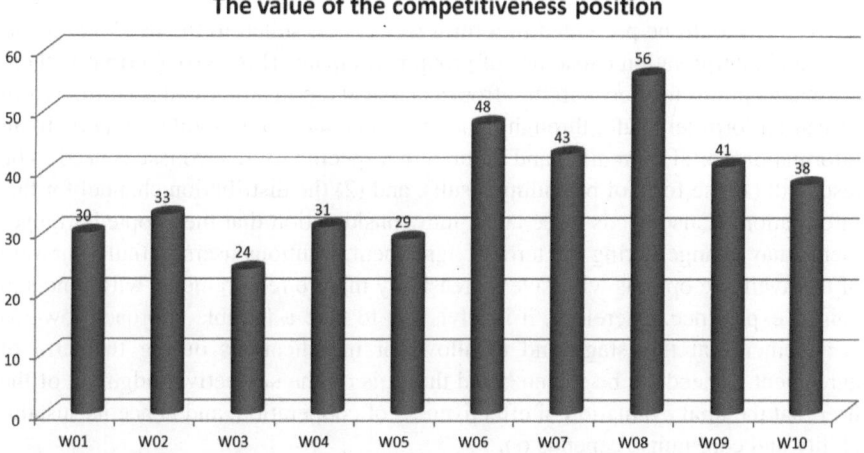

Fig. 4.5 Coding the names of entities (*source*: own research)

Table 4.1 Using the references to the statistics of the entire group

| | | | Statistics for the entire group | | |
Effectiveness indicator	Company indicator (%)	Company's position on the group's ranking list	MAX (%)	AVG (%)	MIN (%)
Net profit as % of sales	3.9	2	5.10	3.15	1.20
Gross profit as % of sales	20.5	1	20.50	13.60	6.70
Change in sales as % of sales in the previous year	14.0	2	14.80	9.00	3.20

Source: own research

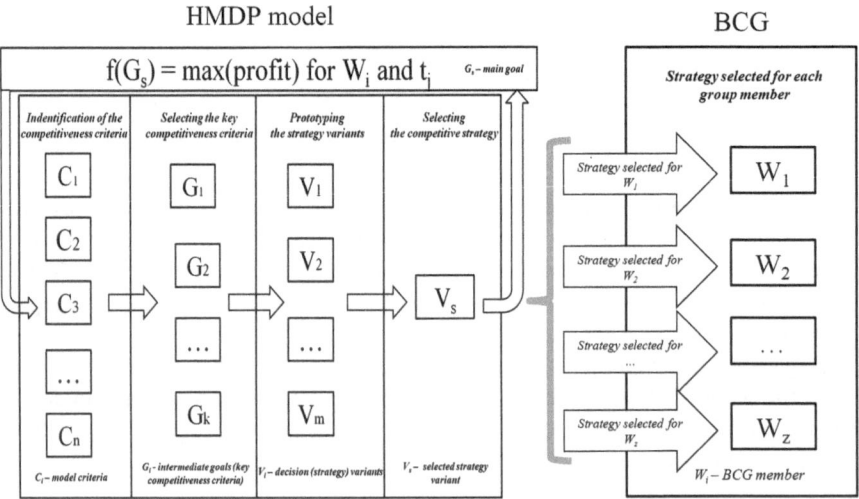

Fig. 4.6 Providing the strategic information for each group member (*source*: own research)

Results should be presented in a form that is best suited to the needs, expectations and interpretation capacities of group participants (Fig. 4.6). Currently, there are many options to choose from—from a classical report structured according to an agreed uniform template, through dynamically created and modified reports to an information portal accredited and tailored to a specific user. Two issues need to be resolved: (1) the form of providing results, and (2) the distribution channel for this information. It also needs to be taken into consideration that the adopted arrangements may change during the term of agreement. Cautious users initially unaware of the available options will have increasingly mature requirements with time and gained experience. Therefore, it is advisable to take a flexible approach towards arrangements at this stage and to allow for modifications during the term of agreement. It needs to be remembered that it is on the subjective judgment of the user that the final evaluation of effectiveness of cooperation, and hence its sustainability and continuity, depends on.

Similarly to stage AM3b, it is necessary to establish a schedule for submission of the results (stage AM4b). It may be consistent or inconsistent with the schedule of providing source data (stage AM3b). The consistency of these two schedules is motivated by the psychological impact on the user, who will submit data and at the same time receive information on the recommended tailor-made competitive strategy in exchange (Figs. 4.4 and 4.6). Providing feedback in longer intervals than the intervals of data submission is, in turn, motivated by the specifics of management since verification of the effectiveness of the implemented changes requires time for the evaluation to be reliable. Therefore, the optimum periods of data submission and feedback receipt for a given group should be determined during the first year of cooperation.

4.3 Benchmarking Collaboration: Case Study and Utilities Verification

The experiment verifying the utility of the BCM was carried out on the same BCG group that was characterised in Sect. 3.3. The present chapter presents additional information which indicates the need to organise a benchmarking group and the resulting benefits. The course of the presented experiment is described in accordance with the stages of the BCM.

4.3.1 AM1: Creating the Benchmarking Collaborative Group

4.3.1.1 AM1a: Determining the Information Needs of the Group

As was already mentioned in Sect. 3.3, the experiment involved 10 dental clinics selected from among a group of 150 clinics covered with a survey. The characteristics of these companies were as follows:

- all clinics were located in Warsaw,
- seven of them provided only dental services, and three offered additional medical services,
- all of them were SMEs since they employed from 6 to 85 people, and their annual revenues did not exceed PLN eight million,
- they were digitised—they had between 1 and 12 computers, but employed no more than one computer specialist to operate the hardware and maintain the IT resources,
- they used specialist IT applications to support specific areas of conducted activity, including:

- ProDentis—a complex tool dedicated to dental practices and clinics;
- Symfonia System—integrated solution supporting management in small and medium enterprises including modules supporting the following divisions: accounting and finances, human resources and payroll, fixed assets management, sale of services, financial analyses and billing;
- Simple Business—an application supporting the keeping of accounts and books in small and medium enterprises;
- InsERT—a package of applications supporting financial and bookkeeping settlements as well as the management of payroll and human resources;
- KS-PPS—Basic Provider's Programme, which is obligatory if contracts are settled with the National Health Fund, covering also electronic data exchanged between a clinic and the National Health Fund.

– the software used usually belonged to the clinic; outsourcing was rarely resorted to.

Each of the clinics invited to this stage of research declared its interest and willingness to cooperate within the framework of the experiment and assessed its level of competitiveness as insufficient. None of the entities had any experience related to coopetition and benchmarking as effective tools supporting the development of competitive advantage.

The conducted analysis of the use of IT tools demonstrated that accountancy and finances are most often supported, followed by human resources and payroll, fixed assets management and the sale of services. Analyses supporting decision making in the field of strategy and planning were used marginally. As the clinic owners explained to us, management consists in solving contemporary problems and focusing on what is happening now because tomorrow is too distant and unpredictable. As a result, as has been mentioned before, 4 companies from among 20 invited to the experiment, could not take part in it either because they had declared bankruptcy or because they had been acquired by a stronger company. Therefore, it was determined that clinics expect information concerning:

– the assessment of their competitiveness against the background of the group;
– characteristics of factors with the strongest impact on market competitiveness;
– tips concerning the implementation of strategic measures resulting in improved competitiveness at a desired level.

4.3.1.2 AM1b: Signing the Benchmarking Collaborative Contract

The concluded agreement specified the purpose of cooperation, the terms of its execution and the principles of data and information security during the term of cooperation.

The purpose of the cooperation included dedicated benchmarking analyses and cyclically submitted reports assessing competitiveness and guidelines on competitiveness development strategies. Reports were prepared and submitted to each clinic in the group individually.

The terms and conditions of cooperation specified:

- the term of the collaborative agreement—6 months from 1 January 2010 to 30 June 2010;
- lack of any form of payment for the provided service during the specified term;
- a declaration on the submission of data feeding the HMDP model throughout the term of agreement with frequency specified by the data submission schedule;
- a declaration on the submission of analytic reports dedicated to a specific clinic and its needs throughout the term of agreement with frequency specified by the analyses' results submission schedule;
- a declaration on the assessment of utility of provided strategic information on the basis of a prepared survey no later than 6 months after the end of collaboration.

Data security principles were also agreed upon:

- source data were submitted per e-mail or in person in the form of standardised MS Excel tables;
- source data were stored in a single computer protected with the Kaspersky Internet Security anti-virus software;
- collaborating clinics familiarised themselves with the general group characteristics (described in stage S1a) but did not contact each other, so they did not know the names or addresses of other companies and had no direct access to data provided by other companies;
- analytical reports in PDF formats submitted to individual clinics were the only channel of information exchange. The reports did not make it possible to identify the entities collaborating within the group in more details (than described above).

4.3.2   AM2: Providing the Technology Platform

4.3.2.1   AM2a: Project

Since it was decided that the BI technology was the optimum tool to support the diversified, changing and evolving needs of the BCN, reference architecture of a DBI tool (Dedicated Business Intelligence) was developed (Fig. 4.7). The tool is dedicated to serve the HMDP model and the HRMP/FHRPM method. It also takes into account the characteristics of the companies forming the BCG group.

In the prototype version prepared for the purpose of the experiment, the above model was limited only to elements required to implement the HMDP model and the HRMP/FHRPM method in accordance with the scheme presented in Fig. 4.8.

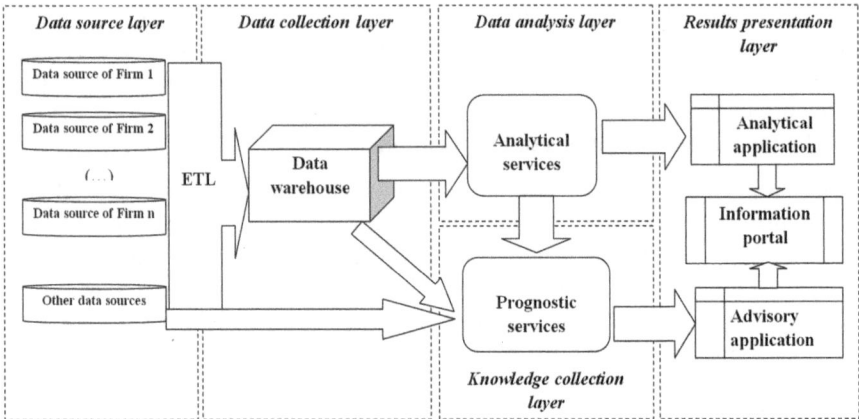

Fig. 4.7 The reference architecture of the DBI system (*source*: own research)

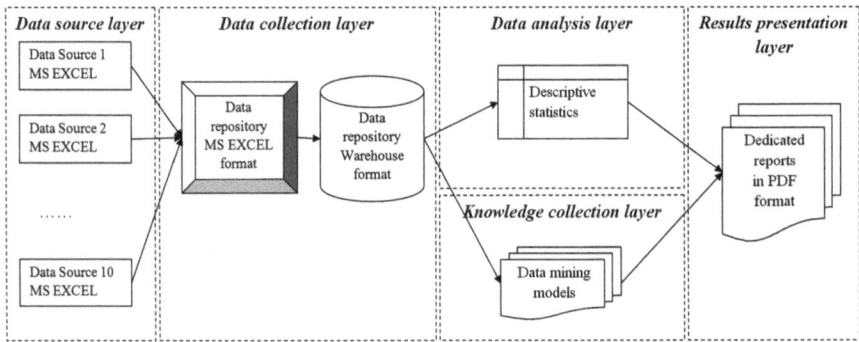

Fig. 4.8 The architecture of the DBI prototype (*source*: own research)

The extent to which the proposed solution changes the typical situation of solutions applied in SMEs is shown in Fig. 4.9.

Usually companies operate with isolated individual sets of source data. They limit themselves to preparing only basic statistics required by accountancy and legal requirements. In this perspective, even a simplified model of the DBI prototype (Fig. 4.8) is a significant change that improves the analytical potential of processed data and utility of strategic feedback.

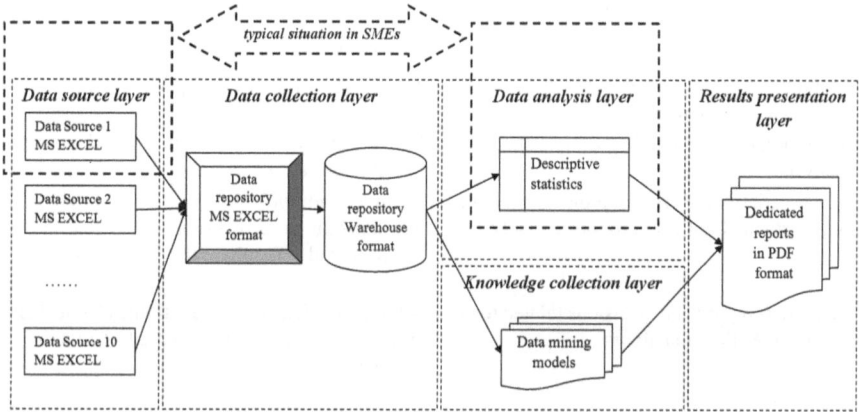

Fig. 4.9 Typical analytical situation in SMEs (*source*: own research)

4.3.2.2   AM2b: Implementation

The functionality specified in the previous chapters and conditions to be met by the BI system dedicated to a selected group of SMEs require:

– ensuring appropriate amount and scope of data for analysis;
– providing a broad variety of analytical tools enabling not only statistical but also prognostic analyses;
– comparing obtained results and relating them to the relevant market;
– providing support as regards the decisions related to the obtained results of analyses.

The above requirements call for introducing changes in relation to the classical implementation of the BI, as presented in Table 4.2.

The above requirements also determine the choice of technology which on the one hand has to ensure the implementation of the HRMP/FHRPM method, and on the other hand should be available in organisational and financial terms to SMEs. The approach to overcoming these limitations will be presented in Chap. 5. In the experiment, SAS Institute technology was applied, which makes it possible to achieve all set objectives and adhere to the identified conditions and limitations (Fig. 4.10).

Table 4.2 Changes introduced to the Dedicated Business Intelligence system

SME's needs	Changes to DBI
Comparing obtained results and relating them to the relevant market	The BI system that serves not one but several SMEs
Appropriate amount and scope of data for analysis	Feeding the system with data from all companies that use the BI system
Broad variety of analytical tools enabling not only statistical but also prognostic analyses	Team and not individual financing of system development, construction and maintenance, which will also facilitate the purchase of hardware
Support as regards the decisions related to the obtained results of analyses	Adding an advisory module to the classical BI system, tailor-made or purchased as a ready product

Source: own research

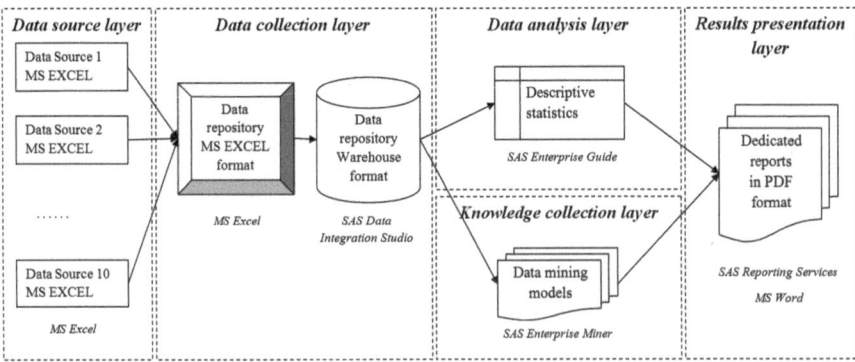

Fig. 4.10   Implementation of DBI system (*source*: own research)

4.3.2.3   AM2c: Exploitation

System exploitation by users consisted in cyclical submission of a set of source data specified in the agreement and the receipt of dedicated analytical reports. The reports contained:

– the assessment of the clinic's achievements as compared to the entire group;
– the indication of changes that occurred in relation to previous periods of analysis;
– the specification of competitive strategy measures that should improve the current situation.

At the end of the experiment (after 30 June 2010), all clinics were asked to assess the usefulness of the analyses in relation to the amount of work related to the preparation and submission of source data. The evaluation was positive and indicated group participants' interest in further exploitation of the DBI.

4.3.3   AM3: Supplying the Source Data

4.3.3.1   AM3a: Establishing Safety and Confidentiality Rules of Data

Data fed to DBI encompassed the values that were necessary to specify the identified competitiveness criteria. The data was broken down into four areas related to (Table 4.3): registered patients, achieved results of sale of services, employed medical and administrative staff members and borne costs.

On the basis of the above data, values of competitiveness criteria for the HMDP were calculated (Table 4.4).

The results from the lists provided above, showed that the data obtained from clinics included financial data, as well as data related to productivity and efficiency of the conducted activity. Therefore, strict rules of protecting them against unauthorised access and dishonest use had to be specified. These rules were described in the collaborative benchmarking agreement (stage AM1b) and were strictly observed throughout the term of agreement and after its expiry. Therefore, scientific publications describing the present experiment do not contain information that would enable linking of this data to any specific clinic.

4.3.3.2   AM3b: Determining the Schedule of Supplying the Data

Seven reporting periods were envisaged. They included:

1) January–June 2008;
2) July–December 2008;
3) January–June 2009;
4) July–December 2009;
5) January–February 2010;
6) March–April 2010;
7) May–June 2010.

Data was subsequently stored in a repository of the DBI system and identified by means of: (1) the period they related to, (2) the numerical code of the company they belonged to (Table 4.5).

Because of this conducted analyses could refer to the subject of research (clinic) and the point in time (the period that the data related to). This enabled predicting the value of the objective function in subsequent reporting periods, which is one of the most important tasks of the HRPM/FHRPM method.

As results from Table 4.5 show, various reporting periods were used for analysis—6 and 2 months. According to the users, 2 month periods were better because these obtained results of analyses were more accurate, and their reliability and utility greater.

Table 4.3 Structure of source data in the HMDP model

Source data acronyms	Source data descriptions
Patients-related data:	
LPO	Total number of patients
LSP	Number of patients that resorted to company's services at least three times a year
L3L	Number of patients who have been company's patients for at least 3 years
LPZM	Number of patients residing over 100 km away from Warsaw
LPZG	Number of foreign patients
Services-related data:	
SB	Gross value of sold services in PLN 1,000
SN	Net value of sold services in PLN 1,000
SUN	Gross value of sold innovative services in PLN 1,000
ZS	Profit
LWO	Number of visits in the specified period
SCO	Average time of waiting for a visit in days
SCT	Average duration of a visit in minutes
LR	Number of complaints
WR	Gross value of complaints in PLN 1,000
Staff-related data:	
PO	Total number of employees
PM	Number of medical staff members
PA	Number of administrative staff members
PS	Number of staff members under any form of training
LRM	Number of man hours of medical personnel
LRA	Number of man hours of administrative personnel
SPM	Average wage of the medical staff
SPA	Average wage of the administrative staff
KRM	Labour cost of the medical staff in PLN 1,000
KRA	Labour cost of the administrative staff in PLN 1,000
Cost-related data:	
KM	Cost of medical materials in PLN 1,000
KN	Cost of inspection and repair of medical equipment in PLN 1,000
WS	Value of medical equipment in PLN 1,000
WZM	Value of spare medical materials in PLN 1,000
KMR	Costs of marketing and promotion in PLN 1,000
WIR	Investment and development expenditure in PLN 1,000
CWST	Total value of fixed assets in PLN 1,000
WB	Value of buildings in PLN 1,000

Source: own research

Table 4.4 Method of calculation of the values of competitiveness factors in the HMDP model

Criterion symbol	Criterion name	Formula to calculate criterion's value
C_1	Value of sold innovative medical services as % of the value of sold services	=SUN/SB
C_2	Investment and development expenditures as % of the value of sold services	=WIR/SB
C_3	Number of complaints as % of the number of provided medical services	=LR/LWO
C_4	Value of complaints as % of the value of sold services	=WR/SB
C_5	Number of registered patients per one employed medical staff member	=LPO/PM
C_6	Average time of waiting for a visit	=SCO
C_7	Average duration of a visit	=SCT
C_8	Number of patients repeatedly resorting to company's services as % of the total number of patients	=LSP/LWO
C_9	Number of loyal patients resorting to company's services as % of the total number of patients	=L3L/LWO
C_{10}	Number of visiting patients resorting to company's services as % of the total number of patients	=LPZM/LWO
C_{11}	Number of foreign patients resorting to company's services as % of the total number of patients	=LPZG/LWO
C_{12}	Number of sold services per one employed member of medical staff	=LWO/PM
C_{13}	Value of sold medical services per one employed member of medical staff	=SB/PM
C_{14}	Sales profitability	=ZS/SN
C_{15}	Average wage of the medical staff	=SPM
C_{16}	Average wage of the administrative staff	=SPA
C_{17}	Labour cost of the administrative staff as % of the labour cost of medical staff	=KRA/KRM
C_{18}	Labour cost of the administrative staff as % of the value of sold services	=KRM/SB
C_{19}	Promotion and marketing costs as % of the value of sold services	=KMR/SB
C_{20}	Total value of fixed assets as % of the value of sold services	=CWST/SB
C_{21}	Value of medical equipment as % of the value of sold services	=WS/SB
C_{22}	Value of medical equipment per one employed member of medical staff	=WS/PM
C_{23}	Profit per man-hour of a member of medical staff	=ZS/PM
C_{24}	% of employees under any type of training	=PS/PO

Source: own research

Table 4.5 Method of identifying detailed data in the DBI repository

ID	Clinic	Period	Criteria			
			C_1	...	C_{21}	...
W011	W01	January–June 2008	0.000000		0.500000	
W021	W02	January–June 2008	0.000000		0.125000	
W031	W03	January–June 2008	0.000000		0.600000	
...	...	....	....	.....	...	...
W057	W05	May–June 2010	0.000000		0.800000	
W067	W06	May–June 2010	0.006122		1.112245	
W077	W07	May–June 2010	0.000000		0.383333	
...	...	...	...	...	...	...

Source: own research

4.3.4   AM4: Providing the Strategic Information

4.3.4.1   AM4a: Determining Rules and Scope of Sharing the Analysis Results

As has been mentioned before, reports covered three topics:

1) assessment of clinic's achievements in comparison to the group—in order to answer the question: *what is my level of competitiveness?*
2) assessment of changes that occurred in the clinic as compared to the previous analysed period—in order to answer the question *how effective are the undertaken strategic measures?*
3) suggestions of changes that should be implemented in order to further improve competitiveness—in order to answer the question: *what should be done to further improve competitiveness?*

The group 1 analyses contained comparisons of the achievements of individual group members concerning their generated profit (Fig. 4.11) and calculated competitiveness criteria (Fig. 4.12). On the basis of the above analyses, each of the clinics could assess its competitiveness in relation to other group members.

The group 2 included analyses presenting the values of individual competitiveness criteria achieved in time (Fig. 4.13) and the change in these values in relation to comparable periods (Fig. 4.14). On the basis of obtained information, clinics evaluated the value of change, which served as a measurement of effectiveness of previously implemented measures to improve competitiveness.

Predictive analyses from the group 3 were, naturally, the most important component of reports. They referred to further measures, i.e. the selection of the best suited competitive strategy depending on the desired level of profit. In this group, each clinic received the results of the HRPM/FHRPM method for the desired level of profit, as presented in Chap. 3.

The above means of reporting exhausted all information needs of the BCG covered by the agreement. Coding clinic names ensured security and confidentiality

Fig. 4.11 Comparison of
the profit (*source*: own
research)

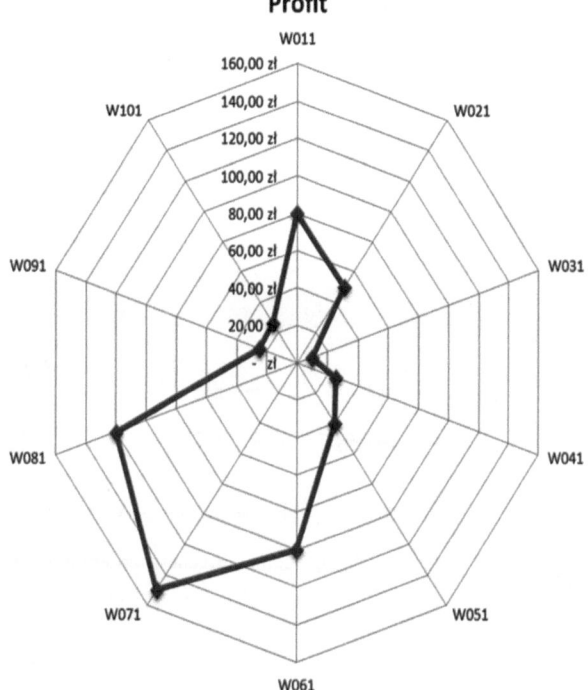

Fig. 4.12 Comparison of
the selected
competitiveness criteria
(*source*: own research)

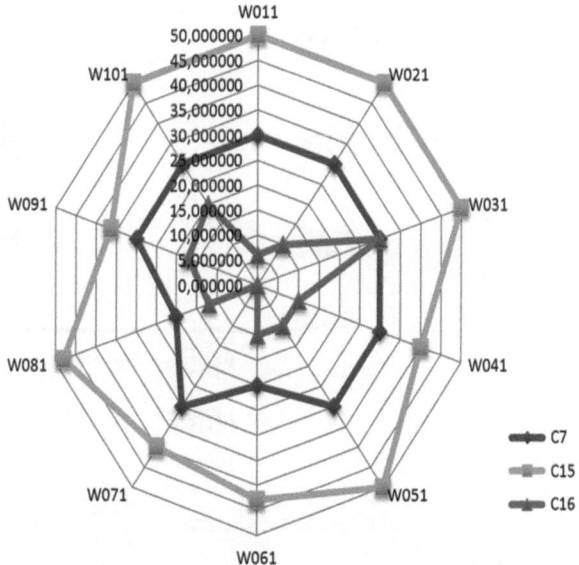

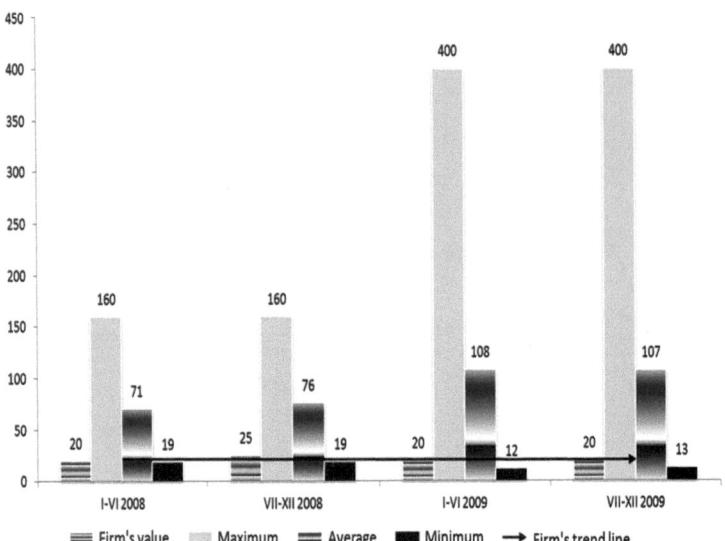

Fig. 4.13 Comparison of the competitiveness criterion over the time period (*source*: own research)

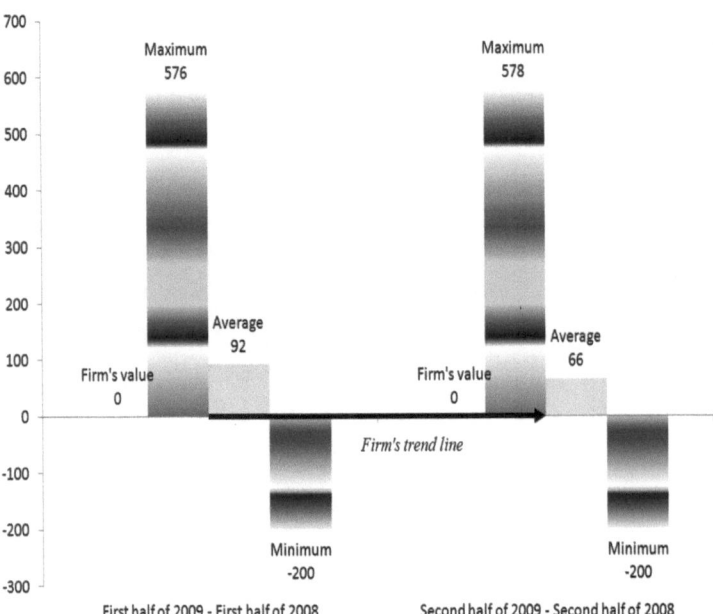

Fig. 4.14 Comparison of the competitiveness criterion change over the time period *(source*: own research)

of acquired information, making it impossible to assign the information to any individual entity.

4.3.4.2   AM4b: Determining the Schedule of Downloading the Analysis Results

The schedule of providing analytical reports was consistent with the one for providing source data. An exchange took place—results of data analysis from the previous reporting period were provided in exchange for new data.

In the case of the conducted experiment, this arrangement proved to be effective since it motivated group members to comply with the terms of the benchmarking collaborative contract.

4.3.5   Summarizing the BCM Method

The results obtained from the research experiment showed that the use of the BCM method is an alternative and an effective tool in the development of competition in the SMEs. It has a substantial impact on reducing the uncertainty in the process of making strategic decisions. It also strengthens the competitive potential of recipients to a level that ensures the feasibility of the competitive analysis implementation to the same level as in the large enterprises.

However, it needs to be remembered that the final effectiveness of the method is strongly determined by the way and extent of using the obtained information and knowledge. And this is conditioned by knowledge, experience and belief in the value and importance of competitive analysis by decision-makers.

Production deployment of the method requires the development of criteria that determine its profitability for the user. These criteria should include the size and diversity of the group of collaborating companies and the period of cooperation.

While the benefits of such collaboration and the need for it are obvious for companies with average market results, it would be desired to attract also market leaders, who would provide knowledge and best practices to be used by weaker entities. The possibility of observation and control of measures undertaken by competitors may serve as arguments for a market leader to enter the group, yet it needs to be remembered that the appeal of this argument depends solely on the size of the BCG.

Too high homogeneity of the group's level of competitiveness, in turn, will considerably contribute to lowering the effectiveness of collaborative benchmarking. Therefore, approaching the set similar level of competitiveness should serve as a signal to search for new group participants or to cancel the group.

In conclusion, the concept of the BCM is not a closed matter and requires further research on the BCG's organisation and management.

4.4   Summarizing: How to Effectively Coordinate the Group?

The proposed BCM method integrates several elements, which hitherto have been implemented independently:

- providing knowledge of the suggested actions for the competitive strategy with a known level of effectiveness, and not exclusively statistical results of competitive analysis;
- enabling the use of advanced information technologies that are not available or cannot be used by a single SME company;
- strengthening the analytical potential of source data by integrating the resources of multiple SME companies;
- teaching entrepreneurs the posture of competitive cooperation in place of rivalry;
- is a flexible form of collaboration in which the company takes the decision to join or leave the group.

Yet it needs to be noted that the use of the BCM depends on the introduction of a BI-class IT system that will ensure the implementation of the HRPM/FHRPM method. While the group of SMEs would be able to run such an IT solution through network collaboration, it would be difficult for them to keep it running in the long term due to the lack of qualified personnel.

Moreover, correct cooperation requires security and confidentiality of exchanged data and information, which would be impossible with internal coordination and group's self-service. For this reason, participation of an external entity is necessary, which would provide continuity and functioning coordination within the benchmarking collaborative group (Fig. 4.15).

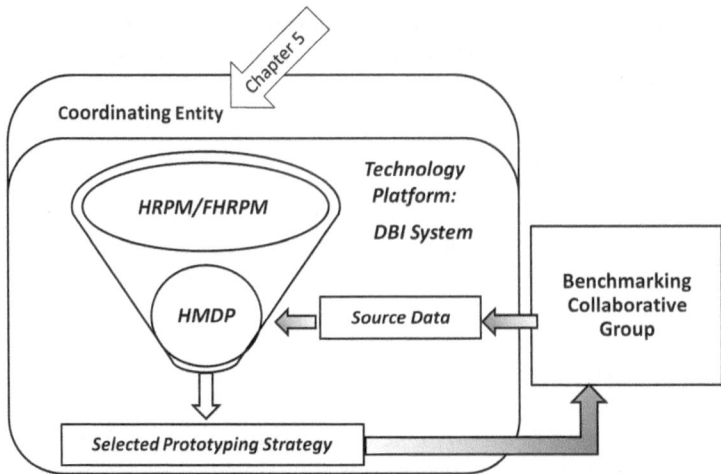

Fig. 4.15 Elements to ensure the coordination of Benchmarking Collaborative Group *(source:* own research)

On the other hand, the participation of an external coordinating entity requires profitability of implementation of the offered service. The method of including the external entity as an coordinator of SMEs group will be shown in the Chap. 5.

References

APQC. (2010). *Benchmarking code of conduct. Guidelines and ethics for benchmarkers.* Houston, Texas: American Productivity & Quality Center.

Dresner, H. (2013). *The Wisdom of Crowds® small and mid-sized enterprise business intelligence market study. The report on the 2013.* Dresner Advisory Services, LLC.

GBN. (2012). *Benchmarking code of conduct.* Berlin: Global Benchmarking Network.

Grabova, O., Darmont, J., Chauchat, J. H., & Zolotaryova, I. (2010). Business intelligence for small and middle-sized enterprises. *ACM SIGMOD Record, 39*(2), 39–50.

Guarda, T., Santos, M., Pinto, F., Augusto, M., & Silva, C. (2013). Business intelligence as a competitive advantage for SMEs. *International Journal of Trade, Economics & Finance, 4*(4), 187–190.

ISO/IEC 27002—*Information technology—Security techniques—Code of practice for information security management.* International Organization for Standardization (ISO) and the International Electrotechnical Commission (IEC).

Rostek, K. (2010). Business intelligence for SME. In E. Lechman (Ed.), *SMEs and enterpreneurship* (Vol. 2, pp. 164–190). Gdańsk: Gdańsk University of Technology Publishing House.

Rostek, K. (2013). Dedicated business intelligence system for SMEs consortium. *African Journal of Business Management, 7*(13), 999–1014.

Chapter 5
Coordinating Benchmarking Collaborative Group

The BCM method, described in Chap. 4, represents SME's perspective in the Benchmarking Collaborative Network approach. The customer's perspective is shown and their needs for access to key strategic information. The current chapter focuses on the service provider's perspective, which is the coordinator of Benchmarking Collaborative Group, who is responsible for the quality, completeness and usefulness of provided strategic information. The coordinator of the BCG is the last element of the BCN structure.

5.1 Model of Benchmarking Collaborative Network

Taking into account the need for SMEs to have access not only to solutions of competitiveness analysis, but also their organizational, financial, technical and personnel limitations of using these, the proposed solution is the use of a Model of Benchmarking Collaborative Network (MBCN, Fig. 5.1) comprising the following elements:

- Benchmarking Collaborative Group (BCG)—group of SMEs—services recipients have a contract of brokering strategic information in the range of supplying the source data to HMDP model and joint exploitation of the results obtained from competitiveness analyses;
- Broker of Strategic Information (BSI)—the service provider delivering all resources, knowledge and skills necessary to prepare useful strategic information for the service recipient;
- Contract of Brokering Strategic Information (CBSI)—civil law contract specifying the terms, conditions and procedures for implementation of services of brokering strategic information, including both—the relationship between the service provider and service recipients, as well as mutual benchmarking collaboration within the group;

© Springer International Publishing Switzerland 2015

K. Rostek, *Benchmarking Collaborative Networks*, Contributions to Management Science, DOI 10.1007/978-3-319-16736-7_5

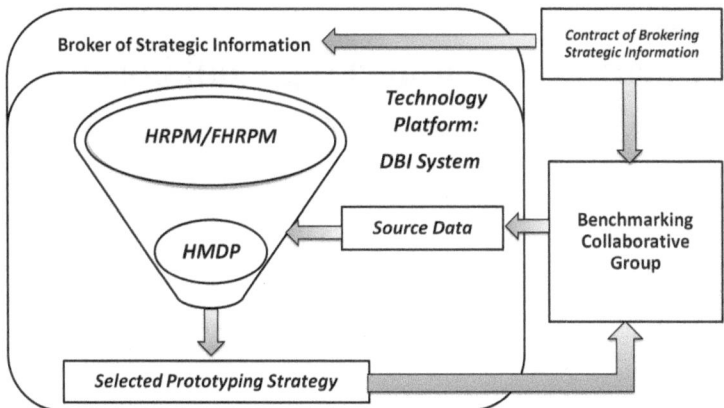

Fig. 5.1 Model of benchmarking collaborative network (*source*: Own research)

– Technology Platform—the area of flexible communication between the service provider and service recipients, through which the information system dedicated for competitiveness analysis operates.

MBCN was prepared considering the following conditions and assumptions:

– the services recipients need the information to achieve a competitive advantage, but cannot prepare such information for themselves;
– the service provider is an expert in the area providing services and also has the organizational, technical and personnel possibilities for implementing them;
– the services recipients are responsible for the timeliness and quality of the source data supplied to DBI system, understanding that the data, determining the final utility and usability of the obtained strategic information;
– the service provider is responsible for the best fit scope and form of available results of DBI system to the needs and abilities of the recipients;
– the service provider is responsible for the confidentiality and security of collected and processed data and the provided information, understanding the liability associated with them;
– the service recipients and the service provider are mutually responsible and have mutual trust that gained knowledge will not use in bad faith.

It follows that the effective functioning of BCN requires, above all, a smooth interaction between two elements of the structure—the BCG and the BSI. The BCG is a group of SMEs who are aware of their expectations, but also undertake the obligations and responsibilities arising from the cooperation. The method of managing the organisation and functioning of the BCG is described in detail in Chap. 4. This chapter is devoted to the use of the BCG by the BSI.

The BSI is the coordinator of the group and an expert in the field of company competitiveness, whose knowledge and experience support the activities of the BCG to improve the competitiveness of its members. The mutual benefit of the cooperation lies in the preparation of useful strategic information by the BSI and its subsequent delivery to the BCG, for a fee. This service is carried out with the support of the DBI class system. Proper use of the provided information will result in the improvement of the competitiveness for the BCG's participants.

From the BSI's perspective, it is evident that providing a chargeable service results in benefits. They will be the greater, the larger the number of serviced customers. The above statement leads to the concept of the Method of Brokering Strategic Information, which goes beyond the coordination of a single BCG and constitutes providing chargeable information services in the field of company competitiveness.

5.2 Method of Brokering Strategic Information

The implementation of the MBCN raises the need for a definition of the *brokering service of strategic information,* understood as: *payable and ensuring organized and safe access to strategic of high quality and useful information to the recipient, with the support of specialized information technology and with the principles established by the contract.*

In order to ensure the realization of this, the Method of Brokering Strategic Information (MBSI) was developed, specifying the terms and conditions for the implementation of brokering service of strategic information (Fig. 5.2).

Certain steps of the MBSI method, such as arranging the BCG group or concluding a cooperation contract, are identical with the corresponding stages of the BCM method (presenting the perspective of the group's participant—the service

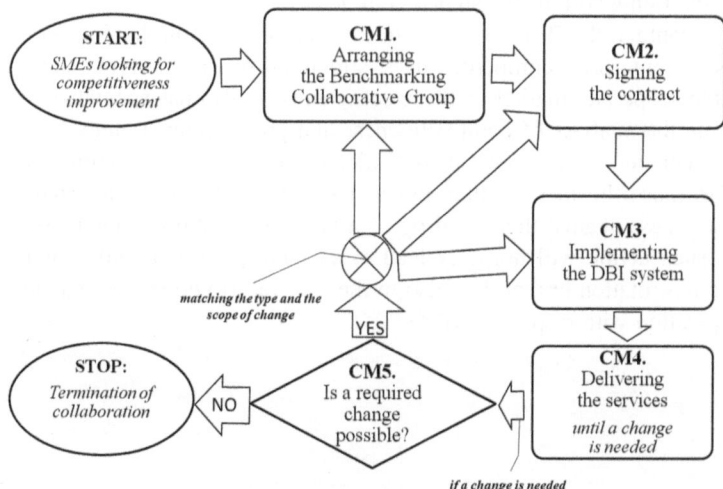

Fig. 5.2 Method of brokering strategic information (*source*: Own research)

recipient), so this chapter will only introduce elements relevant to the coordinator—
the service provider.

5.2.1 CM1: Arranging the Benchmarking Collaborative Group

The need for BSI support occurs when a group of SMEs look for ways to improve
their competitiveness is ready to join a Benchmarking Collaborative Network in
order to achieve it. The conditions for the formation of a BCG have been described
in detail in the framework of the BCM method in Chap. 4. Looking at them from the
perspective of the coordinator, one should include the profitability indicators of
such an organisationally and technologically complex venture in their characteristics. In other words, it is necessary to specify the (minimal) number of businesses
and the (minimal) period of cooperation required for the service provider to achieve
expected benefits. No research leading to the designation of the BSI profitability
indicators has been made within this work. However, a simulation that shows the
profitability of such a project from the perspective of a BCG was carried out
(as shown in Sect. 5.3).

Defining the provided service as strategic information brokering imposes possible solutions and a broader context of the BSI functioning. It indicates that the
coordinating body generates a valuable database of information and knowledge
through long-term cooperation with various types of enterprises in diverse and
changing markets, forming different groups of the BCG, and thanks to the aforementioned database can provide strategic information brokering services to businesses outside of given BCGs. Of course, subject to the rules agreed upon with the
BCG in the framework of the signed contract.

In this context, the BSI is seen as an external service unit, having access to the
expertise of enterprise competitiveness, structured due to the type, size, industry
sector, the scope and market of these companies. It also has specialized IT tools,
facilitating the analysis of competitiveness and prototyping strategy for competitiveness. This allows untapped possibilities of accessing information and knowledge for those businesses that never had the opportunity to analyse their
competitiveness against the backdrop of a competitive environment. As a consequence, such action will not only lead to an increase in material benefits of the
strategic information broker, but also to the transfer of knowledge gained through
the cooperation with respective BCGs.

5.2.2   CM2: Signing the Contract

The cooperation agreement within the BCG has been described in detail in the BCM method in Chap. 4. Looking at it from the service provider's perspective, one should emphasize the importance of the following elements:

- general rules for offering information brokerage services, including the description of the provider and the recipient of the service, the scope and form of the service and its duration;
- detailed description of the content and quality of the source data provided by the service recipient, together with information on the frequency of delivery;
- rules on the collection of source data in the DBI system and rules on access by other users of the cooperation group;
- a detailed description of available results of competitiveness analysis together with the designation of the form, manner and frequency of their collection and the eventual opportunities to create additional analysis—on explicit request of the service recipient;
- detailed rules concerning the security and confidentiality of sharing and processing data and the ethical use of obtained results;
- financial arrangements in relation to services covered by the contract, concerning the costs associated with the implementation of the schedule and charged fees;
- detailed rules for the conclusion of the contract (at a date specified in the contract), the eventual termination of the contract (at an earlier date than projected in the agreement) and the consequences of non-compliance with the memorandum of agreement with financial penalties and legal consequences.

The aim of the agreement is, on the one hand, to ensure the continuity and the usefulness of the results of the analyses provided and, on the other hand, to guarantee the safety and ethics of the results obtained and used by the recipients. Critical elements of cooperation, which should be determined with due diligence in the contract are:

- timeliness and quality of data (i.e. the completeness, truthfulness, accuracy) supplied by the recipients;
- safety, reliability and usefulness of the results of competitiveness analyses performed by service providers.

The service recipient must understand that without his data the analysis results will be either incomplete or impossible to obtain. The service provider must recognize however that meeting the expectations of the BCG members is the only way to ensure the viability of the undertaken cooperation.

5.2.3   CM3: Implementing the DBI System

The structure of the supporting DBI system is presented in Chap. 5. As part of the MBSI method, an implementation method will be presented. For SMEs, it will constitute an organisational and financial challenge that is beyond their individual capabilities. Literature mentions many success factors in implementing a BI class system, and the most important are (Moss and Atre 2003; Yeoh and Koronios 2010; Sangar and Iahad 2013):

- experience and knowledge of the designing and implementation team;
- intensive cooperation between designers and users in the whole of the design and implementation period;
- use of proper implementation methodology, which includes the process break down into smaller projects.

Therefore, the need to support the BCG in implementing a DBI system is obvious. An implementation company that has experience in the BI technology implementation will perform this task. However, the transfer of responsibility for implementation to the BSI, in addition relieves the BCG group members, who do not have the skills to coordinate such a complex undertaking. The method of implementation should consist of the steps shown in Fig. 5.3. For the BCG it involves a limitation associated with the ownership form of the system. The DBI system is offered as a service to the BCG. The DBI system is the property of the BSI, whereas BCG members can have access to it only in the time and scope regulated by the concluded contract.

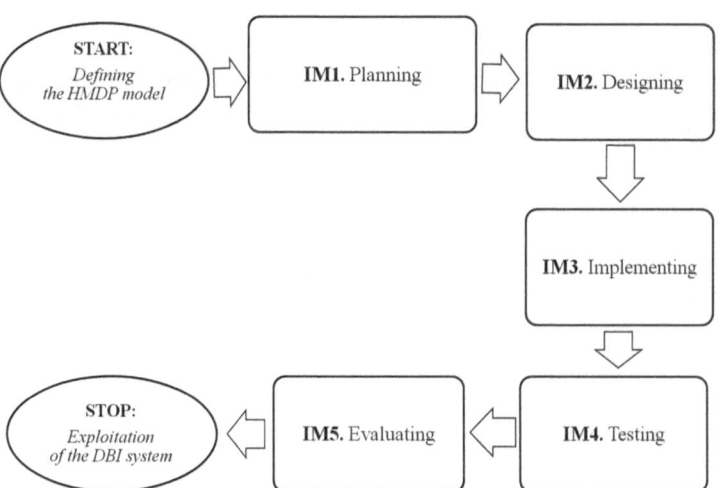

Fig. 5.3 Method of DBI implementation (*source*: Own research)

5.2.3.1   IM1: Planning

Planning the DBI system is an important step in the implementation process. It determines the scope of its adaptation to the ever changing BCG groups and their needs. It is assumed that the created tool will be used differently by different BCGs, as well as by other external BSI clients.

The minimal structure of the system must be conceived in such a way to handle various HMDP models, as well as the implementation of all analyses within the scope of the HRPM/FHRPM method. It should also allow the creation of such statements and reports that the user expects and can make use of. Thus, both technical capabilities and visual qualities of the implementation tool will be of importance. Additionally, one should reckon with a variable load on the system, dependent on the number and count of supported groups of BCG. In this context, both the technology and the DBI system architecture itself must be chosen accordingly.

Given the above, and given the expected profits from the provision of the service within the BCN, one should plan:

– system infrastructure:

  • technical infrastructure—hardware, software, network cables, peripherals, database systems, operational systems, network components, metadata repository, user applications etc.;
  • non-technical infrastructure—metadata standards, data mining standards, logical database model, methods, textbooks, testing procedures, change control procedures, change management procedures etc.;

– system structure—adapted to implement the HMDP model and HRPM/FHRPM method, but also to the organizational, personal, budget, technological, services sales and collaboration possibilities within the BSI.

5.2.3.2   IM2: Designing

The scope of the DBI system structure project includes the following parts:

– data model—consistent with the structure of the HMDP model;
– ETL process—the process of extracting, transforming and loading the data from the resources (BCG group members databases) to the DBI system data model.
– data processing—the projects of the analyses implemented under the HRPM/FHRPM method;
– user applications—all statements, reports and accounts received by the BCG members;
– system security measures—very important if the application is provided to the users via network.

As the knowledge and experience accumulates, the project can also be expanded with a knowledge base and mechanisms for the effective use of this knowledge in the form of inference and explanation modules. It is now, however, a transition from an analysis-and-reporting system to an expert system. It requires a substantial amount of work and an effectiveness that is difficult to ascertain at this stage of testing.

5.2.3.3   IM3: Implementing

While the preparation of the project is carried out with the significant participation of the BSI, an IT company with experience and skills in this area should carry out its implementation. However, it is important to take into account that the DBI system:

- will have different variants of the HMDP model for BCG groups of various characteristics implemented and, subsequently, updated.
- there must be an easy way of adding and modifying the required statistical summaries and analytical reports
- the available methods and analytical techniques should not be limited only to those that are required in the HRPM/FHRPM method, as the possibility of developing the method and its analytical tools is assumed.
- the propagation of analyses results will use various distribution channels and different forms of result reporting;
- there is a need to ensure the security and confidentiality of data and information transmitted within the network access.

Today, there are many possibilities and options for the implementation of BI technologies (cf. Sect. 2.4). One should choose such a formula that—while taking into account the above conditions and limitations—will be the most flexible and the most advantageous for both the BCG (the service recipient), as well as the BSI (the service provider).

5.2.3.4   IM4: Testing

Putting the tool into operation is conditioned by the positive results of verification and validation testing.

Verification tests check the correct operation of the individual elements of the structure, the process of supplying the system with data, as well as access security and user experience. They certify that the functional requirements are met, check the technical efficiency of the system and the security of its use.

Validation tests are based on an assessment of the system by its users. They reflect meeting user expectations, and in the case of the DBI system, primarily evaluate the intuitiveness of use and clarity of collected information.

5.2.3.5   IM5: Evaluating

The implementation assessment carried out at the end of the cycle is important for two reasons.

Firstly, it is important to summarize the experience gained, in order to use it during the development of the system for another HMDP model, created for a new group of BCG.

Secondly, because of the quality of cooperation within the BCN, the assessment of the tool by members of the BCG is very important. The negative attitude of a future user can significantly hinder or even prevent the functioning of the BCN. Hence, taking into account the comments and concerns of BCG members is also an important element in the development of a DBI system.

Putting the tools to operate only partially completes the process of its implementation. If such a solution is to be a profitable investment for the BSI, it should be a kind of skeletal solution that can be easily extended and adapted to a new HMDP model, defined for new groups of BCG. In time, there will be a need for analyses and reports beyond the scope of the HRPM/FHRPM method, which is a natural process of growth and awareness among members of the BCG.

5.2.4   CM4: Delivering the Services

The provision of information brokerage services performed by the BSI for the BCG is based on the contract of cooperation (Fig. 5.4). It involves cyclic sharing the results of competitiveness analyses provided under the HRPM/FHRPM method, implemented by the DBI system. Analyses are performed based on the source data supplied by the members of the BCG. The results of the analyses provided include strategic information on:

- determining the competitive position of a business in the group;
- conclusions on the variations of the competitiveness position in time;
- conclusions on the strengths and weaknesses of the company from the perspective of a potential opportunity to achieve a competitive advantage in the group;
- scenarios of strategic actions for the improvement of the competitive position occupied in the group.

The form of providing the above information must be tailored to the needs and skills of its use by the user, and can be done by: dedicated reports, authenticated access to the information site, direct expert consultation.

The scope of the information made available within the service is determined in the contract. However, over time the need for information and the conditions of service will change. The flexibility of the service provides for the possibility of its adaptation over the course of time specified in the contract by entering into individual annexes to the contract. The new range of services not covered by the

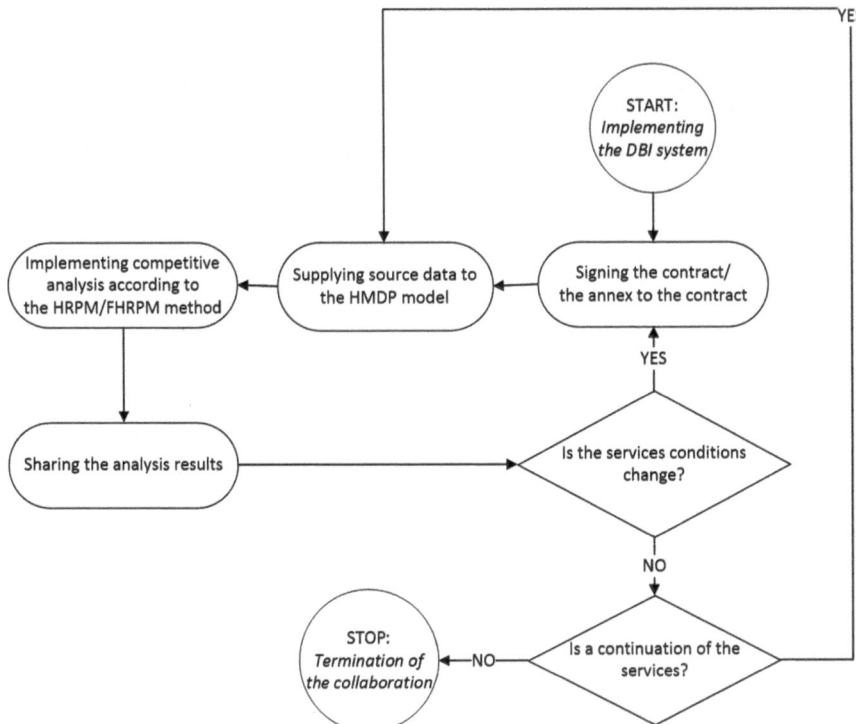

Fig. 5.4 Services delivering process (*source*: Own research)

basic agreement, shall be re-valued. In this way, the customer can shape the range of benefits and cost services without stepping out of the dedicated budget. In turn, along with the development of the solution and the sales process, the service provider acquires experience and skills that can be used when providing similar services to other groups of recipients

5.2.5   CM5: Is a Required Change Possible?

Any change in the conditions of service affects the usefulness of its results. It may then be necessary to make changes that will restore the expected efficiency and quality of service. The decline in the quality of the service, which is carried out properly and with due care, is affected by four basic elements:

– low quality of data for the HMDP model;
– too little diversity of the BCG group;
– insufficient features of the IT tool;
– gaps and deficiencies in the cooperation contract.

The poor quality of source data, caused by deficiencies, errors or falsification of data, is the most common cause of low reliability in the analytical results. The only effective remedy at this stage is to constantly raise the awareness of the responsibility of the recipient, which lies on them when entering a BCG group. Each competitive cooperation involves the mutual trust and responsibility of individual participants for the success of the entire group. Cooperation in BCN is based on the same principles. The inability to provide the required level of data quality supplying the HMDP model is equivalent to the lack of ability to provide strategic information brokering services.

The appropriate diversity of the BCG provides the possibility to benefit from the mutual learning process through the use of patterns developed and tested in group practice. If this diversity is non-existent because its members, adhering to the obtained guidelines and recommendations, became similar to each other in terms of competitiveness, it is an indication of the expansion of the group. Inviting new members will affect the diversity of the source data and increase the utility of provided analytical results. In contrast, the persistent lack of diversity in the level of competitiveness of individual members of the group will consequently lead to its dissolution and termination of cooperation within the framework of BCN.

The on-going cooperation should lead to increasing knowledge and awareness of the members of the BCG. With time, this means the need to expand the scope and form of services provided. Requirements of the recipient will grow both in relation to information obtained from the system and the format of their presentation. DBI system should be able to meet those expectations. However, this is not always possible under the concluded contract. The expansion and upgrade of the system may be associated with costs for the BSI and will require an annex to the agreement, or even to conclude a new contract. It is, however, worth investing in modern technology and maintaining the efficiency, accuracy and validity of information tool, which is the main communication platform between the recipient (members of the BCG) and the provider (BSI) and largely determines the continuity and sustainability of the BCN cooperation.

Changes made to the above elements will affect the timeliness and consistency of the contract of cooperation. Thus, most of them will require the conclusion of annexes, and perhaps the need to reconsider the payments for the services. Regardless of changes in the scope, form and organization of the services, the agreement itself may eventually prove to be insufficiently detailed or even not properly fulfilling its tasks, which is to ensure continuous, efficient and secure collaboration within the BCN. Then it is necessary to re-negotiate the terms and conditions of the contract concluded with all members of the BCG. It is not a comfortable situation for the BSI, as it undermines its credibility as a reliable and competent partner in the BCN. It is therefore important to use the best practices and carefully draft the first version of the contract. Such drafts can be found in benchmarking cooperation codes and civil-law contracts on the provision of results benchmarking services (cf. Sect. 2.2).

5.2.6   STOP: When Is the Time for Termination of Collaboration?

The proper functioning and utility of the DBI system is conditioned by the regularity and the quantity of source data supplied by the recipients. Therefore, the termination shall be in accordance with agreed arrangements, ensuring the continuity of service throughout the life of the cooperation group.

From the point of view of the recipient the opportunity to leave the group is a very important part of the contract. Especially when continued membership in the group does not result in the expected development of its competitiveness, because:

- the group was improperly selected and common the HMDP cannot be used;
- the group is not diversified enough in terms of the assessed level of competitiveness, so the effect of mutual learning is also negligible;
- the customer remains as the group leader for several consecutive periods of time, so he does not use the results of the cooperation, but is the teacher himself;
- the customer has acquired sufficient knowledge about the factors influencing the competitiveness and activities conditioning the increase of their competitiveness in the market and does not see the need to further deepen this knowledge.

The entrepreneur can use the benefits of cooperation within the BCG even after leaving it. Acquired knowledge brings measurable and tangible results in a competitive market, as an element of advantage over those companies that did not have access to such knowledge. It is important to improve the competitiveness of those companies that did not have neither the financial resources nor the technical and organizational capabilities to benefit from the results of the analysis of competitiveness in relation to the results of their own, and the more to the performance of their market competitors.

The BSI, service provider, with every business relationship and supported BCG group acquires knowledge and experience that can be used with other BCG groups and non-members of the BCN. This significantly improves the range of benefits that can be derived and allows maintaining such prices for the services that will be available for every interested SME.

5.3   Brokering Strategic Information: Case Study and Utilities Veryfication

5.3.1   CM1: Arranging the Benchmarking Collaborative Group

Verification of the usefulness and effectiveness of the MBSI was simulated on the base of the research programme described in Chap. 3. For its realization it was necessary to implement a DBI system supporting competitiveness analyses prepared in the HRPM/FHRPM method. The BSI (service provider) was the experiment performer.

5.3.2   CM2: Signing the Contract

As part of the experiment the contract of brokering strategic information was included. The key elements of the contract (described in Chap. 4) were patterned on the recommendations of the MBSI method, such as:

– deadline for terminating the experiment and the validity of the contract;
– range, quality and scheduled delivering of the source data;
– safety and confidentiality of collected source data and shared strategic information;
– range of information and schedule of result reports sharing;
– safety and confidentiality of accessing and sharing analyses results.

5.3.3   CM3: Implementing the DBI System

At this stage, the key is to answer the question of whether and how a service provider can benefit from the implementation of the MBSI method. Let's look at this from the perspective of profit that the recipient received in the reporting period (Table 5.1).

If we assume that about 50 % of the increase in sales and gross profit in 2010 was the result of the strategic use of information obtained and that this trend will be maintained over time, it is on this basis the optimal size of a BCG can be determined, for which the costs of the information brokerage services established by the service provider will be acceptable to the service recipient from the SME group.

In the description of the methods, the role and importance of the use of properly selected executive technology was highlighted. Based on the results shown in Table 5.1, ROI[1] values were calculated for a group of ten users of the DBI system in different variants of BI technologies (Table 5.2).

The data shown in Table 5.2 indicate that the clinic operating individually would be able to implement only the cheapest BI solutions (Microsoft, QlikTech, Pentaho). Whereas Table 5.2 takes into account only the financial capacity of the clinic, omitting the lack of knowledge, skills and qualified staff, who would be able to handle such a solution and use it effectively.

---

[1] ROI—return on investment factor, determined as the ratio of profit to invested capital.

Table 5.1 The observed effects of the use of strategic information brokerage services

Analysis period		No. of patients	Gross sales	Profit	No. of patient visits
2008–2009	Two-month average (thousands of PLN)	4,714.00	319.00	28.00	2,011.00
	For each patient visit (PLN)		158.64	13.73	
2010	Two-month average (thousands of PLN)	18,742.00	603.00	97.00	3,760.00
	For each patient visit (PLN)		160.28	25.68	
Difference: 2010– (2008/2009)	Two-month average (thousands of PLN)	14,028.00	284.00	69.00	1,749.00
	For each patient visit (PLN)		1.64	11.95	

Source: Own research

Table 5.2 ROI for implementing BI solutions

Software developer	BI tool[a]	ROI (1 year, single clinic) [%]	ROI (1 year, a group of ten clinics) [%]	ROI (3 years, single clinic) [%]	ROI (3 years, a group of ten clinics) [%]
Microsoft	SQL server 2008 R2 enterprise edition	35.64	1,256.38	306.91	3,969.13
QlikTech	QlikView	−14.49	755.11	68.58	1,585.78
Pentaho	Pentaho business intelligence gold edition	35.64	1,256.38	35.64	1,256.38
SAP	SAP BusinessObjects edge professional edition	−74.46	155.42	−43.54	464.62
MicroStrategy	MicroStrategy 9	−81.53	84.67	−59.31	306.91
IBM	Cognos 8 business intelligence	−82.75	72.52	−63.24	267.62
Oracle	Oracle business intelligence suite Enterprise Edition plus	−87.35	26.48	−72.10	178.97

Source: Own research
[a]Prices of individual tools have been based on (Burns 2009; Madsen 2010)

However, if we combine the financial potential of ten clinics, then each solution produced by any software developer presented in Table 5.2 becomes financially available. The presented example shows the extent to which the creation of a BCN can strengthen the financial potential of the SME sector. In contrast, the inclusion of a BSI removes other limitations (such as the lack of knowledge, skill or experience).

5.3.4 CM4: Delivering the Services

During an experimental strategic information brokerage servicing, the clinics obtained knowledge on:

- the competitive position occupied within the group;
- competitive factors critical to achieving competitive advantage;
- suggested strategic actions enabling the achievement of the assumed competitive position.

This knowledge could be used to achieve the goals set in the field of competitive strategy. For example, the W08 clinic was originally the leader of the group in terms of the achieved profit (Table 5.3). However, the problem with this clinic was the relatively low turnover coupled by high costs of sales of services, which was used by W10 clinic, who became the group leader in the subsequent periods. In response W08 clinic decided to use the results of the analyses developed within the information brokerage service. It has identified those factors of competitiveness that have the strongest impact on its competitiveness and which values of these factors will provide the expected level of growth. Afterwards, it implemented a competitiveness strategy matched to its capabilities and regained the leading position.

The data contained in Table 5.3 show that these clinics that actually used the obtained strategic information had a chance to increase their competitiveness. The presented W08 and W10 clinics significantly increased their profits through the use of tailored competitiveness strategies. This justifies the usefulness of the method in relation to the recipient and creates the possibility of reaping a profit for the service provider.

Table 5.3 History of the W08 and W10 clinic results

Clinic	Time period	Profit value (thousands of PLN)	Time period	Profit value (thousands of PLN)	Time period	Profit value (thousands of PLN)
W08	2008 I–VI	120.00	2008	75.00	2010 V–VI	250.00
W10		26.00	VII–XII	85.00		230.00

Source: Own research

5.3.5   CM5: Finalization of the Experiment

The experiment ended in July 2010 and received very high usefulness marks from its participants. On this basis, it should be noted that the strategic information brokerage service is useful and financially accessible to SMEs, provided the allocation of costs within the BCG group. Thus, the proposed MBSI method is a good alternative, as compared to currently used methods for improving the competitiveness of SMEs, limited by the organization, costs and scope of knowledge necessary for their application. The introduction of the BCN concept, taking into account the participation of the BCG group and a BSI coordinating body significantly reduces these limitations, equating the capabilities of SMEs with the capabilities of large enterprises.

References

Burns, M. (2009, December). BI/CPM survey 2009. Using technology to improve the way you do business. *CA Magazine*. Canada.

Madsen, M. (2010). *Lowering the cost of business intelligence with open source*. White Paper, Third Nature, Rogue River, USA.

Moss, L. T., & Atre, S. (2003). *Business intelligence roadmap: The complete project lifecycle for decision-support applications*. Boston: Addison Wesley.

Sangar, A. B., & Iahad, N. B. A. (2013). Critical factors that affect the success of Business Intelligence Systems (BIS) implementation in an organization. *International Journal of Scientific & Technology Research, 2*(2), 176–180.

Yeoh, W., & Koronios, A. (2010). Critical success factors for business intelligence systems. *Journal of computer information systems, 50*(3), 23–32.

Chapter 6
Benchmarking Collaborative Network: Summarizing

Limited potential of financial, organizational, personal and technology resources doesn't give SMEs sufficient opportunities to access information and knowledge necessary in the complete process. Observing the methods and tools used by large companies, posed the question—*under which conditions would it be possible to provide SMEs support at the same level, but at a lower cost and with greater methodological and organizational support?*

It is obvious that a small company acting alone will not be able to achieve the capabilities possible for its much larger competitors. Hence, small businesses are less focused on development, and much more on daily survival. To change the orientation, it would take creating the conditions for increasing competitiveness through the provision of an access to sources of resources, knowledge and skills.

At the moment, even while assuming the acquisition of funding and support from government organizations, it is difficult to imagine that individual representatives of SMEs resorting to the methods, tools and technologies used by large enterprises. However, what is unattainable by one becomes available, if such actions are taken by a group.

The proposed solution is the Benchmarking Collaborative Network, which results in the enhancement of individual potential thanks to cooperation between market competitors with different levels and opportunities for development. The functional structure of BCN is presented in Fig. 6.1. The BCN provides SMEs access to information about its level of competitiveness, the key areas for the creation of competitive advantage and the activities required to achieve this advantage.

The functional structure of BCN consists of three basic functional elements, which form the perspectives of (Fig. 6.1):

- service recipient—Benchmarking Collaborative Method—a new method of organization of SMEs collaboration leading to improvement with their competitiveness;

© Springer International Publishing Switzerland 2015
K. Rostek, *Benchmarking Collaborative Networks*, Contributions to Management
Science, DOI 10.1007/978-3-319-16736-7_6

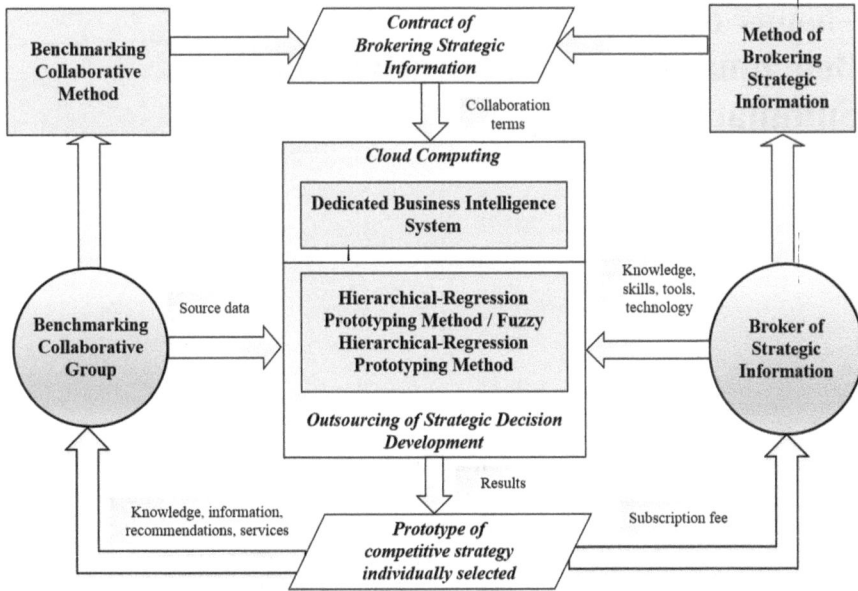

Fig. 6.1 Functional structure of Benchmarking Collaborative Network (*source*: own research)

- service provider—Method of Brokering Strategic Information—a new method of coordination of SMEs collaboration ensuring improvements to their competitiveness;
- analytical—Hierarchical-Regression Prototyping Method/Fuzzy Hierarchical-Regression Prototyping Method—a new method of competitive strategy prototyping in the situation of a lack of expert knowledge.

Due to the structure of the BCN, the participants of the BCG group gain access to knowledge on the competitive position they occupy, factors determining the market competitiveness and the possible ways to improve upon this. The scope and value of the acquired information is determined by the size and diversity of the BCG, but it will always be significantly higher than the potential of information data collected by a single member of the group.

The BSI group coordinator, beyond direct financial benefits from subscription fees, creates its own knowledge base that allows it to expand the range of services provided. In this way, the BCN brings to its participants financial and intangible benefits in the form of knowledge and experience. These benefits are felt even after the end of collaboration and leaving the BCG group.

Although the proposed approach is dedicated to SMEs, it can be applied to companies of any size, as long as it is possible to include them in the BCG group to develop a common model of the HMDP. In turn, the formation of subsequent and different BCG groups will have a significant impact on the competitive environment. On the one hand the experience and skills acquired by collaborating companies has a strong influence on the actions taken by their competitors. On the other hand the need for changes in group structure, guaranteeing the ability to develop effective and useful patterns of strategic actions, opens the BCN to the participation of new members. As a result of the positive effects of acquired knowledge, experiences and skills in a natural way propagate into the environment and help to improve the competitiveness of the whole market in the long term.

The phenomenon of knowledge transfer to the environment is currently being intensively studied in business (Maurer et al. 2011), scientific (Braun and Hadwiger 2011) and social (Gooderham et al. 2011) contexts. Studies suggest a significant impact on the improvement of both the organization and its environment. Knowledge transfer is often seen as the primary cause and the purpose of the formation of cooperation networks, in which the units are set to improve their competitiveness (Capó-Vicedo et al. 2011; Zonooz et al. 2011). The concept of the BCN also fits into this context.

The BCN, as a concept, is still open. There are still areas that require further research and refinement. One such unclosed research area is the analysis of perspective determined by the greatness of SMEs collaboration group. Thus the number and diversity of collaborating companies, determines the usefulness of information obtained from the brokering services. This implies a need for further research in order to determine the requirements for such structure within a collaborative group that will allow its members to obtain the assumed benefits.

Another issue is to consider that further research, necessary in the commercialization process of the solution, is the answer for the question of cost-effectiveness criteria in the proposed approach from the point of view of SMEs (as the member of the BCG and the services recipient) and the BSI (the unit of coordinating collaboration, the services provider). From the SMEs point of view, this is very important to determine which companies and under which conditions of collaboration have a chance to significantly improve its competitiveness. When a participant should withdraw from the group and no longer count on this interaction, the achieved benefits will outweigh services costs. From the BSI point of view, it is important is to determine how large a group of collaborating companies should be in order to ensure that the brokering services will be effectively provided and will be financially profitable for the coordinating unit.

Seeing the BSI in a broader context than just a body coordinating BCN activities, the possibility of using developed tools, analytical methods and report templates for greater audience, not necessarily associated in the BCN should be considered. There is also an untested direction within the context of this study; that involving social knowledge (Su 2011; Yu et al. 2013) and crowd knowledge [e.g. in the formula of crowdsourcing (Garrigos-Simon et al. 2014; Maskell 2014)], as a representative source of knowledge and solutions provided to BCN. This would be particularly important with regard to such problems, which cannot be solved using proven algorithms or if the quality of results obtained in such a way is lower than expected.

In summary, BCN is a new approach to improve the competitiveness of SMEs, using the methods and tools known and used previously in large enterprises. It is also an innovative approach (organizational innovation) to develop the strategic decisions. The BCN thus creates a plane that equalises all types of businesses in strategic opportunities to prepare them to compete in the market. In addition, the existence of the BCN has an impact on the competitive environment. It is located in the stream of service customization. Using the capabilities of outsourcing of the development of strategic decisions makes to compete more sustainable and effective.

The use of a functioning the BCN with a diversified member structure in different markets and in the long run, will result in the transfer of awareness, knowledge and skills within market competitiveness. From this it follows that this form of competitive cooperation can bring benefits not only locally but also globally. This is a prerequisite for further research in the field of networking, connecting different environments and different communities, with the potential and knowledge to contribute to the development of the organization.

References

Braun, S., & Hadwiger, K. (2011). Knowledge transfer from research to industry (SMEs)–An example from the food sector. *Trends in Food Science & Technology, 22,* S90–S96.

Capó-Vicedo, J., Mula, J., & Capó, J. (2011). A social network-based organizational model for improving knowledge management in supply chains. *Supply Chain Management: An International Journal, 16*(5), 379–388.

Garrigos-Simon, F. J., Narangajavana, Y., & Galdón-Salvador, J. L. (2014). Crowdsourcing as a competitive advantage for new business models. In I. G. Pechuán, D. Palacios-Marqués, M. Peris-Ortiz, E. Vendrell, & C. Ferri-Ramirez (Eds.), *Strategies in E-Business* (Positioning and social networking in online markets, pp. 29–37). New York: Springer.

Gooderham, P., Minbaeva, D. B., & Pedersen, T. (2011). Governance mechanisms for the promotion of social capital for knowledge transfer in multinational corporations. *Journal of Management Studies, 48*(1), 123–150.

Maskell, P. (2014). The creation of knowledge: Local building, global accessing and economic development—toward an agenda. *Journal of Economic Geography, 14*(5), 869–882.

Maurer, I., Bartsch, V., & Ebers, M. (2011). The value of intra-organizational social capital: How it fosters knowledge transfer, innovation performance, and growth. *Organization Studies, 32* (2), 157–185.

Su, C. (2011). Can social networking improve individual competitiveness? Exploring the effects of social network centralities on knowledge acquisition and work efficiency in organizational work teams. *Competition Forum, 9*(2), 247–259.

Yu, Y., Hao, J. X., Dong, X. Y., & Khalifa, M. (2013). A multilevel model for effects of social capital and knowledge sharing in knowledge-intensive work teams. *International Journal of Information Management, 33*(5), 780–790.

Zonooz, B. H., Farzam, V., Satarifar, M., & Bakhshi, L. (2011). The relationship between knowledge transfer and competitiveness in "SMES" with emphasis on absorptive capacity and combinative capabilities. *International Business and Management, 2*(1), 59–85.

Annex 1. Results of the Survey

Part 1. The Respondent: Characteristics

Question category	Question subcategory	Answer quantity
The respondents number	*Total*	*150*
The clinic localisation	Gdańsk	11
	Gdynia	5
	Katowice	11
	Kraków	9
	Lublin	13
	Łódź	9
	Poznań	21
	Sopot	1
	Warszawa	50
	Wrocław	20
The annual income	Up to 100 thousand. PLN	40
	100–250 thousand. PLN	39
	250–500 thousand. PLN	19
	500 thousand. to 4 million PLN	19
	4–210 million PLN	8
	No answer	25
The services type	Stomatological only	65
	Stomatological and other medical	35
The employees general number	2–5	66
	6–15	40
	Above 15	44
The stomatological employees number	2–3	83
	4–9	44
	Above 9	23

(continued)

© Springer International Publishing Switzerland 2015
K. Rostek, *Benchmarking Collaborative Networks*, Contributions to Management
Science, DOI 10.1007/978-3-319-16736-7

Question category	Question subcategory	Answer quantity
IT employees number	0	114
	1	27
	2–4	7
	Above 4	2
The computers number	1	63
	2	28
	Above 2	59

Part 2. The Decision Process: Characteristics and Decision-makers' Expectations

Question category	Answer quantity				
How often the management decisions are based on:	*1–25 %*	*26–50 %*	*51–75 %*	*76–100 %*	*0 %*[a]
Experience and knowledge of decision-maker	9	27	22	80	12
Consultations with other employees	63	47	11	16	13
Analytical reports delivered to the decision-maker	80	26	10	18	16
Results obtained from decision support systems	113	'0	4	10	13
Other, not mentioned above	17	12	1	6	114

[a]It means that this method is not used

Question category	Answer quantity				
How often the management decisions are made:	*1–25 %*	*26–50 %*	*51–75 %*	*76–100 %*	*0 %*[a]
"By feel" and with a deficit or complete lack of the necessary information?	84	29	6	10	21
To what extent the management decisions made "by feel" are the cause of:	*1–25 %*	*26–50 %*	*51–75 %*	*76–100 %*	*0 %*[b]
Management failures and financial losses	111	4	2	3	30
Unused or loss market opportunities	88	9	3	1	49

[a]It means that this problem does not exist
[b]They are not at all

Question category	Answer quantity						
To what extent would help to reduce the number of wrong decisions:	Not at all 0	1	2	3	4	Very significantly 5	Don't know
Organisational changes	32	21	26	35	8	7	21
Financial controlling	40	22	16	32	14	14	12
Employees selection	52	9	19	21	16	20	13
Internal sharing of knowledge and experience[a]	34	12	19	25	25	23	12
External sharing of knowledge and experience[b]	26	8	21	41	26	18	10
IT development	63	–	–	–	–	47	40
Analytical reports[c]	35	21	26	33	18	12	5
Use of decision support system	39	12	18	34	17	14	16
Other, not mentioned above	137	–	–	–	–	13	–

[a]It means sharing of knowledge and experience within the organization
[b]It means sharing of knowledge and experience with other organizations
[c]The analytical reports—more accurate and more frequently generated

Question category	Answer quantity		
Would the benchmarking data are able to help in improving the quality of decisions?	*Yes*	*No*	*Don't know*
	49	53	48

Question category	Answer quantity						
What kind of the benchmarking data are important:	*Not at all 0*	*1*	*2*	*3*	*4*	*Very significantly 5*	*Don't know*
Characteristics of patient population	31	10	16	29	33	20	11
Characteristics of patient population demographics	43	16	13	37	14	17	10
Characteristics of the services	19	14	12	39	30	27	9
Characteristics of supply and inventory	49	16	19	25	20	14	7
Employment characteristics	51	19	19	33	8	11	9
Financial results	31	12	19	31	27	20	10
Other, not mentioned above	139	–	–	–	–	11	–

Part 3. The IT Software: Characteristics and Users' Expectations

Question category	Answer quantity			
Is there used in the organisation:	*Yes, ourselves*	*Yes, but in outsourcing*	*No, not at all*	*Don't know*
Database system	67	4	66	13
Sales service system	29	3	106	12
Financial and accounting system	44	41	52	13
HR (Human Resources)	32	26	77	15
CRM (Client Resources Management)	19	4	112	15
ERP (Enterprise Resources Management)	9	8	118	15
Analysis and reporting system	42	6	89	13
DSS (decision support system)	14	–	129	7
Other, not mentioned above	36	–	114	–

Question category	Answer quantity		
Is the implementation of a specialized IT system (e.g. DSS) would help influence the effectiveness of decision-making?	*Yes*	*No*	*Don't know*
	47	63	40

Question category	Answer quantity				
What costs would be acceptable in scope of:	*None*	*Up to 5 thousand. PLN*	*5–10 thousand. PLN*	*Above 10 thousand. PLN*	*Don't know*
Implementation of IT system	70	35	6	3	36
Annual maintenance of IT system	67	37	6	3	37

Question category	Answer quantity		
The method of reducing IT costs is to implement a common system not individually, but for a group of organisations. Is it an attractive offer?	*Yes*	*No*	*don't know*
	32	66	36

Question category	Answer quantity					
Comparing the two types of IT systems: 1) individual (supports only one entity), and 2) group (supports many entities)—which one would be better?	*Definetly type 1*	*Rather type 1*	*Equally good*	*Rather type 2*	*Definetly type 2*	*Don't know*
	37	25	10	35	21	22

Question category	Answer quantity						
How important in the decision support system is the following feature:	*Not at all 0*	*1*	*2*	*3*	*4*	*Very significantly 5*	*Don't know*
Simplicity and convenience of use	11	2	9	20	36	68	4
Efficiency and flexibility of data access	9	4	12	28	32	62	3
Automation of analysis and management reporting	16	10	20	29	24	45	6
Possibility of self analysis and reporting (ie. ad-hoc analysis)	20	8	15	33	35	36	3
Possibility of forecasting and simulation	10	9	14	30	33	47	7
Improving communication and information flows in group decision making	25	12	15	27	26	41	4
Improving communication and information flows in collaboration with contractors and cooperators	12	7	19	38	32	38	4
Other, not mentioned above	77	–	–	–	–	5	68

Annex 2. Results of the Analysis

Part 1. The HRPM Analysis

Section A. Regression Analysis

The selected model based on the errors degree of validation data, consists of the following regression coefficients:

Intercept	C_{12}	C_{13}	C_{15}	C_{16}	C_{17}	C_{21}	C_{22}	C_{23}	C_{24}	C_7	C_8

Analysis of variance

Source	Degrees of freedom	Sum squares	Average squares	F statistic	$p > F$
Model	11	599,052	54,459	37.63	<0.0001
Error	37	53,543	1,447		
Corrected total	48	652,595			

Model fit statistics:

Statistic	Value
R-Square	0.9180
Adj R-Sq	0.8936
AIC	366.8246
BIC	378.7372
SBC	389.5264
C(p)	9.3062

© Springer International Publishing Switzerland 2015

K. Rostek, *Benchmarking Collaborative Networks*, Contributions to Management Science, DOI 10.1007/978-3-319-16736-7

Analysis of maximum likelihood estimates:

Parameter	Degrees of freedom	Standard estimate	Error	t statistic	p > |t|
Intercept	1	−51.3335	103.9000	−0.49	0.6243
C_{12}	1	0.1115	0.0302	3.69	0.0007
C_{13}	1	0.1917	0.1482	1.29	0.2038
C_{15}	1	5.5109	1.6876	3.27	0.0024
C_{16}	1	−2.5075	1.0630	−2.36	0.0237
C_{17}	1	89.2236	54.8475	1.63	0.1123
C_{21}	1	76.3225	15.3430	4.97	<0.0001
C_{22}	1	−1.0021	0.2171	−4.62	<0.0001
C_{23}	1	9.2250	0.6019	15.33	<0.0001
C_{24}	1	−42.2789	26.5556	−1.59	0.1199
C_7	1	−10.8349	1.6071	−6.74	<0.0001
C_8	1	22.5100	6.2448	3.60	0.0009

Section B. Decision Tree Analysis

Model fit statistics

Statistic	Training data	Validation data
Sum of frequencies	49.00	21.00
Sum of case weights times freq	49.00	21.00
Maximum absolute error	462.86	87.14
Sum of squared errors	27,2147.69	23,921.21
Average squared error	5,554.03	1,139.11
Root average squared error	74.53	33.75
Divisor for ASE	49.00	21.00
Total degrees of freedom	49.00	21.00

The significance of the variable for the model

Variable	Importance
C_{23}	1.00000
C_7	0.24911
C_{13}	0.14223
C_{12}	0.08985
C_{17}	0.02592

The rules set

ID	Conditional part IF	Conclusion part THEN
1	$C_{23} >= 17.4154$	Predicted: Aim $= 287.1429$
2	$C_7 < 25$ and $C_{23} < 9.58333$ or MISSING	Predicted: Aim $= 93$
3	$C_{23} < 17.4154$ and $C_{23} >= 9.58333$ and $C_{13} < 83.6538$ or MISSING	Predicted: Aim $= 51.7188$
4	$C_{23} < 17.4154$ and $C_{23} >= 9.58333$ and $C_{13} >= 83.6538$	Predicted: Aim $= 99.6000$
5	$C_7 >= 25$ or MISSING and $C_{23} < 9.58333$ or MISSING and $C_{12} < 733.333$ and $C_{12} >= 332.5$	Predicted: Aim $= 44.1667$
6	$C_7 >= 25$ or MISSING and $C_{23} < 9.58333$ or MISSING and $C_{12} >= 733.333$	Predicted: Aim $= 19.8333$
7	$C_7 >= 25$ or MISSING and $C_{23} < 9.58333$ or MISSING and $C_{17} < 0.14741$ or MISSING and $C_{12} < 332.5$ or MISSING	Predicted: Aim $= 14.3333$
8	$C_7 >= 25$ or MISSING and $C_{23} < 9.58333$ or MISSING and $C_{17} >= 0.14741$ and $C_{12} < 332.5$ or MISSING	Predicted: Aim $= 23.6000$

Section C. Hybrid AHP Analysis

Input data

Clinic	Time start	Competitiveness criteria				Profit [thousand PLN]
		C_7	C_{12}	C_{13}	C_{23}	
W03	2009 VII	30.000000	800.000000	26.666667	5.000000	15
W06	2009 VII	20.000000	538.461538	38.461538	0.861538	56
W09	2009 VII	30.000000	1700.230769	131.153846	3.307692	43

The case of clinic W03

The preference of criteria differentiating the strategy variants					
Regression coefficients		0.0923	0.1115	0.1917	9.2250	
Criterion value achieved by the clinic		C_7	C_{12}	C_{13}	C_{23}	Criterion preference
30.0000	C_7	325.0470	269.0583	156.4945	3.2520	0.0348162
800.0000	C_{12}	8667.9200	7174.888	4173.1873	86.7209	0.9284333
26.6667	C_{13}	288.9307	239.1629	139.1062	2.8907	0.0309478
5.0000	C_{23}	54.1745	44.8431	26.0824	0.5420	0.0058027

The preference of strategy variants in relative to defined criterion C_7				
	Profit value	15.00	25.57	
Profit value	Strategy variant	S_{52}	S_{44}	Strategy/criterion preference
15.00	S_{52}	1.000000	0.586625	0.369731329
25.57	S_{44}	1.704667	1.000000	0.630268671

The preference of strategy variants in relative to defined criterion C_{13}				
	Profit value	51.72	15.00	
Profit value	Strategy variant	S_{52}	S_{44}	Strategy/criterion preference
51.72	S_{52}	1.000000	3.448000	0.775179856
15.00	S_{44}	0.290023	1.000000	0.224820144

The preference of strategy variants in relative to defined criterion C_{23}				
	Profit value	39.52	39.52	
Profit value	Strategy variant	S_{52}	S_{44}	Strategy/criterion preference
39.52	S_{52}	1.000000	1.000000	0.500000
39.52	S_{44}	1.000000	1.000000	0.500000

The preference of strategy variants in the individual selection					
Criterion preference:	0.034816	0.928433	0.030947776	0.005802708	Strategy preference
Strategy variant:	C_7	C_{12}	C_{13}	C_{23}	
S_{52}	0.369731	0.447761	0.775179856	0.500000	0.455480
S_{44}	0.630269	0.552239	0.224820144	0.500000	0.544519

The case of clinic W06

The preference of criteria differentiating the strategy variants

Regression coefficients		0.092294	0.1917	9.225	
Criterion value achieved by the clinic		C_7	C_{13}	C_{23}	Criterion preference
20.000000	C_7	216.6980	104.329700	2.168022	0.33713693
38.461538	C_{13}	416.7269	200.634000	4.169272	0.64834025
0.861538	C_{23}	9.3347	4.494202	0.093392	0.01452282

The preference of strategy variants in relative to defined criterion C_7

	Profit value	56	93	
Profit value	Strategy variant	S_{99}	S_{93}	Strategy/criterion preference
56	S_{99}	1.000000	0.602151	0.375838926
93	S_{93}	1.660714	1.000000	0.624161074

The preference of strategy variants in relative to defined criterion C_{13}

	Profit value	51.72	56.00	
Profit value:	Strategy variant	S_{99}	S_{93}	Strategy/criterion Preference
51.72	S_{99}	1.000000	0.923571	0.48013368
56.00	S_{93}	1.082753	1.000000	0.51986632

The preference of strategy variants in relative to defined criterion C_{23}

	Profit value:	39.52	39.52	
Profit value	Strategy variant:	S_{99}	S_{93}	Strategy/criterion preference
39.52	S_{99}	1.000000	1.000000	0.500000
39.52	S_{93}	1.000000	1.000000	0.500000

The preference of strategy variants in the individual selection

Criterion preference	0.337137	0.64834	0.014522822	
Strategy variant	C_7	C_{13}	C_{23}	Strategy priority
S_{99}	0.375839	0.480134	0.500000	0.445261
S_{93}	0.624161	0.519866	0.500000	0.554739

The case of clinic W09

The preference of criteria differentiating the strategy variants

Regression coefficients		0.092294	0.1917	9.225	
Criterion value achieved by the clinic		C_7	C_{13}	C_{23}	Criterion preference
30.000000	C_7	325.0470	156.4950	3.2520	0.182413471
131.153846	C_{13}	1421.0390	684.1620	14.2170	0.797474275
3.307692	C_{23}	35.8390	17.2550	0.3590	0.020112254

The preference of strategy variants in relative to defined criterion C_7

Profit value	Profit value:	43.00	25.57	
	Strategy variant:	S_{99}	S_{93}	Strategy/criterion preference
43.000000	S_{99}	1.000000	1.681658	0.627096398
25.570000	S_{93}	0.594651	1.000000	0.372903602

The preference of strategy variants in relative to defined criterion C_{13}

Profit value:	Profit value:	99.60	43.00	
	Strategy variant:	S_{99}	S_{93}	Strategy/criterion preference
99.60	S_{99}	1.000000	2.316279	0.698457223
43.00	S_{93}	0.431727	1.000000	0.301542777

The preference of strategy variants in relative to defined criterion C_{23}

Profit value:	Profit value:	39.52	39.52	
	Strategy variant:	S_{99}	S_{93}	Strategy/criterion preference
39.52	S_{99}	1.000000	1.000000	0.500000
39.52	S_{93}	1.000000	1.000000	0.500000

The preference of strategy variants in the individual selection

Criterion preference	0.182413	0.797474275	0.020112254	
Strategy variant	C_7	C_{13}	C_{23}	Strategy priority
S_{99}	0.627096	0.698457	0.500000	0.681448
S_{93}	0.372904	0.301543	0.500000	0.318551

Output data

Clinic	Time end	Competitiveness criteria				Profit
		C_7	C_{12}	C_{13}	C_{23}	[thousand PLN]
W03	2010 VI	30.000000	257.500000	15.000000	2.500000	10
W06	2010 VI	20.000000	237.704918	16.065574	2.459016	150
W09	2010 VI	30.000000	923.076923	92.307692	10.000000	130

Part 2. The FHRPM Analysis

Section A. Regression Analysis

The selected model based on the errors degree of validation data, consists of the following regression coefficients:

C_{12}	C_{15}	C_{16}	C_{17}	C_{18}	C_{21}	C_{22}	C_{23}	C_{24}	C_7	C_9

Analysis of variance

Source	Degrees of freedom	Sum squares	Average squares	F statistic	p > F
Model	11	1254218	114020.000	93.100	<0.0001
Error	59	72256	1224.685		
Corrected total	70	1326474			

Model fit statistics

Statistic	Value
R-Square	0.9455
Adj R-Sq	0.9354
AIC	507.7637
BIC	515.9440
SBC	532.4971
C(p)	6.3272

Analysis of maximum likelihood estimates

Parameter	Degrees of freedom	Standard estimate	Error	t statistic	p > |t|
C_{12}	1	0.0811	0.0184	4.41	<0.0001
C_{15}	1	3.9670	0.6169	6.43	<0.0001
C_{16}	1	−3.2047	0.9245	−3.47	0.0010
C_{17}	1	154.5	39.9392	3.87	0.0003
C_{18}	1	71.3622	32.4548	2.20	0.0318
C_{21}	1	37.2122	11.1573	3.34	0.0015
C_{22}	1	−0.3819	0.1308	−2.92	0.0050
C_{23}	1	9.0261	0.4535	19.90	<0.0001
C_{24}	1	−59.2092	28.2119	−2.10	0.0401
C_7	1	−9.1394	1.1074	−8.25	<0.0001
C_9	1	13.2035	2.6268	5.03	<0.0001

Section B. Fuzzy Decision Tree Analysis

Model fit statistics

Statistic	Training data
Sum of frequencies	70.000
Sum of case weights times freq	280.000
Misclassification Rate	0.114
Maximum absolute error	0.800
Sum of squared errors	9.533
Average squared error	0.034

(continued)

Model fit statistics	
Statistic	Training data
Root average squared error	0.185
Divisor for ASE	280.000
Total degrees of freedom	210.000

The significance of the variable for the model:	
Variable	Importance
C_{23}	1.00000
C_{21}	0.86221
C_{17}	0.69172
C_9	0.58379
C_{22}	0.45481
C_{12}	0.21956

The rules set:

ID	Conditional part IF	Conclusion part THEN
1	$C_9 < 1.18206$ and $C_{23} < 2.47951$	Predicted: Aim =quartile $4 = 0.00$ Predicted: Aim =quartile $3 = 0.00$ Predicted: Aim =quartile $2 = 0.50$ Predicted: Aim =quartile $1 = 0.50$
2	$C_9 < 2.81$ and $C_9 > = 1.18206$ or MISSING and $C_{23} < 2.47951$	Predicted: Aim =quartile $4 = 0.00$ Predicted: Aim =quartile $3 = 0.40$ Predicted: Aim =quartile $2 = 0.60$ Predicted: Aim =quartile $1 = 0.00$
3	$C_9 > = 2.81$ and $C_{23} < 2.47951$	Predicted: Aim =quartile $4 = 1.00$ Predicted: Aim =quartile $3 = 0.00$ Predicted: Aim =quartile $2 = 0.00$ Predicted: Aim =quartile $1 = 0.00$
4	$C_{23} < 8.91667$ and $C_{23} > = 2.47951$ and $C_{17} < 0.08981$	Predicted: Aim =quartile $4 = 0.00$ Predicted: Aim =quartile $3 = 0.00$ Predicted: Aim =quartile $2 = 1.00$ Predicted: Aim =quartile $1 = 0.00$
5	$C_{23} > = 8.91667$ or MISSING and $C_{21} < 0.45$ and $C_{21} > = 0.205$	Predicted: Aim =quartile $4 = 0.00$ Predicted: Aim =quartile $3 = 1.00$ Predicted: Aim =quartile $2 = 0.00$ Predicted: Aim =quartile $1 = 0.00$
6	$C_{23} > = 8.91667$ or MISSING and $C_{21} > = 0.45$	Predicted: Aim =quartile $4 = 1.00$ Predicted: Aim =quartile $3 = 0.00$ Predicted: Aim =quartile $2 = 0.00$ Predicted: Aim =quartile $1 = 0.00$
7	$C_{23} < 8.91667$ and $C_{23} > = 2.47951$ and $C_{17} < 0.15741$ and $C_{17} > = 0.08981$ and $C_{12} < 560$	Predicted: Aim =quartile $4 = 0.00$ Predicted: Aim =quartile $3 = 0.00$ Predicted: Aim =quartile $2 = 0.00$ Predicted: Aim =quartile $1 = 1.00$

(continued)

The rules set:

ID	Conditional part IF	Conclusion part THEN
8	$C_{23} < 8.91667$ and $C_{23} >= 2.47951$ and $C_{17} < 0.15741$ and $C_{17} >= 0.08981$ and $C_{12} >= 560$ or MISSING	Predicted: Aim =quartile $4 = 0.00$ Predicted: Aim =quartile $3 = 0.00$ Predicted: Aim =quartile $2 = 0.25$ Predicted: Aim =quartile $1 = 0.75$
9	$C_{23} < 8.91667$ and $C_{23} >= 2.47951$ and $C_{22} < 14.875$ and $C_{17} >= 0.15741$ or MISSING	Predicted: Aim =quartile $4 = 0.00$ Predicted: Aim =quartile $3 = 0.75$ Predicted: Aim =quartile $2 = 0.25$ Predicted: Aim =quartile $1 = 0.00$
10	$C_{23} < 8.91667$ and $C_{23} >= 2.47951$ and $C_{22} >= 14.875$ or MISSING and $C_{17} >= 0.15741$ or MISSING	Predicted: Aim =quartile $4 = 0.00$ Predicted: Aim =quartile $3 = 0.00$ Predicted: Aim =quartile $2 = 1.00$ Predicted: Aim =quartile $1 = 0.00$
11	$C_{23} >= 8.91667$ or MISSING and $C_{21} < 0.205$ or MISSING and $C_{12} < 335$ or MISSING	Predicted: Aim =quartile $4 = 1.00$ Predicted: Aim =quartile $3 = 0.00$ Predicted: Aim =quartile $2 = 0.00$ Predicted: Aim =quartile $1 = 0.00$
12	$C_{23} >= 8.91667$ or MISSING and $C_{21} < 0.205$ or MISSING and $C_{12} >= 335$	Predicted: Aim =quartile $4 = 0.67$ Predicted: Aim =quartile $3 = 0.33$ Predicted: Aim =quartile $2 = 0.00$ Predicted: Aim =quartile $1 = 0.00$

Section D. Hybrid AHP Analysis

Input data

Clinic	Time start	Competitiveness criteria					Profit [thousand PLN]
		C_9	C_{12}	C_{17}	C_{21}	C_{23}	
W03	2009 VII	0.208333	800.000000	0.100000	0.812500	5.000000	15
W06	2009 VII	1.364114	538.461538	0.000000	0.436000	0.861538	56
W09	2009 VII	0.904855	1700.230769	0.468493	0.371848	3.307692	43

The case of clinic W03

The preference of criteria differentiating the strategy variants						
Regression coefficients		13.2040	0.0811	154.5000	9.0260	
Criterion value achieved by the clinic		C_9	C_{12}	C_{17}	C_{23}	Criterion preference
0.208	C_9	0.016	2.569	0.001	0.023	0.00026
800.000	C_{12}	60.588	9864.365	5.178	88.633	0.99341
0.100	C_{17}	0.008	1.233	0.001	0.011	0.00012
5.000	C_{23}	0.379	61.652	0.032	0.554	0.00621

The preference of strategy variants in relative to defined criterion C_9					
	Profit value	1.000	1.000	1.500	
Profit value	Strategy Variant:	S_1	S_2	S_{12}	Strategy/criterion preference
1.000	S_1	1.000	1.000	0.667	0.286
1.000	S_2	1.000	1.000	0.667	0.286
1.500	S_{12}	1.500	1.500	1.000	0.429

The preference of strategy variants in relative to defined criterion C_{12}					
	Profit value:	1.000	1.000	1.000	
Profit value	Strategy variant	S_1	S_2	S_{12}	Strategy/criterion preference
1.000	S_1	1.000	1.000	1.000	0.333
1.000	S_2	1.000	1.000	1.000	0.333
1.000	S_{12}	1.000	1.000	1.000	0.333

The preference of strategy variants in relative to defined criterion C_{17}					
	Profit value	1.143	2.000	1.000	
Profit value	Strategy variant	S_1	S_2	S_{12}	Strategy/criterion preference
1.143	S_1	1.000	0.572	1.143	0.276
2.000	S_2	1.750	1.000	2.000	0.483
1.000	S_{12}	0.875	0.500	1.000	0.241

The preference of strategy variants in relative to defined criterion C_{23}					
	Profit value	1.884	1.884	2.571	
Profit value	Strategy variant	S_1	S_2	S_{12}	Strategy/criterion preference
1.884	S_1	1.000	1.000	0.733	0.297
1.884	S_2	1.000	1.000	0.733	0.297
2.571	S_{12}	1.365	1.365	1.000	0.406

The preference of strategy variants in the individual selection

Criterion preference	0.00026	0.99341	0.00012	0.00621	
Strategy variant	C_9	C_{12}	C_{17}	C_{23}	Strategy preference
S_1	0.286	0.333	0.276	0.297	0.33309
S_2	0.286	0.333	0.483	0.297	0.33312
S_{12}	0.429	0.333	0.241	0.406	0.33380

The case of clinic W06

The preference of criteria differentiating the strategy variants

Regression coefficients		13.2040	0.0811	37.2122	9.0260	
Criterion value achieved by the clinic		C_9	C_{12}	C_{21}	C_{23}	Criterion preference
1.364114	C_9	0.103	16.820	0.037	0.151	0.00252
538.461538	C_{12}	40.780	6639.476	14.470	59.657	0.99490
0.363333	C_{21}	0.028	4.480	0.010	0.040	0.00067
1.030769	C_{23}	0.078	12.710	0.028	0.114	0.00190

The preference of strategy variants in relative to defined criterion C_9

Profit value		4.000	2.500	2.500	2.500	Strategy/criterion
Profit value	Strategy variant	S_{4a}	S_{4b}	S_{43}	S_3	preference
4.000	S_{4a}	1.000	1.600	1.600	1.600	0.348
2.500	S_{4b}	0.625	1.000	1.000	1.000	0.217
2.500	S_{43}	0.625	1.000	1.000	1.000	0.217
2.500	S_3	0.625	1.000	1.000	1.000	0.217

The preference of strategy variants in relative to defined criterion C_{12}

Profit value		2.500	2.500	3.670	2.500	Strategy/criterion
Profit value	Strategy Variant	S_{4a}	S_{4b}	S_{43}	S_3	preference
2.500	S_{4a}	1.000	1.000	0.681	1.000	0.224
2.500	S_{4b}	1.000	1.000	0.681	1.000	0.224
3.670	S_{43}	1.468	1.468	1.000	1.468	0.329
2.500	S_3	1.000	1.000	0.681	1.000	0.224

The preference of strategy variants in relative to defined criterion C_{21}

Profit value:		2.500	4.000	3.670	3.000	Strategy/criterion
Profit value	Strategy variant	S_{4a}	S_{4b}	S_{43}	S_3	preference
2.500	S_{4a}	1.000	0.625	0.681	0.833	0.190
4.000	S_{4b}	1.600	1.000	1.090	1.333	0.304
3.670	S_{43}	1.468	0.918	1.000	1.223	0.279
3.000	S_3	1.200	0.750	0.817	1.000	0.228

The preference of strategy variants in relative to defined criterion C_{23}:

Profit value		4.000	4.000	3.670	3.000	Strategy/criterion
Profit value	Strategy variant	S_{4a}	S_{4b}	S_{43}	S_3	preference
4.000	S_{4a}	1.000	1.000	1.090	1.333	0.273
4.000	S_{4b}	1.000	1.000	1.090	1.333	0.273
3.670	S_{43}	0.918	0.918	1.000	1.223	0.250
3.000	S_3	0.750	0.750	0.817	1.000	0.204

The preference of strategy variants in the individual selection

Criterion preference:	0.00252	0.99490	0.00067	0.00190	
Strategy variant:	C_9	C_{12}	C_{21}	C_{23}	Strategy preference
S_{4a}	0.348	0.224	0.190	0.273	0.224
S_{4b}	0.217	0.224	0.304	0.273	0.224
S_{43}	*0.217*	*0.329*	*0.279*	*0.250*	*0.328*
S_3	0.217	0.224	0.228	0.204	0.224

The case of clinic W09

The preference of criteria differentiating the strategy variants

Regression coefficients		13.2040	0.0811	37.2122	9.0260	
Criterion value achieved by the clinic		C_9	C_{12}	C_{21}	C_{23}	Criterion preference
0.905	C_9	0.069	11.158	0.024	0.100	0.00053
1700.154	C_{12}	128.761	20963.673	45.688	188.362	0.99844
0.374	C_{21}	0.028	4.609	0.010	0.041	0.00022
1.385	C_{23}	0.105	17.073	0.037	0.153	0.00081

The preference of strategy variants in relative to defined criterion C_9

Profit value:		4.000	1.000	1.000	1.000	Strategy/criterion
Profit value	Strategy Variant	S_{4a}	S_{4b}	S_{43}	S_3	preference
4.000	S_{4a}	1.000	4.000	4.000	4.000	0.571
1.000	S_{4b}	0.250	1.000	1.000	1.000	0.143
1.000	S_{43}	0.250	1.000	1.000	1.000	0.143
1.000	S_3	0.250	1.000	1.000	1.000	0.143

The preference of strategy variants in relative to defined criterion C_{12}

Profit value:		1.000	1.000	3.670	1.000	Strategy/criterion
Profit value	Strategy variant	S_{4a}	S_{4b}	S_{43}	S_3	preference
1.000	S_{4a}	1.000	1.000	0.272	1.000	0.150
1.000	S_{4b}	1.000	1.000	0.272	1.000	0.150
3.670	S_{43}	3.670	3.670	1.000	3.670	0.550
1.000	S_3	1.000	1.000	0.272	1.000	0.150

The preference of strategy variants in relative to defined criterion C_{21}

Profit value:		1.000	4.000	3.670	3.000	Strategy/criterion preference
Profit value	Strategy variant	S_{4a}	S_{4b}	S_{43}	S_3	
1.000	S_{4a}	1.000	0.250	0.272	0.333	0.086
4.000	S_{4b}	4.000	1.000	1.090	1.333	0.343
3.670	S_{43}	3.670	0.918	1.000	1.223	0.314
3.000	S_3	3.000	0.750	0.817	1.000	0.257

The preference of strategy variants in relative to defined criterion C_{23}

Profit value		4.000	4.000	3.670	3.000	Strategy/criterion preference
Profit value	Strategy variant	S_{4a}	S_{4b}	S_{43}	S_3	
4.000	S_{4a}	1.000	1.000	1.090	1.333	0.273
4.000	S_{4b}	1.000	1.000	1.090	1.333	0.273
3.670	S_{43}	0.918	0.918	1.000	1.223	0.250
3.000	S_3	0.750	0.750	0.817	1.000	0.204

The preference of strategy variants in the individual selection

Criterion preference:	0.00053	0.99844	0.00022	0.00081	
Strategy variant	C_9	C_{12}	C_{21}	C_{23}	Strategy preference
S_{4a}	0.571	0.150	0.086	0.273	0.150
S_{4b}	0.143	0.150	0.343	0.273	0.150
S_{43}	0.143	0.550	0.314	0.250	0.550
S_3	0.143	0.150	0.257	0.204	0.150

Output data

Clinic	Time end	Competitiveness criteria					Profit [thousand PLN]
		C_9	C_{12}	C_{17}	C_{21}	C_{23}	
W03	2010 VI	1.310680	257.500000	0.100000	2.750000	2.500000	10
W06	2010 VI	3.055172	237.704918	0.000000	1.112245	2.459016	150
W09	2010 VI	2.291667	923.076923	0.468493	0.528333	10.000000	130

Bibliography

Rostek, K. (2009). Business intelligence for insurance companies. *Foundations of Management. International Journal, 1*(1), 65–82.

Rostek, K. (2010). Integration of business intelligence technology and benchmarking analyses for SME. In J. Kałkowska (Ed.), *Applications of information technologies in management* (pp. 49–68). Poznań: Publishing House of Poznan University of Technology.

Rostek, K. (2011). Information technologies supporting the development of SMEs competitiveness. In A. Adamik & S. Lachiewicz (Eds.), *Methods and concepts of small and medium-sized enterprises management* (pp. 62–81). Łódź: Technical University of Lodz Press.

Rostek, K. (2012). Methodology of BI implementation in SME sector on the example of dental clinics group. In L. Kiełtyka, W. Jędrzejczyk, R. Kucęba, K. Smoląg (eds.) *Use of selected communications technologies in value management organization* (Monographs no. 234; pp. 169–184). Czestochowa: The Publishing Office of Czestochowa University of Technology.

Rostek, K., & Sitarski, K. (2007). Information management vs knowledge Management. In J. Lewandowski, S. Kopera, & J. Królikowski (Eds.), *Innovation and knowledge in innovative enterprises* (pp. 11–18). Łódź: Łódź University of Technology Publishing House.

Rostek, K., & Wiśniewski, M. (2012). The role of benchmarking method in reorganization of logistics processes on the case of uniformed institutions. In K. Grzybowska (Ed.), *Logistics—selected concepts and best practices* (pp. 73–90). Poznań: Publishing House of Poznan University of Technology.

Rostek, K., Wiśniewski, M., & Kucharska, A. (2012). Cloud business intelligence for SMEs consortium. *Foundations of Management, 4*(1), 105–122.

© Springer International Publishing Switzerland 2015   165
K. Rostek, *Benchmarking Collaborative Networks*, Contributions to Management
Science, DOI 10.1007/978-3-319-16736-7

Index

A
Analytical hierarchical process (AHP),
    17, 61, 91
  crisp variant, 71
  fuzzy judgment matrix, 85
  fuzzy variant, 85
  judgment matrix, 71
ASTRA, 16

B
B4B, vii
BCG. *See* Benchmarking Collaborative
    Group (BCG)
BCM. *See* Benchmarking Collaborative
    Method (BCM)
BCN. *See* Benchmarking Collaborative
    Network (BCN)
Benchmarking, 37
  analysis, 36
  code of conduct, 104
  definition, 33
  European Benchmarking Procedure, 36, 37
  European Secretariat for Cluster Analysis,
    37
  Open Method of Coordination, 36
  process, 35
Benchmarking Collaborative Group (BCG),
    102, 109, 111, 125, 126, 129, 136, 142
Benchmarking Collaborative Method (BCM),
    101, 121, 122, 127
Benchmarking Collaborative Network (BCN),
    viii, 51, 100, 131, 133, 136, 139, 141
Benchmarking Collaborative Paradigm, 100
Big Data, 46

Broker of Strategic Information (BSI),
    125, 128, 130, 132, 133, 137, 142, 143
Business application monitoring, 44
Business intelligence, 41
  ETL, 43, 45
  in-cloud, 47
  in-memory, 45
  metadata, 44
  OLAP, 43
  technology, 41–44
Business process management (BPM), 44

C
Chicago School, 2
C-I-A, 106
Cloud Computing (CC), 47
  Infrastructure as a Service, 47
  Platform as a Service, 47
  Software as a Service, 47
Competition, 30
Competitive
  advantage, 5, 11, 15, 64
  collaboration, 31
  position, 11
  strategy variants, 62
Competitive analysis, 15–19
  qualitative analysis, 17
  quantitative analysis, 18
  strategic analysis, 15
Competitiveness
  choice, 3
  criteria, 13, 14
  definition, 2–4
  efficiency, 3

© Springer International Publishing Switzerland 2015
K. Rostek, *Benchmarking Collaborative Networks*, Contributions to Management
Science, DOI 10.1007/978-3-319-16736-7

Competitiveness (*cont.*)
key criteria, 62, 65
macro perspective, 3
micro perspective, 3
model, 10–15
objectives, 3
potential, 11
resources, 3
structure, 3
Competitive strategy
collaboration strategy, 7
concentration strategy, 6
confrontation strategy, 7
cost advantage strategy, 8
definition, 5, 59
diversification strategy, 7
dodge strategy, 8
prestige advantage strategy, 9
process, 5
Computer Assisted Personal Interviewing
(CAPI), 72
Confidence interval, 73
Confidence level, 73
Cooperation, 30
Coopetition
adapter, 32
contender, 32
definition, 31
monoplayer, 32
partner, 32
Crowdsourcing
definition, 38
resources, 38

D
DBI. *See* Dedicated Business Intelligence
(DBI)
Decision making model, 12
Decision tree
crisp variant, 68
fuzzy variant, 84
test splitting, 68, 85
Dedicated Business Intelligence (DBI),
105, 111, 113, 126, 129, 131, 133, 137
Defuzzification, 86
Delphi method, 17

E
Entropy function, 69
Evolutionary School, 2

F
Five-R's cycle, 44
F-test statistic, 74, 87
Fuzzy Hierarchical-Regression Prototyping
Method (FHRPM), 84, 87

G
Gartner business analytics framework, 41

H
Hadoop, 46
Harvard School, 2
Heuristic methods, 17
Hierarchical Model of Decision Problem
(HMDP), 60, 62, 63, 73, 100, 104,
105, 111, 115, 131, 142
Hierarchical-Regression Prototyping Method
(HRPM), 60, 63, 73, 77, 83

I
Industry 4.0, vii
Information broker, 37
Information brokering, 37

K
Key performance indicators (KPIs), 44
Knowledge broker, 40
Knowledge brokering, 40

M
MapReduce, 46
Maximum permissible error, 73
Mean square error, 67, 69
Method of Brokering Strategic Information
(MBSI), 127, 130, 136
Model of Benchmarking Collaborative
Network (MBCN), 125, 127

N
Null hypothesis, 67

P
Porter's Five Forces Model, 10
p-value, 67

Q
Quartile, 87

R
Regression
    coefficients, 66
    function, 65
Return On Investment (ROI), 44
Risk management, 50
Rivalry, 1, 2
R-squared statistic, 74, 87

S
SME
    definition, 19
    limitations, 21
    significance, 20
Social capital, 48

SPACE, 16
Strategic analysis
    competitive-environment analysis, 16
    macro-environment analysis, 16
    strategic potential analysis, 16
Student's T-test, 67
SWOT, 16, 17

T
Trapezoid fuzzy function, 89
Trust management, 48
    cognitive-based dimention, 49
    institutional-based dimention, 49
    knowledge-based dimension, 49

U
Ultra-Liberal School, 2